Philosophy and
Psychotherapy

Perspectives on Psychotherapy

editor: Colin Feltham
Sheffield Hallam University

Each book in this challenging and incisive series takes a particular perspective on psychotherapy to place it in its intellectual and cultural context. Disciplines which will be brought to bear in this series will include sociology, anthropology, philosophy, psychology, science and feminism.

Philosophy and Psychotherapy

Razing the Troubles of the Brain

EDWARD ERWIN

SAGE Publications
London • Thousand Oaks • New Delhi

First published 1997

 SAGE Publications Ltd
6 Bonhill Street
London EC2A 4PU

SAGE Publications Inc
2455 Teller Road
Thousand Oaks, California 91320

SAGE Publications India Pvt Ltd
32, M-Block Market
Greater Kailash − I
New Delhi 110 048

British Library Cataloguing in Publication data

A catalogue record for this book is available
from the British Library.

ISBN 0 8039 7520 1
ISBN 0 8039 7521 X (pbk)

Library of Congress catalog card number 96-071787

Typeset by Mayhew Typesetting, Rhayader, Powys
Printed in Great Britain by Redwood Books, Trowbridge, Wiltshire

To Adolf Grünbaum

Contents

Canst thou not minister to a mind diseas'd;
Pluck from the memory a rooted sorrow;
Raze out the written troubles of the brain;
And with some sweet oblivious antidote
Cleanse the stuff'd bosom of that perilous stuff.

Macbeth, Act V, Scene III

Preface

When Joseph Breuer used his "talking cure" in treating Anna O in the late nineteenth century, there were few alternative psychological therapies available. Today, in contrast, there are more than 400 distinct types of psychotherapy. Some closely resemble the original talking cure, at least as it was transformed by Sigmund Freud, but many are quite different. Consequently, the term "psychotherapy" has come to denote virtually any kind of psychological treatment.

As the list of therapies has expanded, the number of types of professionals dispensing psychotherapy has also increased. Practitioners now include psychiatrists, social workers, clinical psychologists, members of the clergy, psychiatric nurses, and counselors, working in hospitals, prisons, corporations, schools, outpatient clinics, private offices, and many other settings in numerous countries around the world. This book is addressed to these professionals and to anyone who has an interest in psychotherapy.

It is also addressed to my fellow philosophers, who, until recently, have written comparatively little about the field. Although some (most notably, Adolf Grünbaum, 1984, 1993) have written about the theories of Sigmund Freud, most philosophers of psychology have focussed in recent decades on cognitive science. It is not surprising that philosophers are attracted to cognitive science given its close connections to logic and philosophy of mind, but the time is right for more philosophers to pay attention to psychotherapy, and some in fact are now doing so – see, for example, the papers in Graham and Stephens (1994), the new journal *Philosophy, Psychiatry & Psychology*, and recent philosophic works on multiple personality. Psychotherapy, after all, is a huge field (in the United States, clinical psychology, for example, includes more psychologists than all other areas of psychology combined), and it is rich in theory and in issues that ought to be of interest to philosophers. For example, philosophers have written a great deal about the nature of the self, but there is a parallel literature that discusses numerous psychotherapeutic theories of the self, as well as related clinical phenomena.

To take another example, meta-analysis has produced a revolutionary change in the way outcome literature is now evaluated. The use of meta-analysis, however, has engendered significant epistemological discussions that philosophers of science can both learn from and contribute to. Other psychotherapeutic examples of philosophic interest include: questions about basic criteria for evaluating psychotherapeutic goals and outcomes, the postmodernist epistemology that is becoming increasingly influential in the field of psychotherapy, the new behaviorism, the proper epistemological standards for evaluating clinical work, and various philosophic issues raised in the cognitive-behavior therapy literature.

If psychotherapy should be of interest to philosophers, what about the reverse question? Why should psychotherapists take a professional interest in philosophy? One can, quite obviously, do psychotherapy without paying much attention to philosophic questions. Yet, at least occasionally, it is useful for psychotherapists to reflect on the field as a whole, or to think through particular questions that are basic to the enterprise. Is the field developing in the right direction? Is progress being made? What are the proper standards for evaluating psychotherapies and therapeutic theories? Many psychotherapy theories talk about the self. What sort of thing is this supposed to be? Are the goals of psychotherapists jointly realizable? For example, is it possible to provide genuine autonomy for the client and yet develop a science of psychotherapy?

There are many different ways to deal with such questions. One could examine the works of particular philosophers, such as Wittgenstein, Sartre, Foucault, or Nietzsche, and see what implications their work has for psychotherapy, or try to determine whether the contributions of psychotherapists bear on the work of the philosophers. Another approach would be to concentrate on a single topic of joint interest to psychotherapists and philosophers, such as multiple personality disorder (now commonly referred to as dissociative identity disorder) or various forms of irrationality. This book adopts neither approach. It is not about the work of any one philosopher, nor is it about any single issue. It is, rather, about many different issues concerning autonomy, value, the self, epistemic justification, and other philosophic matters relevant to psychotherapy.

Except for the applied ethics questions discussed in Chapter 2, the issues of Part I are examples of "pure philosophy." Part II discusses issues in applied philosophy as they arise within some of the main paradigms of psychotherapy. Empirical issues here are interwoven with various evaluative, conceptual, and epistemological questions.

In discussing issues associated with the main paradigms, I have not aimed for completeness. In particular, I do not discuss a "humanistic paradigm" partly because I doubt that there is such a single coherent paradigm (Carl Rogers' views, however, are briefly discussed in Chapter 3).

I have also included descriptions of various theories and therapies. In some cases, these accounts are very brief, too brief to be of interest to the specialist. I have included them partly because even a superficial statement of certain theories of psychotherapy helps to ground the philosophic discussion, and partly because the field is so fragmented that people working in one area often complain that their work is unknown to those working in separate areas.

As the reader has no doubt noticed, the subtitle of the book is borrowed from *Macbeth*; it reflects neither a commitment to nor a rejection of philosophic materialism.

Part I
Foundational Questions

1

Autonomy, Free Choice, and the Possibility of a Psychotherapeutic Science

In this chapter, I discuss some of the connections between autonomy, free choice, and science. The main goal is to answer the question: Can there be both client autonomy and a science of psychotherapy?

SCIENCE AND THE AIMS OF PSYCHOTHERAPY

What should be the aims of psychotherapy? That question is discussed in Chapter 2. Here, I want to discuss one goal that *in fact* is widely accepted: promotion of the client's autonomy.

For many psychotherapists, this goal is not just one among many equals; it is the *primary* goal. As one writer puts it, "If there is a single, overriding purpose of psychological counseling and psychotherapy, it is the promotion of Autonomy" (Thompson, 1990: 13). The pursuit of free autonomous choice, another writer notes (Kovel, 1978), is the one value that can be emphasized in the selection and conduct of a therapy. The primary reason for expanding the field of psychotherapy, Holmes and Lindley argue (1989: 42–3), is that it aims not merely at symptom relief but also at the enhancement of the client's autonomy. They also argue that because psychotherapy offers this benefit, a moral case can be made for its being subsidized by taxpayer money.

Bringing about client autonomy is a therapeutic goal, but there is a second goal that concerns the field itself: the transformation of psychotherapy into a scientific discipline. Not all psychotherapists share this goal, but it arguably *ought* to be accepted. Despite much laborious work, a case can be made that the field is in a state of disarray (see Chapter 8). There is widespread disagreement about most of the fundamental elements of the discipline. Psychotherapists disagree not only about the proper aims of psychotherapy and the criteria for improvement, but also about the field's diagnostic categories, the underlying clinical theories, and, perhaps most disturbingly, what, if anything, produces substantial therapeutic benefits. What needs to be done? The discipline needs to become a science. Or, if it is already a science, it needs to become *more* scientific; at least, that is what many argue.

How does this goal for the discipline fit with the therapeutic goal of helping the client to become autonomous? Carl Rogers, long a supporter of both the promotion of client autonomy and the scientific study of psychotherapy, held that determinism holds true in the psychological world just as it does in the physical world, but that freedom exists along side it as a "paradox" (Rogers, 1989a: 85). He never did, however, resolve the paradox. Many followers of B.F. Skinner will reply that it cannot be resolved: the conditions for achieving the one goal prevent the achievement of the other. Science requires determinism; autonomy requires free will, which in turn requires the absence of determinism.

Outside the field of psychotherapy, there is a more general anxiety shared by many who aim to develop a cognitive science. Such a science would appear to require that human thinking and action be caused in the same sense that events studied by chemists and physicists are caused. The worry is that if this precondition is met, it seems to leave no room for such things of fundamental human concern as human dignity, creativity, free choice, autonomy, or moral responsibility.

Construed a bit more narrowly, to fit the concerns of psychotherapists *qua* psychotherapists, the issue becomes: Can the twin goals of achieving client autonomy and transforming the field into a science be jointly met? Here is an argument – call it the "dilemma of determinism" – that says they cannot:

1 Either determinism is true or it is not.
2 If it is true, then there is no free choice.
3 If there is no free choice, there is no genuine autonomy.
4 If there is no genuine autonomy, it is futile to make the achievement of autonomy a goal of psychotherapy.
5 If determinism is not true, most human actions are not caused.
6 If most human actions are not caused, there can be no science of psychotherapy.
7 Therefore, either it is futile to make the achievement of autonomy a goal of psychotherapy or there can be no science of psychotherapy.

What is meant by "determinism" in the above argument? I take it to mean that all macro events (that is, events above the quantum level) are caused. We could mean that *all* events are caused, but that more ambitious, traditional doctrine appears to be refuted if modern quantum theory is approximately true; for, the theory postulates uncaused events at the quantum level. The existence of uncaused quantum events could have an impact on the free will debate – see the very nice discussion of Fine (1993) – but this possibility raises a different sort of issue than the one I want to discuss, and so I will set it aside and interpret "determinism" as a thesis about macro events, especially human action. With this understanding in mind, let us briefly examine the above argument.

Some humanistic therapists will not be troubled by the conclusion. They will simply point out that psychotherapy cannot be a science. Human beings, unlike comets and electrons, are autonomous, or at least they have the capacity to become so through psychotherapy. Being autonomous, they can freely choose to act counter to whatever seeming laws of behavior that social scientists formulate.

Those who doubt the conclusion will reject at least one premise (I assume that the reasoning is correct), but which one? An obvious target is premise 5. Even if determinism is not true, it does not follow that *most* actions are uncaused. It could be that only one or two are. Still, this may not be a viable line of attack. Some of the arguments against (macro) determinism, if sound, also seem to show that few if any actions are caused. So, even if premise 5 is not *necessarily* true, it might be true anyway. Before deciding which premise, if any, is in error, it will be useful to take a look at the key issues.

COMPATIBILISM

Most of the major philosophers who have discussed the issue of free will and determinism have supported the common-sense view that only in unusual circumstances, such as cases of extreme mental illness or coercion, are we unfree. The nineteenth-century philosopher Arthur Schopenhauer is an exception. In a rather odd comparison, he describes the apparent choices of a man and a body of water. The man says to himself:

> It is six o'clock in the evening, the working day is over. Now I can go for a walk, or I can go to the club; I can also climb up to the tower to see the sun set; I can go to the theater; I can visit this friend or that one; indeed, I also can run out of the gate, into the wide world, and never return. All of this is strictly up to me, in this I have complete freedom. But still I shall do none of these things now, but with just as free a will I shall go home to my wife. (Schopenhauer, 1960)

Schopenhauer comments that this is exactly as if water spoke to itself and said: I can make high waves, or rush downhill, or rise freely into the air; but I am doing none of these things, and instead am voluntarily remaining quiet and clear water in the reflecting pond. What the man overlooks is that he is like the water in that he can do any of the various things that appear open to him *only when* the determining causes operate for one thing or the other. Until the causes begin to operate, it is impossible, Schopenhauer notes, for him to do any one of these things, but once they do begin to operate, he *must* act as he does, just as the water must, as soon as it is placed in the corresponding circumstances.

Many contemporary philosophers, commonly referred to as "compatibilists" (or sometimes as "soft determinists"), challenge Schopenhauer's argument. There can be, they say, both causal determination of human action and free choice. The two things are perfectly compatible.

A decade or so ago, compatibilism was probably the most dominant view of the free-will issue among philosophers. That may still be true today, but the theory has had to face incisive criticisms, and now appears to be on somewhat shaky foundations, as we shall see shortly.

PROBLEMS WITH COMPATIBILISM

Some traditional compatibilists, most notably David Hume, rested their case on a controversial account of the causal relation, one that in effect made causation nothing more than correlation. Most contemporary compatibilists reject that approach. Instead, they tend to argue that the sort of free choice required for moral responsibility is not categorical but is conditional upon something else. If that is true, it is further argued, causation can be more than constant conjunction, and yet determinism and free will can still be reconciled.

For example, suppose we say that a client has begun drinking again, and that he freely chose to do so. On one so-called "conditional" analysis, all this means is that he could have refrained from drinking *if he had chosen to*. If this account is correct, the man might have been free to remain abstinent even if his drinking was caused (say, by his desire for immediate alcoholic gratification and his belief that he could handle the drinking), and that cause was caused by a prior event, and that event was caused, and so on. That is, even if every event is caused, including the man's action, it might still be true that he met the conditions sufficient for free choice. That can be true even if, contrary to Hume, there is a necessary connection between a cause and its effect. For, it might still have been true of the man that he could have acted differently *if he had so chosen*.

There is a problem with the above analysis, however, if it purports to capture what is generally meant by saying that someone acted freely. Suppose that our client were an alcoholic who had been abstinent for two days, and who then drank to the point of drunkenness. Even after he finished his fourteenth drink of scotch, he might have been able to stop *if only he could have so chosen*. Yet he might have been so drunk at this point that he could not have freely declined another drink. Yes, if he had chosen to, he would have stopped, but by then, let us suppose, that choice was beyond him. So, it is true of this client that he could have refrained from ordering his fifteenth scotch if he had so chosen. That this is true, however, hardly guarantees his freedom: after finishing his fourteenth drink, he was too drunk to make that choice.

Compatibilists have provided more subtle sorts of "conditional" analyses of free choice than the one considered above, but it is by no means clear that any single such analysis is immune from counter-examples (see van Inwagen, 1983: 114–26). A second problem is that it is not enough to give such an analysis. Unless it is self-evidently correct, one also has to show that it is right; otherwise an incompatibilist need not accept it. A third, and perhaps more serious, problem is that incompatibilists have now mounted strong, direct attacks on compatibilist doctrine. If any one of these attacks is right, two things follow. First, it will prove impossible to find the sort of conditional analysis needed to establish compatibilism. Second, no other strategy will work either; for compatibilism will have been shown to be false. I turn next to the most powerful incompatibilist arguments.

INCOMPATIBILISM

Some incompatibilists claim that free action requires the ability to do otherwise, to do something different from what we in fact do. They then argue that we lack this ability if determinism is true. This argument, however, is itself vulnerable to certain objections. First, many compatibilists reply that the ability-to-do-otherwise condition is only a conditional one, which can be met even if determinism is true.

If a drunken man strikes his wife, for example, some compatibilists will say that he acted freely only if had the ability to do something different *if certain conditions had prevailed*. So, the man might very well have been free and morally responsible for his action even if it were caused, say, by his being in a drunken rage. Given his personality, his drunken state, his anger, and all other causally relevant factors, he had to do what he did; but if certain factors had been different, if, say, he had had more respect for his wife or if he did not drink so much, he could have acted differently. Therefore, the compatibilist will conclude, compatibilism can withstand the challenge that freedom requires the ability to do otherwise. Freedom does require this, but it is not the *categorical* ability that Incompatibilists insist on. Free will does not require that the agent could have acted differently even if everything, including his or her beliefs, desires, attitudes, decisions, character, and so on, were exactly the same. It requires, rather, a conditional ability to do otherwise; the capacity to do something different if one had wanted to, or had believed something different, or had decided differently, or was a different sort of person, and so forth.

I doubt that compatibilists have established that the conditional ability to do otherwise is enough for freedom; as I noted earlier, their analyses of freedom have all encountered problems. However, neither have incompatibilists proved the reverse: that free action does require a categorical ability to do otherwise. So, the argument of the incompatibilist has a weak spot. Furthermore, it has another problem. There is a powerful line of argument that seems to show that there is no logical connection at all between being free (and morally responsible) and having any sort of ability to do otherwise (Frankfurt, 1969).

For the above two reasons, I do not think that the appeal to the ability-to-do-otherwise requirement constitutes the strongest case for incompatibilism. To make the argument cogent, two things would have to be done: first, it would have to be shown that free choice really does require the ability to do otherwise; and second, it would have to be shown that if there is such a requirement, it is categorical rather than conditional. Whether or not the argument can be made to work, there is, as some incompatibilists point out (Klein, 1990), a stronger argument available that concerns the inevitability of human action if determinism is true.

One version of this argument appears in a well-known paper on free will and psychoanalysis by the philosopher John Hospers (1950). He constructs a deductive argument to show that someone is not responsible for his or her neurotic behavior if such behavior was inevitable. The argument contains a controversial empirical assumption, that all neuroses result from events occurring in one's babyhood, but that assumption is not needed if our goal is merely to establish a hypothetical conclusion of interest to incompatibilists: namely, if our neurotic behavior results from events that occurred in our infancy, then we are not responsible for it.

The premise in Hospers' argument that does matter here concerns moral responsibility and the inevitable consequences of things beyond our control. I will refer to this assumption as the "inevitability thesis," and any argument employing it as the "inevitability argument." The thesis says that we are not responsible for any of our behavior that inevitably results from events for which we were not responsible. All we need add is that if determinism is true, then our present behavior is the inevitable consequence of events occurring in our infancy, *and* we had no control over these events. Thus, even if events in one's adult life are the immediate cause of one's neurosis, it will still be true that one is not responsible for one's neurotic behavior. In fact, it does not matter whether the behavior is neurotic or not. We will not be responsible for *anything* we do, even if we are not neurotic at all, if determinism is true.

Several philosophers sympathetic to incompatibilism have given arguments very similar to Hospers', although without making any reference to neuroses. Here is one succinct version of the inevitability argument:

> If determinism is true then our acts are the consequences of the laws of nature and events in the remote past. But it is not up to us what went on before we were born and neither is it up to us what the laws of nature are. Therefore, the consequences of these things (including our present acts) are not up to us. (van Inwagen, 1983: 16)

Of course, another step is required: If none of our present acts is up to us, then we are not free and are not morally responsible. We can then infer that if determinism is true, we are neither free nor morally responsible. Not only is the inevitability argument, in all its forms, the main argument for incompatibilism, it may also be what incompatibilists really have in mind when they link the free-will issue to the categorical ability to do otherwise; see Klein (1990) on this point. Whether this speculation is true or not, if the inevitability argument is cogent, there is no need to rely on the controversial assumption that freedom and moral responsibility require the categorical ability to do otherwise. The inevitability argument, if it is cogent, would by itself establish incompatibilism. I take up the question of its cogency next.

As I noted earlier, John Hospers' (1950) argument relies on the inevitability thesis: "But if there is something we cannot be held responsible for, neither can we be held responsible for something that inevitably results from it" (Hospers, 1950: 710).

Is this thesis true? Hospers gives no reason to think so; he presumably thought that it was sufficiently obvious that it required no supporting argument. But is it just *obviously* true?

Suppose that my brother and I are undergoing psychotherapy but quit on the same day. He is making real progress with his therapy but ends it for no apparent reason. Unknown to him, the reason he quits has something to do with the transference relation. He projects on to his therapist feelings of hatred that were formerly directed to our father. His motive for terminating therapy is not the one he subsequently makes up for himself. The main motive lies deeply buried in his unconscious: he wants to punish our deceased father.

Is my brother's act of quitting therapy a free act, and is he responsible for it? Both Hospers and I would be inclined to say "no" (although more details might have to be filled in). If the act is unfree, why is that so? Is it because my brother has no access to his unconscious motivation, or is it because, assuming the truth of determinism, a causal chain links the motive through a series of preceding events back to childhood events outside of my brother's control?

Hospers is apparently undecided about which answer he wants to rely on. Most of his (1950) paper is designed to spell out the consequences of psychoanalytic doctrine for issues about human freedom. As he puts it, "we are not masters of our fate," not always but quite often, because our very acts of volition are so often but façades for the expression of our unconscious wishes (1950: 706). It is unconscious motivation, according to Hospers, that takes away our freedom, at least if we have not gained insights through psychoanalysis into what really motivates us. When he constructs his inevitability argument, however, he makes no mention of unconscious motivation. If the latter argument were sound, it would show that we are never responsible for our neurotic behavior *whether or not* it results from unconscious motivation. The inaccessibility of the agent's motive becomes irrelevant.

Regardless of which answer Hospers would pick — he might choose both — I am inclined to give only the first: My brother's termination of his therapy was unfree because his real motive lay deep in his unconscious.

Contrast his case with mine. I know, let us assume, why I quit. I was paying a high price for therapy that was clearly not helping me with my problem. After reading virtually all of the relevant research, I concluded, on quite rational grounds, that this particular type of therapy almost never works with my sort of problem. In order to conclude that I was responsible for my act, do I first have to rule out the possibility that its causal antecedents can be traced to some event in my childhood that was beyond my control, and which led inevitably to my terminating the therapy? For reasons to be given shortly, I doubt that this is necessary. Consider what my brother did next.

After leaving therapy, let us imagine, my brother joined a religious cult, and after much indoctrination, he began selling religious items at the local airport. Convinced that he was acting in a zombie-like manner, we kidnaped him and forced him to submit to deprograming. Because he had often acted in erratic, irrational ways even before joining the cult, we decided to go further: we forced him to undergo a kind of cognitive therapy. In order to receive food, he was forced to read books on logic, statistics, decision theory, and other subjects relevant to the making of calm, calculated, rational decisions. The inevitable result of this successful treatment was that he reflected on his decision to join a cult, weighed all of the pros and cons, and decided that his continuing in the cult was not in his best interest, and that he certainly had no moral obligation to continue. What followed was also inevitable: he quit the cult and rejoined his old law firm.

Suppose that a strict determinism does not hold true of the world I am describing. There are causal sequences of various sorts but *none* of my brother's behavior prior to his joining the cult was the inevitable consequence of the combination of the laws of nature and prior events. So, his quitting therapy and his other irrational acts *might* have been free. At least, we cannot infer the lack of freedom from the inevitability thesis plus the facts of the case; for his behavior, I am stipulating, was not the inevitable result of events over which my brother had no control. The situation changes, however, once my brother joins the cult. When he later quits, his decision and the act itself, I will now stipulate, are the inevitable consequences of his learning how to make rational decisions. Is it just obvious that all of his earlier behavior, including his quitting therapy because of his unconscious hatred of our father, was free, but his quitting the cult was unfree? Neither one of these things is obvious.

To return to my case, it just so happens (let us assume) that I was forced by my tyrannical father, a famous logician, to learn how to make rational decisions. I resisted, but I was very young, and had no choice but to learn. I also learned the power and attractions of rationality, and inevitably made decisions that were always rational. In fact, my decision to quit therapy became inevitable once my father indoctrinated me in the ways of rationality. Other events subsequently followed, and the causal chain led inexorably to my weighing all of the evidence concerning my psychotherapy, and then quitting.

Is it obvious, then, that my act of terminating the therapy was unfree? Suppose that I had violated a contract with the therapist by quitting earlier than promised. Would it be a valid excuse to point out that I had done so as a result of weighing all of the costs and benefits, and that this sort of cool, calculating behavior was the inevitable consequence of my father's training? I do not find that obvious at all. I conclude, then, not that the inevitability thesis is false, but that there is no good reason to accept it in the absence of a supporting argument.

Let me sum up the disagreement here about the inevitability thesis. If my brother's termination of his therapy was due mainly to a repressed desire, the inaccessibility of the desire, according to the incompatibilist, does *not* prevent his quitting from being free. If the unconscious cause made the action extremely probable but not inevitable, and nothing else made it inevitable, then the action was free, according to the inevitability doctrine. The kind of cause, whether it was unconscious or not, is not the crucial factor; it is, rather, the inevitability of the action that matters. Even if the unconscious wish can be traced to an act of repression in infancy that was automatic, free choice is still not ruled out, according to the inevitability thesis, if there is a little play in the long causal chain, if there is probabilistic causation but also a tiny bit of spontaneity. To be unfree, the action has to be *inevitable* given the operation of prior causes.

In contrast, even though I quit because I wanted to, and my preference survived rational reflection, and no one coerced me, I acted unfreely according to the incompatibilist: because my father's teaching me how to think clearly made it inevitable that I would later make the rational choice, the very choice that I did make.

It seems to me that the incompatibilist's theory dictates the wrong decision about these cases. It was I, not my brother, who freely chose to quit therapy. The incompatibilist who relies on the inevitability doctrine is forced to say just the reverse.

The implausibility of this viewpoint becomes even clearer as the case develops. Suppose, as I stipulated, there was probabilistic causation, but there was no inevitability about my brother's quitting therapy or joining the cult. Inevitability sets in only after we kidnap him. Once we train him how to think rationally, he inevitably does the rational thing, the very thing he wants to do after calm reflection: he quits the cult. The defender of the inevitability thesis has to say: Now, for the first time in his life, he is genuinely *unfree*. It seems to me that just the opposite is true. Whether or not he made any free choices before, he is now capable of making such choices.

In his defense of incompatibilism, Peter van Inwagen (1983) might appear to avoid all problems with the inevitability thesis. In spelling out his argument (he has three versions of a single argument), he nowhere explicitly appeals to the thesis. Instead, he relies on a certain metaphysical rule of inference (page 222), noting that the assumption of its validity comes very close to being the single premise upon which the argument of his book is based (page 229, note 17). How do we know that the rule is valid? Van Inwagen provides no argument that it is. Instead, he claims that the proposition that it is valid "disposes the mind to assent," and that the proposition seems to be a truth of reason (1983: 222). The rule, however, although it does not use the term "inevitable," is simply another version of the inevitability thesis. I doubt that it will dispose the minds of most compatibilists to assent; it clearly gains no assent from me. The proposition that the rule is valid may be more likely to be correct, as van Inwagen claims (page 222), than any conditional analysis of "free will," but that is because all such analyses, as shown by him and others, are problematic. We can concede the correctness of van Inwagen's criticisms of these analyses, but still ask: Is his rule valid?

Not only is the rule not self-evident, it appears to be invalid if my descriptions of my brother and me are correct. Assume that it is a law of nature that if he undergoes the cognitive therapy and that certain other events occur, then he quits the cult, and that no one has had, or ever will have, a choice about whether this is a law of nature. Assume further that neither he nor anyone else had a choice about his under-going the cognitive therapy. If van Inwagen's rule (page 222) were valid, it would have to be true that my brother had no free choice about quitting the cult. That does not appear to be correct. It is not self-evident that the event that transformed my brother into a rational decision maker, and made it inevitable that he would quit the cult, took away his freedom or his responsibility for his action. If anything, it appears that my brother gained the capacity for free choice when he shook off the conditioning effects of the cult-therapy, and learned to think logically.

We get the same result – true premises and a false conclusion – if we substitute in van Inwagen's schema a description of the causes of my quitting therapy, and then apply his rule. That could not happen if his rule were valid.

I conclude that van Inwagen's rule is not obviously correct; instead it appears to me, at least, to license reasoning that is obviously incorrect. Without some argument to support the contention that the rule is valid, van Inwagen has no case at all in favor of incompatibilism.

I return now to the inevitability thesis. Is there some way to demon-strate its correctness, that is, to show that if my current action was made inevitable by events outside of my control, then I am not responsible for it? Here is one sort of argument.

There are imaginary problematic cases used by philosophers to test our intuitions about responsibility and free will. These include cases of brain damage, hypnosis, brain washing, and even cases where an evil demon has implanted something in us that controls our actions. Are we not inclined to say in such cases, that the victim is not free and not responsible? Cannot the incompatibilist provide a satisfactory *unified* account of our reactions to such cases? We do not blame the victims in such cases, it might be said, because they are not responsible for their motivations. The fact that this account provides the only satisfactory, unified explanation of our intuitions lends some support to the inevitability thesis, it could be argued, assuming that our intuitive reactions are not due to some systematic error. The account, moreover, not only explains our intuitions in such cases, it also justifies them; at least that is what some incompatibilists claim.

Martha Klein (1990) uses the above argument to support what she calls the "U-condition" for blameworthiness. Agents are responsible for their decisions or choices, according to this condition, only if they are "ultimately responsible" in the sense that nothing for which they are not responsible is the source of their decisions or choices (Klein, 1990: 51). Assuming that by the "source" Klein means an event that not merely made a difference but made inevitable the agent's choices, decisions, and behavior, then her U-condition is just a variant of the inevitability thesis. Her argument, then, if cogent, will support both the thesis that the U-condition must be met if the agent is responsible and (what comes to the same thing) the truth of the inevitability thesis.

The most important question to ask about Klein's argument is this: Does her account provide a satisfactory explanation of the entire range of imaginary cases? If it does not, then she cannot correctly claim to have provided a satisfactory unified explanation. Does her theory explain, for example, our different reactions to why my brother and I terminated psychotherapy? On her theory, our reactions to both cases will be the same if we think that the ultimate source of our decisions is an event that was beyond our control. We should be inclined to say that neither of us made a free, responsible decision. Although neither Klein nor I know how other people would generally react, my reactions are different in the two cases. I am inclined, as made clear earlier, to say that I was responsible but my brother was not. Klein's theory does not explain this difference.

Furthermore, it does not satisfactorily explain our reactions even in my brother's case taken by itself. I, and, I suspect, many others, will agree that his decision was not free because it was "outside of his control," but not in the sense that the ultimate source was beyond his control. It was outside of his control in the sense that it — the desire to strike back at our father — was completely inaccessible to consciousness. My brother, then, was in no position to step back and reflect calmly on his motivation. He could not just say to himself: "This is a silly reason to quit therapy, especially given that the therapy is producing good results." On Klein's theory, this total inaccessibility to consciousness is not enough reason to doubt my brother's responsibility. We also need reason to think that his motive could be traced to causes for which he was not responsible. I deny this. I would doubt my brother's responsibility even if I thought that his unconscious motivation was uncaused.

Klein could reply that even if his unconscious motive were uncaused, he was not responsible for it. Whether or not this is right, the key point is that Klein's theory points to the wrong item in trying to explain our intuitions (mine at least). It fixes on my brother's motive being either uncaused or causally traceable to events outside of his control, whereas, given my intuitions, I need not have any opinion about such things. It is enough that I believe that my brother's motivation lay deep in his unconscious. Even if I believed that he would be responsible for his motive if it were generated within him spontaneously and that is what happened, I would still believe that he was not responsible for his quitting therapy.

The unsatisfactory nature of Klein's explanation becomes even clearer when we apply it to my brother's quitting the cult. If we believe that his being forced to undergo cognitive therapy made it inevitable that he would make a rational decision, and given the facts of the case, it became inevitable that he would quit, then Klein's theory predicts that we will judge his decision to be unfree and conclude that he was not responsible. After all, the ultimate source of his motive was something beyond his control.

My intuition, however, is that he was responsible for his decision. What does it matter whether his undergoing cognitive therapy was caused by factors beyond his control, or whether it was completely uncaused, or whether it was caused by factors within his control? However he got to his state of sanity and clarity of mind, once he arrived there, he weighed all of the evidence and made the decision he did because on balance the evidence supported that decision. Could he excuse himself later, if he were criticized, by saying, "Yes, I did make the decision in a calm, lucid frame of mind, *but* my very lucidity was the result of what others did"? I would find that excuse unacceptable, and I believe that many others would as well.

Even in a case such as brain damage, Klein's theory does not always provide the most plausible explanation of our intuitions. We normally think of such cases as involving damage that clearly takes away a person's freedom to choose. For example, a man suffers a brain trauma and, as a consequence, climbs a tower and begins shooting people. Not all cases of brain damage, however, need be like that.

Consider the case of George, who is an exemplar of what people would have to be like in order for B.F. Skinner's operant conditioning theory to be generally true of human beings. In short, he responds to his environment the way an average rat or pigeon does. When an environmental cue appears (a so-called "discriminative stimulus"), he responds automatically and mechanically, depending on his previous history of reinforcement and punishment. No reflective thought or rational calculation mars the automaticity of his responses. Make a political remark and

George will give his stereotypical response; repeat an often-told joke and he will respond always in the same way. He has no more freedom to respond differently than does a rat in a maze.

One day poor George slips and smashes his head against a marble floor. Something happens to his brain circuitry; he becomes like a normal human being who can think about what he is doing, evaluate his choices, and modify them if they appear to be wrong given the best available evidence. The next time George acts, his motive results from his brain damage, but if he were making an obviously wrong decision, he would be caused to reflect and to alter his course of action. On Klein's theory, because his motive is due to his brain damage, whereas before his motives were caused by environmental cues, we should say that his capacity for free choice has not improved. I, however, am inclined to say that the brain alteration has helped (do not call the change "damage" if doing so implies a change for the worse). He now has the same capacity to make free choices as the rest of us.

Suppose, for example, that the head trauma causes a recurring severe headache and a corresponding desire to relieve the pain. In the past, Jones probably would have acted ineffectively, depending on what cue just happened to have been in his immediate environment. Now, however, armed with his newly found rationality, he thinks things over and decides that he ought to see a neurologist. Would most of us be inclined to say that he is not responsible for this decision because it is based on a desire that ultimately resulted from brain injury? I see no reason to think that most of us would have that inclination. I clearly do not.

I conclude, then, that Klein has not made a satisfactory case for either the U-condition or the inevitability thesis, and neither has anyone else. Furthermore, the strongest arguments for incompatibilism all rely on a premise that is neither supported nor self-evident: they depend on either the inevitability thesis or a categorical I-could-have-done-otherwise requirement. Without adequate support for either premise, these arguments lack cogency. Unless there are better arguments, we have no good reason to think that incompatibilism is true.

I return now to the dilemma of determinism.

The Dilemma Revisited

1 Either determinism is true or it is not.
2 If it is true, then there is no free choice.
3 If there is no free choice, there is no genuine autonomy.
4 If there is no genuine autonomy, it is futile to make the achievement of autonomy a goal of psychotherapy.
5 If determinism is not true, most human actions are not caused.
6 If most human actions are not caused, there can be no science of psychotherapy.

7   Therefore, either it is futile to make the achievement of autonomy a goal of psychotherapy or there can be no science of psychotherapy.

Without support for incompatibilism, we have no reason to believe premise 2. The argument, therefore, collapses. Unfortunately, pointing this out fails to resolve the relevant issues. Premise 2 may lack support, but do we know that it is false? We do not unless we know that incompatibilism is false, and I doubt that we know that, despite my arguments and the arguments of other compatibilists (see Dennett, 1984). Perhaps our evidence is not quite sufficient for knowledge, but do we at least have *some* good reason to disbelieve incompatibilism? I, at least, have not provided any reason that is not question begging. I have shown at most that there is no good reason to accept the incompatibilist doctrine. In showing that, I have relied on intuitions of myself, and presumably of many others, about whether someone would be responsible under certain conditions. Incompatibilists are likely to respond that they, however, do not have the same intuitions about the cases of my brother or myself. Unless there is some other evidence, the issue is a stand-off.

Suppose we were to search the entire compatibilist literature, would we find at least one argument that ought to convince us all that incompatibilism is false, one that in the end does not rest on intuitions that incompatibilists reject? I will not try to rule that out, but my reading of that literature is that such a search would yield no such argument, even though I agree with compatibilism. In the end, the arguments of compatibilists also turn on premises about sufficient conditions of freedom and responsibility that have no support beyond intuitions, intuitions not shared by incompatibilists. In short, neither compatibilism nor incompatibilism has been established.

If my verdict is correct, it would be reasonable to look for some other flaw in the determinist dilemma besides the frailty of premise 2. We might, as I noted earlier, question premise 5. If determinism is false, it does not follow that most human actions are uncaused; all that follows is that one action (or one macro event of some kind) is uncaused. The reply to this point was noted earlier. It is possible that there is only one uncaused action but that is unlikely; if there is good reason to believe that there is one, there will also be reason to think that most human actions are uncaused. For example, if, as some philosophers have argued, reasons are not causes, and reasons but not causes explain some human actions, then probably most human actions can be explained non-causally. In any event, I will not pursue the objection to premise 5, for I think that it leads nowhere.

We could also challenge premise 6, and I believe that the issue here is of some importance. When philosophers speak of "determinism," they generally mean that all events (or at least all macro events) are caused by events that together with the laws of nature and all initial conditions are causally *sufficient* for the occurrence of their effects. A cause (combined with certain conditions), then, *necessitates* its effect. If we were to postulate a weaker type of causal relation, then it would not even seem that determinism and free will are incompatible.

Incompatibilists are drawn to incompatibilism because what is being envisioned is a state of the universe such that a cause and the laws of nature make it *inevitable* that certain subsequent events occur. If a cause does not generally necessitate its effect, then the inevitability factor disappears, and with it the attractions of incompatibilism.

Suppose, then, the term "cause" in both premises 5 and 6 is interpreted to mean an event (together with other relevant factors) that is sufficient for its effect. In that case, premise 6 is dubious. If human actions, psychological problems, and the workings of psychotherapy are explainable in terms of causally relevant factors – factors that make an important difference even if they are not causally sufficient – then the failure of most actions to have causally sufficient conditions would not automatically doom attempts to transform the psychotherapy enterprise into a science.

Consider, for example, Freud's explanation of the etiology of psychoneuroses in terms of repressed wishes. As Grünbaum points out (1984), Freud claimed that such wishes are causally relevant but not causally sufficient. Constitutional factors of an unknown sort were also said to be of causal importance. Suppose that we were to confirm Freud's view about the etiological role of repressed wishes, but it turned out that there were no other factors that in combination with them necessitated psychoneuroses. Would we still not have the beginnings of a science of psychotherapy? Some philosophers would say that it would not be much of a beginning, that without uncovering causally sufficient conditions we would only have an explanation sketch, not a genuine scientific explanation. If we say that, however, then we rule out widely accepted explanations in other scientific areas in which the explanations are sometimes, even typically, probabilistic in nature. The history of this controversy, which concerns the requirements of the so-called "deductive-nomological" model of explanation, is reviewed by Salmon (1989), who makes a strong case that this model is too stringent. Probabilistic causation is sufficient for scientific explanation. There are other reasons why one might doubt that there can be a science of psychotherapy, but I will discuss them later (Chapter 4). My conclusion here is merely that the falsity of (macro) determinism does not by itself guarantee that there cannot be a science of psychotherapy.

Let me pick up the thread of the argument. I began with the question of whether we can have both autonomy and a science of psychotherapy. The argument that I called the "dilemma of determinism" concludes that we cannot have both. Its key second premise (that if determinism holds, there is no free choice) appears to have received powerful support in recent years from the writings of the incompatibilists. In reply, I argued that, contrary to appearances, they have a weak case, but I also doubt that compatibilists have made a better case. There is, as far as I can determine, a stalemate. If, however, premise 6 is false, if a science of psychotherapy does not require determinism (probabilistic causation is enough), then why not resolve the problem without paying any attention to the incompatibilism–compatibilism controversy? Why not save free choice and autonomy by rejecting determinism, without thereby posing any threat to the possibility of a science of psychotherapy? It is by no means clear, however, that this solution works either.

Suppose that there are causally relevant factors that explain human actions, but that in most cases there are no causally sufficient conditions for these actions. Determinism, then, would be false. One might think that this would guarantee the existence of freedom, but some philosophers have argued just the opposite. On this view, freedom and responsibility *require* the truth of determinism.

As an illustration of this view, Bergmann (1977) asks us to imagine Raskolnikov walking up the steps to kill the old pawnbroker of Dostoevsky's novel *Crime and Punishment*. Raskolnikov thinks to himself, "I shall kill her," but as he pushes the door open, his last thought is "no, I shall not do it." *Now* indeterminacy sets in. The thinking of this latter thought is the last link in a causal chain, but a gap occurs between the thought that he will not kill her, and the next event: he kills the woman. Would the causal gap, Bergmann asks, render Raskolnikov's act free? If his last thought is "no, I shall not do it," but the thought is disconnected from the next event, so that it has no causal influence on it, and then he kills, the indeterminacy would appear to have rendered his will ineffective. Instead of giving the agent more power, the causal gap, Bergmann suggests, has *decreased* or eliminated the agent's capacity to refrain from killing.

One problem suggested by Bergmann's example concerns the location of the alleged indeterminacy. If there were indeterminacies, where in the causal chain of events would they typically occur? Suppose that I decide to move to a different part of town. Are we to envision a chain of causes leading up to my deciding, but stopping just before I make up my mind, leaving my choice undetermined by prior causes? Or are we to assume that my choice is caused, but that indeterminacy sets in after I decide but before I act?

A more basic problem for those who believe in indeterminism and freedom is to explain how the absence of causation would contribute to my freedom. If my decision to act or the act itself is uncaused, does that mean that either or both just happen randomly? If it does, why would indeterminism give me freedom? Raskolnikov decides not to kill the old woman, but then a random event occurs: he kills her. Was he free not to kill her *because* his act was random?

One response to such questions is to speak of a new type of causation: agent causation. On this view, actions are typically not caused by prior events and yet they are not uncaused either. Rather, in so far as they are free, they are caused by the agent. What *events* caused Raskolnikov to murder the old woman? None. He himself caused his own action. Philosophers disagree, however, about whether the idea of agent causation helps resolve anything.

In fact, they still disagree about most of the central issues surrounding free will and responsibility. Fifteen years ago or so, some incompatibilists promised a solution to the traditional problems of free will and determinism along the following lines. Incompatibilism was to be established, determinism refuted, and free will and moral responsibility vindicated. That promise has not been kept. As I argued earlier, incompatibilism has *not* been established, although I also doubt that it has been refuted. Furthermore, it remains unclear whether the truth of incompatibilism would help establish freedom, not only because the truth or falsity of determinism is still unclear but also because of doubts about whether indeterminism would be sufficient for freedom. One leading incompatibilist now argues that if, as he believes, incompatibilism is true, then we have free choice, at most, in relatively rare cases (van Inwagen, 1989).

Despite much rigorous philosophizing on both sides of the issues, it is fair to say that recent philosophical work on free will and determinism has failed completely to resolve any of the *major* issues. It is not just that philosophers continue to disagree about compatibilism, determinism, and whether free will requires determinism. That could happen even if the arguments clearly supported only one side, but, alas, they do not.

Where does that leave the dilemma of determinism? We still have at least one more option: to deny premise 3, which reads, "If there is no free choice, then there is no genuine autonomy."

AUTONOMY WITHOUT FREE CHOICE

In some sense, there are obvious connections between freedom and autonomy. What is it to be free, one might ask, but to have the ability to be the author of one's own actions? But if one meets this condition is one not autonomous? Conversely, to the degree that one is autonomous, to the degree that one can be the author of one's own actions, one has the capacity for free choice. Because of these connections, philosophers often equate freedom and autonomy. Should we accept this equation? That depends on the kind of autonomy we are talking about.

Let us call the sort of autonomy that presupposes the freedom needed for moral responsibility "metaphysical autonomy," and that sort of freedom "metaphysical freedom." It may be, for all that anyone has ever proved, that this kind of autonomy will always remain beyond our reach. There is another kind of autonomy, however, that may be attainable by psychotherapeutic methods, although it may also be possible to gain or enhance it through other means as well.

I will refer to this second kind of autonomy as "inner autonomy," or sometimes just "autonomy." Inner autonomy should be contrasted with an external type of autonomy, the lack of which is caused by such factors as extreme poverty, the oppression of the state, or the coercion of individuals. Psychotherapy is not the treatment of choice for the lack of external autonomy, and it is generally not what psychotherapists have in mind when they support autonomy as a main goal of psychotherapy.

The presence of inner autonomy may also be due to external causes, or it may result from a mixture of both internal and external factors, but it involves a greater psychological component than does external autonomy. What, then, is inner autonomy? There are numerous accounts in the philosophic and psychotherapy literature, although they are called by different names. Here, I will merely cite some important elements, and return to the subject in the next chapter.

Inner autonomy is not an all-or-nothing state; it comes in degrees. One has it to a greater degree to the extent that one has certain capacities and skills, such as the capacity to reflect on one's preferences, desires, and wishes, and the capacity to change them in the light of higher-order preferences or values – see Dworkin's discussion (1988: 20).

It is doubtful, however, that having such capacities and skills is enough. An individual might have them but still be autonomous only to a very small degree because of dysfunctional desires and preferences. He or she might have the capacity to get rid of these desires and preferences, but may never exercise the capacity. Some philosophers try to handle this factor solely in terms of irrationality, but for reasons given in the next chapter, I believe that a wider notion is needed. Some desires and preferences are "defective," whether or not they are irrational, and their presence contributes to a diminishment of the agent's autonomy. (For an explanation of "defective," see the section on defective desires and rationality in the next chapter.)

A third important element is self-control. Sometimes I judge that it is best to do such and such – say, to begin working or to stop eating – but I cannot bring myself to do it. If I do something else, say, continue eating, I may be "the author of my actions," but I may still have little autonomy. If I generally act on impulse and lack the ability to control myself, I may lack the ability to fulfill goals that I deem more important than immediate gratification. To the degree that I am like this, my autonomy is diminished.

Increasing inner autonomy, then, includes these three things (although it may include more): (1) enhancing the capacity to reflect on one's preferences, wishes, and values, and to change them when rational considerations indicate the need for change; (2) actually eliminating one's defective desires, wishes, and values; and (3) increasing the capacity for self-control.

A philosopher primarily interested in the traditional problem of free will and determinism will be unimpressed by the thought that inner autonomy is obtainable. Unless it is shown that autonomy of this sort is sufficient for moral responsibility, such a philosopher will point out, establishing its existence does nothing at all to solve the traditional problem of freedom of the will. I agree, of course, with this point. I also assume that many psychotherapists have some interest in the traditional problem, which is one reason that I have spent time discussing it. However, the traditional problem is not the only one of interest.

Many psychotherapists agree that enhancing the client's autonomy is one desirable goal of psychotherapy; many, not necessarily the same ones, also agree that transforming the field into a science is also a desirable aim. Are these two aims reconcilable? The dilemma of determinism suggests "no." My counter reply is that either premise 3 is false or premises 2 and 3 contain an ambiguity that renders the reasoning invalid. On either option, the argument is unsound.

Let me remind the reader what the relevant two premises say:

2 If it (i.e., determinism) is true, then there is no free choice.
3 If there is no free choice, there is no genuine autonomy.

There is an ambiguity if "free choice" refers in premise 2 to metaphysical freedom (the sort required for moral responsibility) and to a non-metaphysical freedom in premise 3. If, however, "free choice" is used in the metaphysical sense in both premises, then premise 3 is false. For one can pretty clearly have genuine inner autonomy without having metaphysical autonomy or metaphysical freedom. Whichever option is taken, the argument fails to support its conclusion.

I return now to the opening question of this chapter: Can there be both client autonomy and a science of psychotherapy? My answer is "yes." Even if the traditional free will and determinism problem is presently unresolvable, we have good reason for believing that the conditions required for a psychotherapeutic science do not preclude the attainment of the sort of inner autonomy that many psychotherapists seek for their clients.

Even if inner autonomy is attainable to some degree through psychotherapy, *should* that be the main goal of psychotherapy? I take up that question in the next chapter.

2

Values and Morals

Some of the issues that most divide the field of psychotherapy concern therapeutic values. What, for example, should be the primary aim of psychotherapy? As suggested in Chapter 1, many psychotherapists hold that if there is a single, overriding purpose of psychological counseling and psychotherapy, it is the promotion of the client's autonomy, or, as some would say, the client's freedom (Thompson, 1990; Holmes and Lindley, 1989; Ryle, 1982; Kovel, 1978).

Many other psychotherapists, however, emphasize rival values. For example, many cognitive-behavior therapists and cognitive therapists will argue that the primary aim should be the elimination of symptoms (understood in a non-medical sense), or what is sometimes called the client's "presenting problem."

Behavior analysts (those who use operant-based behavior modification techniques) might agree about the desirability of eliminating symptoms, but are likely to stress above all the modification of behavior as opposed to changing cognitions or feelings. Some of them will also argue that autonomy is either in principle unobtainable or is of little clinical value.

Many dynamic therapists, in contrast, do not agree that the primary aim should be the elimination of symptoms. Some would aim mainly at enhancing client autonomy, others at resolution of unconscious conflicts, others at character change, others at the achievement of insight, and still others at getting clients in touch with their feelings. These other goals might be linked to the goal of a more permanent cure, or they might be seen as having value in their own right.

Disagreements about the proper aims of psychotherapy are likely to lead to disagreements about the evaluation of outcomes. Holmes and Lindley (1989) give the following illustration. Suppose that a client emerges from analysis with her symptoms controlled but not eliminated. If she feels and really is more autonomous, realizes her own limitations, and understands some of the causes of her problems, this would be a positive outcome. Yet, if we neglected autonomy and insight, and made symptom remission the sole criterion of success, the therapy would be judged a failure.

Many behavior therapists and cognitive therapists would, in fact, judge the therapy in the above case a failure. Many take the position that even if other benefits are provided, a treatment *is* a failure if there has been no improvement in dealing with the client's presenting problem. As Hans Eysenck puts it (1992: 119), even if the elimination of symptoms is not sufficient for therapeutic success, it is necessary.

The choice of criteria for evaluating aims and outcomes often correlates, not surprisingly, with the theoretical framework of the therapist. Behavior therapists favor one criterion, psychodynamic therapists another. For this reason, some researchers take the position that evaluative criteria must be relativized to a paradigm. We cannot, then, ask whether, say, a psychodynamic therapy is effective in treating a certain problem and type of client. Instead, we must ask whether it is effective *relative to the outcome criteria of that paradigm*. In the end we might be forced to adopt this position, but it has the inconvenience of preventing comparisons across theoretical frameworks. For that reason, it is useful to look for a deeper and theory-neutral criterion that can be used to evaluate the various criteria of competing paradigms. Such a criterion can be fashioned, I believe, in terms of satisfaction of certain types of client desires.

IRRATIONAL AND DEFECTIVE DESIRES

What is wrong with the following criterion for evaluating psychotherapeutic aims and outcomes? Put aside cases where the psychotherapy is being done to further the aims of a prison or corporation, and include only those in which the primary aim is to benefit the client. Why not judge results in terms of whether the client's desires are truly satisfied? If the client wanted something from the therapy – say, sobriety – and was given it, that is a benefit. If the client had an aversion to something – say, a deep depression – and is freed from it, that is a benefit. Perhaps the client did not have his heart set on an increase in ego strength or an improved score on a behavioral checklist, but these things too may be of value to him. They are if they correlate with something else he wants, such as improved mental health or the ability to approach a formerly phobic object. We can determine empirically whether such correlations hold, and we can assess intermediate goals of the client by seeing whether meeting them will satisfy more basic desires.

Is anything more subtle needed? Although I believe the above approach is basically correct, more needs to be said. If that were not so, disputes between different schools of psychotherapy about the value of certain outcomes could be settled entirely through empirical inquiry. Although the empirical issues are important, they are not the only issues.

To begin with, psychodynamic therapists are likely to ask: Which are the *real* desires of the client, the ones that she can bring to consciousness or the ones that are repressed? Others will object that after people enter therapy, they sometimes take on the values of the therapist. There is some research supporting this contention (Tjeltveit, 1986; Jensen and Bergin,

1988). When such a conversion takes place, and the client's desires are altered, should outcomes be judged in terms of the original or new desires? An even more serious problem is that people often have desires that they would not retain if they had more information, or if they altered their characters, and became very different people. Which desires should be given primacy: the current ones or the ones that the client would have under certain, and perhaps more ideal, conditions?

There is an old philosophic theory that bears on such issues. It says, roughly, that the things that are of benefit to a person are those that satisfy not just any desire, but rather the desires that are rational. The most sophisticated contemporary version of this view has been developed by the philosopher Richard Brandt.

Although Brandt's theory (1979) is a general theory of the good, it seems ideally suited for discussing psychotherapy benefits, in particular because of its clinical slant. The key idea is that a "good" thing is one that it is *rational* to desire in the sense that one would continue to desire it after undergoing "cognitive psychotherapy." This therapy – which is not identical to any standard form of cognitive therapy – involves the use of logic, the science of today, and propositions supported by publicly accessible evidence in examining one's desires. Roughly, those desires that would survive such critical examinations are rational.

An important virtue of Brandt's account is that its use requires no appeal to other evaluative criteria; subject to certain qualifications, the theory can be applied empirically. Moreover, in deciding which client preferences are rational, we need not actually provide cognitive therapy. We can often appeal to our background evidence to decide which preferences are likely to meet Brandt's criterion. It is likely, for example, that for most clients, the desire to be free from a crippling anxiety or depression is likely to survive cognitive therapy. The desire to be happy and free is likely to remain intact after cognitive therapy, and so on. In some cases, we may not know enough about a particular client to make a prediction about certain basic preferences, but to some degree, this information can be acquired in the initial interview. Additional evidence can be garnered as the therapy progresses.

To see how Brandt's theory may be used, consider its application to some controversial cases. Suppose that a client is satisfied with his therapy because of his improvement on a Rorschach Test. If the evidence, unknown to him, indicates that the test fails to measure anything of value, then his liking the outcome would presumably not survive cognitive therapy and can be criticized. Or, consider a client of a behavior therapist who reduces his problem drinking, but does not like the result because his reading of Freud convinces him that symptom substitution is inevitable. If the evidence tells against this conviction, then the dislike is not likely to survive cognitive therapy.

These sorts of cases do not involve judgments of intrinsic value; they raise primarily empirical issues. However, consider an actual case of a heterosexual accused of having sex with children. With his consent, his therapist trained him to enjoy homosexual sex. Commentators on the case disagreed strongly as to whether this was a good outcome (Davison, 1976). A similar question can be raised by efforts to "cure" gays of their homosexuality; see the work of Feldman and MacCulloch (1971). In questioning such outcomes, one might be raising a moral issue of what ought to be done rather than one about the value of the result. The moral question is: Whether or not the outcome is beneficial to the client, should the therapist try to produce it? That is not the question of interest here. At this point, I am asking only about the value of the outcome, not about the morality of pursuing that outcome. Once again, on Brandt's theory, if the client desires the outcome and that desire would not be extinguished by cognitive therapy (in Brandt's sense) if the client were to undergo it, then the outcome is good for that client.

The idea that we can separate through purely empirical means a client's rational and irrational desires, and in the process determine on objective grounds which therapeutic outcomes are good for him or her, is an attractive one. Brandt's theory about doing this is, as far as I can determine, the best available. Unfortunately, there are problems. Some of these have been addressed in the philosophic literature (for example, Harman, 1982; Gibbard, 1990; Erwin, 1996).

To take but one example, a problem can arise when a client's irrational desires are too solid to be shaken by cognitive therapy. This is a problem for Brandt's theory because surviving cognitive therapy in his sense is supposed to guarantee that the desire is rational. The inability to uproot certain irrational desires and aversions may also arise when using more standard forms of cognitive therapy. In certain phobias, for example, there are emotional components that are immune to rational attacks. Suppose that a traumatic experience causes me to have an irrational desire to avoid riding elevators. If the aversion is long-standing, and attached to some deep fear, it may survive Brandt's cognitive therapy, or any other kind of cognitive treatment. Other irrational desires may be so woven into my personality that no mere repetition of information will extinguish them. A desire, then, can be irrational and yet have the capacity to survive Brandt's cognitive therapy.

In Erwin (1996), in response to such problems, I suggest that we might keep some of Brandt's useful ideas, but do what Harman (1982) recommends: drop the appeal to cognitive therapy. This would, of course, constitute a drastic change, but as a replacement, we could substitute multiple and more finely tuned criteria for deciding which preferences and aversions are rational. Although this would help, I now believe that there is a deeper problem. Rationality does not exactly demarcate those desires that if satisfied would be good for someone from those that would not. Some desires are neither rational nor irrational: they just are. Yet their satisfaction may be beneficial to the person who has them.

Suppose that I collect bottle caps, but a cognitive therapist convinces me that this is a stupid little hobby. As a consequence, I lose my desire and no longer obtain satisfaction from finding new and interesting bottle caps. The original desire was perhaps not rational, but neither was it irrational; the hobby did me no harm, and its successful pursuit gave me great pleasure, a pleasure that is now lost. The satisfaction of that desire was a good for me even though the desire was neither rational nor irrational.

In other cases, I may be better off without a certain desire, but that is no guarantee that it is irrational. Suppose that I want to run through an elaborate, time-consuming routine before I write any philosophy. Perhaps it involves completing some ceremony. Do I enjoy this routine? I do not. Is it that I believe without evidence that the routine serves a useful purpose? No, I do not believe this. In short, I have a mild obsessive-compulsive habit, but the problem is not one of irrationality. No flaw in my reasoning or defect in my information explains my behavior. I try cognitive therapy, including Brandt's idealized version, but none of it helps. My desire to complete this time-consuming routine is defective in some way, but the defect is not due to bad reasoning or lack of information.

The problem, then, with fixing Brandt's theory by substituting different criteria of rationality is that irrationality is only part of the problem. We need a wider notion that covers cases of irrationality but other benefit defeaters as well. Consequently, I will introduce the notion of "defective" desires and aversions.

I will call a desire "defective" if and only if its satisfaction would provide to the individual who has it either no benefit at all, or one that is very minor or very transitory. An aversion is defective exactly if averting its object would produce for the individual no benefit at all, or, again, one that is very minor or very transitory.

In the absence of an overarching theory of defective desires and aversions, we can at least catalogue some of the general types that are relevant to psychotherapy. They include the following:

First, *irrational desires (or aversions)*. These include primarily those that are due at least partly to faulty logic or incorrect information. For example, a client desires some therapeutic outcome only because the therapist has convinced him that it is of great value. He gets what he wants. His score on a certain test improves, and he gets a seeming "insight" (not a correct one) into the cause of his problems, but neither of these things is of any value to him. Another client wants desperately to work at home, but only because of a false belief about the dangers of leaving the house. A third one values total sexual chastity but only because he has an unwarranted belief about religion, politics, or the likelihood of being infected with the HIV virus.

Second, *incoherent desires*. Desires, unlike beliefs, are not propositional and, consequently, cannot be logically inconsistent, but a set of them may be "incoherent" in that they cannot be jointly satisfied. For example, a client may value fame for its own sake, but its pursuit may cause the sacrifice of something valued even more, such as contentment or integrity.

Third, *futile desires*. Some clients want "everybody to love them;" others desire to be perfect in their behavior. The satisfaction of such desires might be of benefit to them, but it may be unreasonable to prefer such ends to more modest ones if their pursuit is bound to be futile and possibly harmful.

Fourth, *neurotic desires*. Without some explication of what counts as "neurotic," it is not illuminating to talk of such desires, but some such category is needed to cover those not falling into any of the above slots, but whose satisfaction provides no benefit to the individual. A man pursues a career in the law but only because of an unconscious desire (it need not be "unconscious" in the Freudian sense) to punish his father, a famous cardiologist. If he were to become aware of this desire, he would have no interest in pursuing a law career. A woman insists on completing a certain daily ritual that provides no benefit, but only because she has an obsessive-compulsive disorder.

I leave open whether the general category "neurosis" is a useful one. Nevertheless, regardless of what we call them, there are uncontroversial examples, such as the above, where the etiology of a desire in some way causes it to be "defective."

I return now to my earlier question: What is wrong with judging therapeutic outcomes in terms of satisfaction of the client's desires? I mentioned several objections that are likely to be raised. One is that a client may not want a certain outcome because he or she is influenced by certain unconscious wishes, some of which may be repressed. However, by itself, the fact that a desire is unconscious is not a problem. At any given time, most of my desires are outside of consciousness. There is no difference in terms of ownership between those in my preconscious and those that I cannot become aware of except with therapeutic help; they are all *my* desires. The real test is not whether the desires are unconscious, but whether they are defective in some way. If they are not, then satisfaction of them is a benefit to me whether or not they are unconscious, and even if they became unconscious because they were repressed.

As to the second "problem," the adoption of the therapist's values, that too is not in itself a problem. Due to maturation, including listening to good arguments and having certain life experiences, people sometimes change their basic values. Perhaps therapists should be wary in trying to induce such changes, but when they occur the satisfaction of the new desires may be a genuine benefit to the client. Again, the proper test is whether the new desires and preferences are defective. If a therapist convinces a client of the value of making rational decisions and getting one's life in order, the adoption of such values may obviously be helpful to the client. The desire to do these things may be free from any defect even if they arise from adopting the therapist's values.

The third problem that I mentioned is that some clients have desires that they would not retain if they had more information or if they became very different people. These two sorts of changes, however, are quite different. If a client were to change radically, he might become a missionary and no longer obtain satisfaction in making large sums of money, but that does not mean that making money is *now* − that is, before his conversion − of no value to him. In contrast, if someone desires a career in show business only because he is greatly misinformed, his current desire may well be "defective": If he gets his wish, he may derive no benefit from realizing his dream.

In sum, a therapeutic outcome is of more than very minor or transitory value to a client if he or she desired it, and the desire is not defective. For the clinical problems most widely treated in psychotherapy, such as depression, anxiety states, and phobias, we have good reason to believe that the desire for symptom remission is generally non-defective; satisfying these desires generally provides a real benefit to the client, assuming no harm occurs. Whether symptom remission in a particular case is good, all things considered, raises a separate issue, one that is typically empirical. If the depression, say, is caused by an underlying conflict that is left unresolved, the client may be worse off. However, that the elimination of the depression would leave the client worse off, all things considered, obviously has to be demonstrated empirically.

Even if the symptom remission is an unmitigated good in a particular case, there may be other outcomes that are also beneficial, such as an increase in autonomy or even an insight not accompanied by symptomatic change. Finally, in some cases, there may be no specific symptom or "presenting problem," other than a general dissatisfaction with life. The increase in life satisfaction, then, may be the only test of therapeutic success or failure.

THERAPEUTIC AIMS

Assuming, then, that we have an objective test for distinguishing good and bad therapeutic outcomes − by appealing to the *non-defective* desires of the client − we can now turn to therapeutic aims. What should they be? Identifying worthwhile outcomes is necessary for answering this question, but it is not sufficient. There are at least two other questions that need to be addressed.

First, *whose* good ought to be of primary importance? Many psychotherapists, perhaps the majority, are not in private practice. They work for the government, private industry, hospitals, rehabilitation programs, and so on. It is arguable that many of these psychotherapists have a primary obligation to benefit their employer, at least in certain cases. One example might be an industrial psychologist who is hired to assist people receiving disability benefits, because of psychological problems, return to work. Where the interests of the employer and the client clash, the therapist may be obligated to protect the employer. Another example might be a psychiatrist working with violent offenders acquitted as a result of a successful insanity defense. The psychiatrist's first responsibility may be to protect society.

Of course, who pays one's paycheck does not by itself determine whose good should be promoted to first rank. If I work in a prison, it may be in the best interest of the warden if I can get a particular prisoner to do such and such, but if the prisoner is likely to become very depressed and perhaps attempt suicide as a result, I should refrain from adopting the warden's aim as a therapeutic goal.

It is difficult to state an informative, defensible general rule here. Sometimes psychotherapists not in private practice should put the welfare of their employers first; sometimes to do that would be morally reprehensible. Those who argue for the primacy of such aims as the enhancement of autonomy or getting in touch with one's feelings, however, are not talking about cases where it is legitimate to place the client's interests second. They are not suggesting, for example, that in treating prisoners we should increase the autonomy of the warden, or try to get him in touch with his feelings. They are talking primarily about psychotherapists in private practice, or at least those, who for whatever reason, are trying mainly to bring about improvement in the client.

Even in these latter cases, why should the good of the client be primary? From the vantage point of utilitarian moral theory, we always have a moral obligation to promote the total amount of good effects. How these good effects are distributed is of no moral relevance unless it affects the total sum. So, it would seem that if I can do more good by sacrificing the client's welfare for the good of his brothers (after all, there are three of them, and only one of him), then that is what I should do.

A plausible response to this line of reasoning is that psychotherapists in private practice typically enter into what lawyers call a "fiduciary relationship" with their clients. The therapist promises to act in the client's best interests, or at least deliberately creates the rational expectation that this will be done. In this respect, the psychotherapist typically acts like a medical doctor; both undertake a special obligation to their patients because of the expectations and trust they deliberately create. The obligation is only what philosophers term "prima facie"; it can be overridden by a higher obligation, such as the obligation to warn the police that the client is planning a murder. Still, the therapist should not demote the client's interests merely because that would help other people, and increase the total amount of good in the world.

In fact, utilitarians rarely, if ever, deny that the client's welfare, at least in private practice, should come first. They argue, rather, that when therapists enter into a fiduciary relationship, the ultimate reason for looking after the client's welfare is that, in the long run, doing so will maximize the total amount of good in the world.

It does not matter here whether the utilitarian or non-utilitarian is right about the ultimate ground of the obligation to place the client's welfare first, so long as there is one. If there is, then we have at least a partial answer to our first question about whose good should be aimed at. Where the therapist enters into a fiduciary relationship with the client (which happens typically in private practice, and sometimes outside of private practice), the main aim of the therapy should be to promote the client's good.

I take this point to be relatively uncontroversial. Now, however, there is a second question to be answered. In cases where the client's welfare should be primary, which of the many possible outcomes that would be good for him or her should dictate the goals of therapy? Here, there is more likelihood of controversy. I will begin with autonomy.

A Critique of Autonomy as the Primary Goal of Psychotherapy

As noted in Chapter 1, autonomy is often recommended as the main, if not the only, legitimate goal of psychotherapy.

What are the arguments for this position? One runs like this. There are no objective values, or at least none that can be established as correct. Consequently, the therapist should increase the client's autonomy so that he or she can better make his or her own value decisions.

This argument is incoherent. The therapist accepts a certain evaluative assumption: that if there are no objectively true value judgments, then autonomy *should* be the main goal. The therapist then tries to defend *this* value judgment on the grounds that no value judgment, including his or her own, is true (or false), or at least is known to be true.

A more plausible approach is to argue that autonomy does have objective value. Thus, Holmes and Lindley argue (1989: 52–64) that pleasurable experience is but one of the constituents of well-being; autonomy, they claim, is one of the most important other constituents. They further claim (page 142) that psychotherapy matters *because* autonomy matters, and that "The crucial evaluative assumption on which the case for psychotherapy depends is that personal autonomy has intrinsic worth as a part of human well-being."

I will assume that they are correct in this one respect: Autonomy does have intrinsic value, at least for many people. Still, without additional premises, nothing follows about the desirable aims of psychotherapy. As Holmes and Lindley concede, there may be other things that have intrinsic value; perhaps one of these should be aimed at, or perhaps, we should not set as a therapeutic goal the achievement of any particular intrinsic good. The argument of Holmes and Lindley, then, fails to show that the primary aim of psychotherapy ought to be enhancement of client autonomy. More is needed than a showing that autonomy is intrinsically good. That might not matter if we can supplement their argument, but there are positive reasons for doubting that autonomy should be the main or only goal.

First, the main objection to making autonomy the main goal is that quite often this is not what the client wants. In some such cases, the client is confused about his own welfare, and it may be reasonable for the therapist to use rational persuasion to convince him of the value of a certain therapeutic outcome, such as autonomy enhancement. Not all cases, however, are like this.

Suppose that I am a scientist and I come to you for treatment of a sleep disorder. You judge that I would be even happier if you treated something else, say my drinking too much alcohol. Perhaps you are right, but at this juncture, I may care little about being happy, and care much more about getting on with my work, which I cannot do if I cannot sleep properly. I came to you for treatment of my insomnia; I am making no mistake in wanting this problem treated; and it is in my best interest that this problem, and not some other one, be treated. You value happiness above all, but you are not the client.

Substitute "autonomy" for "happiness" and the same problem arises. It is not that autonomy or happiness are of no value to me; it is, rather, that doing science is of more importance.

Even if I were to value autonomy a bit more than doing excellent scientific work, it might still be better for me, all things considered, to make the elimination of my insomnia the therapeutic goal. I desire the capacity to sleep, but I also have second-order desires: that this desire for sleep, and not some other desire of mine, be satisfied now; and that the therapist treat the problem that I asked him or her to treat. When the benefits of satisfying these second-order desires are added in, they may tilt the scales against autonomy.

In the above case, if the therapist lets his clinical theory or basic value system dictate a substitute therapeutic goal, one not desired by the client, he is not aiming at what is best for his client. The harder case is where the therapist's judgment is correct; given the client's own values, she is better off with outcome X rather than Y, the one she desires. Even here, the fact that I would be better off is not by itself sufficient for the therapist to override my desires *if*, paradoxically, I have a right to autonomy. Roughly put, if I want some Y – say, good health – and my desire is not defective (it is not due to a false belief, and so on), then I should not be deprived of it *merely* because I would be better off with a substitute. Of course, I may have no right to the means by which to get to that result. Except in special cases, you are not obligated to treat me at all.

Not everyone will grant that we have a right to autonomy. Some utilitarians are driven to an extreme sort of paternalism, which requires (not merely permits) me to choose what is best for you if my choice is correct, and on balance there is no sacrifice in anyone else's good. However, even many utilitarians will agree that each of us, subject to

certain conditions, should choose for ourselves. They explain the desirability of doing so not as due to our having a separate right of autonomy,
but on the grounds that we are more likely to maximize the good if each
of us chooses for ourselves how we wish to live.

Those who believe in the value of autonomy are not logically
compelled to agree to a right of autonomy or to a utilitarian justification
for respecting the client's autonomy. To those who believe in either one,
however, it should be objectionable to make autonomy the goal merely
because the client would be somewhat better off than if his or her
therapeutic aims were satisfied. Those who accept an extreme paternalism
will not be bothered by this objection, but we can still ask: Why should
this particular good – that is, autonomy – be aimed at when the client in
full clarity of mind seeks a different good? In other words, what is the
justification for adopting extreme paternalism?

Second, there are also practical problems in making autonomy the
primary goal. One is that it is often unclear what is meant by "autonomy."
In the last chapter, I explained the idea in terms of three elements: (1) the
capacity for rational reflection; (2) the tendency to eliminate defective
desires; and (3) the capacity for self-control. There are, however, many
different accounts of autonomy in the literature of philosophy and
psychotherapy. Although these accounts often overlap, without some
specification of what is meant, it is hard to know whether different
psychotherapists are talking about the same thing when they endorse
autonomy.

Third, suppose that we fix on a single account of autonomy and
explain the concept in a satisfactory fashion. There is still a measurement
problem, unless our explanation is couched in operational terms. One of
the main barriers to making psychotherapy a science is the difficulty in
measuring outcomes even where we have a relatively clear idea of what
we are aiming at, such as diminishment of depression or anxiety. If we
substitute for symptom relief the idea of autonomy enhancement, we are
likely to make the measurement of outcomes far more problematic.

Fourth, in the United States, at least, psychotherapy is often funded by
health insurance. Another practical problem, then, is that insurance
companies may be unwilling to pay for treatment where the main goal is
to increase autonomy.

Some of the above practical problems may be fixable, but there is still
the primary problem: People who undergo psychotherapy, and who are
not confused, often want something other than autonomy. Very often
what they want is symptom relief. Not to aim at what they want is not to
aim at their good.

Psychoanalytic Goals

Psychoanalysts (including psychoanalytically orientated psychotherapists)
do not all have the same therapeutic values, nor do they all agree about

the proper aims of psychotherapy. Nevertheless, their choice of goals is often influenced by Freudian theory or some newer psychoanalytic variant. For example, intermediate goals often involve improvement on the basis of some psychoanalytic criterion. Thus, in a recent review of the outcome evidence, Bachrach et al. (1991) conclude that patients suitable for analysis derive substantial benefits from their therapy, but the reviewers stress that they evaluate the evidence from a specifically *psychoanalytic* perspective. They, therefore, judge outcomes to be favorable on the basis of a wide variety of specifically psychoanalytic criteria including: insight into core conflicts, transference resolution, change in ego strength, object relations and affect availability, and so on.

Apart from the use of the above criteria, therapists heavily influenced by Freud will often set as one of the main goals of therapy the elimination of unconscious conflicts or the bringing of repressed wishes to consciousness. The result is that the client's so-called "symptom," the problem that motivated the client to undergo therapy, may be intact at the termination of the therapy and yet the treatment may be judged a partial success. For example, in one of the studies reviewed by Bachrach et al. (1991: 880), a client came to treatment because of insecurity and difficulties in dealing with women. There was no indication in the report that *this* problem was resolved to any degree, but the client was judged "moderately improved" on the basis of his acquiring "helpful intellectual insights." Some analysts would go further and hold that eliminating the symptom without eliminating the underlying unconscious conflict makes the client worse off.

The difficulty in adopting specifically psychoanalytic outcome aims is primarily empirical. Is Freudian theory about the origin or maintenance of psychoneurotic problems supported by credible evidence? Does analysis typically yield real (namely, correct) insight into the cause of one's psychological problems? Does symptom substitution typically occur after "cures" that are only symptomatic? I take up such questions in Part II, Chapter 7, where I argue that the Freudian account is generally unfounded. If I am right, that raises serious doubts about adopting specifically psychoanalytic outcome aims. There is, however, another problem. If a client comes to therapy to lose weight, to diminish her drinking, or to overcome her depression, it may be a serious violation of her autonomy if the analyst takes advantage of her vulnerable condition and convinces her to substitute some theory-driven goal for the one that she herself wants met, and wants met for a perfectly good reason.

Pluralism and Client Autonomy

The search for a single legitimate aim of psychotherapy will fail because there is no such aim. That is so for two reasons, one concerning pluralism and the other autonomy.

What is intrinsically good for one client may be different for another. For some people, happiness is the only thing that is good in and of itself. It is not merely that they have a theory about this (although they may); rather, given their personality, character, life plans, and so on, happiness, and happiness alone, really is good *for them* whether or not its possession leads to other goods. They may also value autonomy and good mental health, but only in so far as these things contribute to their happiness. For others, all three are intrinsically good for them. Others may have a much larger list of intrinsic goods, and include most or all of the following: happiness, autonomy, good health, longevity, knowledge, love, friendship, virtue, conscious experience, and so forth.

Given this plurality of intrinsic goods, it would be unreasonable to select one – say, autonomy – as *the* only legitimate goal of therapy. It would be unreasonable, furthermore, even if the achievement of autonomy was always best for the client. Clients do not always want what is in fact best for them.

Suppose, in the case discussed earlier, you argue that I have a serious drinking problem, and that it would be better for me if we tried to eliminate this problem before attacking the insomnia. I agree, but I like good wine, and I do not want to stop drinking it altogether. So, I very much want to aim at becoming a moderate drinker. You believe that total abstinence should be the goal. What should you do?

One option is not to take me on as a client, but suppose you do. Another is to give me a rational argument why abstinence is the preferable goal. That seems reasonable in this case. You are not, after all, coercing me or brainwashing me to accept your point of view. To paraphrase John Stuart Mill, when he objected to the state coercing someone merely for the person's own good, you are merely *remonstrating* with me. However, I tell you that I have read the literature on alcoholism, and found numerous studies in which people with serious alcohol problems were taught social drinking without any additional problems or relapse. I insist that moderate drinking should be the goal for me. Now, what should you do? There are other possible considerations, such as cost-effectiveness and the possibility that achieving my goal will end not just in a lesser good but in a terrible tragedy. Assuming that none of these things is present in this case, surely it is permissible to respect my wishes, even if it is not obligatory, if both outcomes are good but abstinence is slightly better.

In the above case, I assumed that it would be permissible to use rational persuasion to convince me to adopt your goal. It is far from clear, however, that the therapist should always attempt to change the client's mind. Suppose the client's choice is dictated by a deep religious or political conviction. You have evidence that the conviction is mistaken, and that the client would be much better off if he chose a different therapeutic aim. This sort of case raises a difficult issue, one that is particularly troublesome for cognitive therapists who try to cure by eliminating false beliefs and faulty reasoning (see Part II, Chapter 6). However, we need not look for a general rule here. It is enough for my point that, in some cases, the therapist should not try to thwart the desire of the client to hold on to the religious or political belief that gives his life meaning.

The upshot of all this is that, even if the therapist knows that the pursuit of autonomy or some other such aim would be better for the client, it might still be legitimate, perhaps even obligatory, to seek a lesser good out of respect for the client's right to make her own life choices. So, there would be no single legitimate aim of psychotherapy even if only one thing were intrinsically good for all of us, which in fact is not the case.

As I noted earlier, there are practical problems as well in choosing autonomy as the main therapeutic goal. One of these, the measurement of outcomes, will arise if we substitute for autonomy some other intrinsic good. Both in practice and in the study of outcomes, we need a more precise specification of aims than the production of happiness, the reduction of pain, enhancement of autonomy, and so on. Of course, if the only thing that the client ultimately values is, say, happiness, then the *ultimate* goal, in so far as we wish to benefit her, should be to make her happier, but we still need a more precise criterion to determine whether the ultimate goal is met.

"Symptom relief" is one such criterion. The idea can be made precise by explaining it in terms of the particular problem that the client, after adequate reflection and consultation, wants resolved: the depression, anxiety, marital problem, phobia, drug addiction, alcoholism, and so forth. These items, in turn, can often be expressed in either behavioral or quantitative terms, or both. The main reason, however, for using symptom relief as the main intermediate aim is that this is what clients generally desire. In some cases, the desire may be defective, but often it is not.

A therapy may still be partly successful without providing symptom relief; there are other possible outcomes of value to the client, such as insight into the cause of one's problems or increasing one's self-esteem. Nevertheless, where clients have a non-defective desire for symptom relief, and where that ought to be the goal, then the failure even to diminish the severity of the symptom ought to count heavily in judging the therapy a failure.

Some defenders of autonomy as the main therapeutic goal may complain that I have misunderstood their position. They might agree that symptom relief should be the main goal, at least where there is a concrete problem, but claim that the fundamental reason for choosing this goal is that meeting it enhances autonomy. If I relieve your depression, lower your weight, reduce your problem drinking, solve your marital problems, and so on, I make you more autonomous. If that is the position of a particular autonomy advocate, that diminishes our disagreement, but I still have two complaints.

First, many supporters of autonomy contrast it with symptom relief. If they now agree that symptom relief should generally be the main goal, they have seriously misrepresented and now trivialized their position to a large degree. Second, although "autonomy," at least when explained in a certain way, is an important benefit, other things, as I suggested earlier, are also intrinsically beneficial to different people. The therapist may value autonomy above all, but for me, pleasure or happiness may be the only intrinsic good; autonomy may be of value to me only because of its instrumental value. It is not even true, then, that the ultimate justification for all clients for reducing symptoms is the enhancement of autonomy.

3

The Self in Psychotherapy

In recent decades, theories of the self have proliferated in the field of psychotherapy. Some of these theories either raise or purport to answer, or in some other way bear on, traditional philosophic questions about the self.

One reason for this interest in the self is that many think of psychotherapy as essentially an exploration or treatment of the self. To use Michel Foucault's phrase, psychotherapies are said to be "technologies of the self." Whether the ultimate therapeutic goal is autonomy, symptom relief, character change, or something else, the means of getting there is thought to be discovery of the "real" or "true" self, or, as some would say, the integration of the self. Given the popularity of this way of looking at psychotherapy, it is not surprising that the concept of the self has come to play a key role in many psychotherapeutic theories. In addition, there are certain types of clinical phenomena that invite questions about the self, including multiple personality disorder (dissociative identity disorder), pathological narcissism, and self-deception.

Discussions of the many theoretical and clinical issues have generated a psychotherapeutic literature on the self that is extremely rich, chaotic, and difficult to systematize. Adding to the complexities is the existence of a vast body of work on the self in related disciplines such as social psychology and philosophy, as well as an even larger body of work employing related concepts, such as "ego," "soul," "mind," and "psyche."

Given the size of the topic, it would be futile to aim for completeness of coverage here. The theories that are briefly discussed, however, represent some of the most influential work on the self by leading psychotherapists from various research traditions.

PSYCHOTHERAPEUTIC THEORIES OF THE SELF

Psychoanalytic Theories

As with much else in psychotherapy, Sigmund Freud laid the groundwork for much current thinking about the self. Yet he uses the term "self" only sparingly, and not always in the same sense. As his editor points out in the introduction to the *Ego and the Id*, Freud sometimes uses the expression "das Es" to refer to a person's whole self (including, perhaps, his body) and sometimes to part of one's mind (*SE* XIX: 1923–1925). This ambiguity, and others, pervades the psychotherapeutic literature.

Does Freud have a theory of the self? The answer depends on what is meant by "self." If we are referring to part of the mind, namely the ego, then, of course, he has a theory about both how it develops out of the id and of the role it plays in unconscious psychic conflicts. If we mean "person," then again Freud has such a theory; indeed, any psychological theory about people is about selves if "self" is equated with "person." To state his theory about the self in this second sense would require one to state virtually all of Freudian theory (see Chapter 7 for some of the more important elements).

Compared with Freud's formulations, a concept of self attains a greater importance in the writings of British object-relations theorists and American self psychologists. Many of these theorists consider themselves psychoanalysts, but reject, or at least modify, significant parts of Freudian theory. One example is their downgrading the importance of the Oedipal period for the development of psychopathology. Object-relations theorists and self psychologists trace the roots of clinical problems to events occurring in the pre-Oedipal period, especially the first year of life.

A second contested hypothesis is commonly referred to as Freud's "instinct" or "drive" theory. Freud postulates biologically determined sexual and aggressive drives that, together with environmental inputs, basically determine, along with the operation of the mental apparatus, all behavior. This instinct theory serves as a foundation for the further view that psychopathology essentially involves psychic conflict among the id, ego, and superego. Object-relation theorists and self psychologists both reject the instinct theory, and replace it with the idea that the infant's relation to its "objects" are crucial in determining whether or not psychopathology develops.

Some of the main ideas of the British object-relations theorists were developed by Melanie Klein, others by a group of analysts who either were under her influence or were reacting to her modifications of Freudian theory. The group includes among others: W.R.D. Fairbairn, D.W. Winnicott, Harry Guntrip, and John Bowlby.

Besides rejecting Freud's instinct theory and his emphasis on Oedipal events, object-relations theorists stress the relationship of a human being to his or her "objects." As one such theorist puts it, psychology becomes on this view "the study of the relationships of the individual to his objects, whilst, in similar terms, psychopathology may be said to resolve itself more specifically into a study of the relationships of the ego to its internalized objects" (Fairbairn, 1952: 137).

The key concept, that of an "object," applies to physical objects in the infant's immediate environment, or to parts of an object, such as the mother's breast, or, more usually, to persons, especially the mother but also the father. The term is also used by some writers to refer as well to mental objects, such as the baby's image of the mother. Some analysts influenced by the object-relations theorists, however, restrict the use of the term to human beings (Cashdan, 1988: 3; Kernberg, 1976: 58).

A second influential hypothesis, formulated by Fairbairn, concerns the splitting of the ego – some would say "self"; see Cashdan (1988: 44–8) on the splitting of the self. The infant, on this view, initially relates to external objects, especially the mother, but then divides the object, or rather its perception of it, into a good and bad object, internalizing the latter in order to gain control of it. The "bad" object is then split into an exciting and rejecting object, both of which are repressed by the ego. Because parts of the ego remain attached to the repressed objects and part do not, there is a "splitting" of the ego – see Eagle's useful discussion (1984: 77–9).

Other major theses pertain to the development of the true and false self. According to Winnicott (1960), if, soon after birth, the infant's spontaneous responses are met by the "good enough" mother in such a way that it develops a sense of "omnipotence," it begins to accept external reality as if it were not threatening. This feeling leads to the development of the "true self," or what Winnicott sometimes calls "the central self" (1960: 590). If the mother's responses are not adequate, the infant experiences anxiety and develops a "false self." In some adults, the false self exists as a massive defense against painful environmental stimuli, and hides the true self. Psychopathology then develops in the form of what Winnicott terms a "false self disorder." Viewing psychopathology in this way leads naturally to the theory that psychopathology is essentially a disorder of the self rather than a reflection of unconscious conflicts.

The writings of the object-relations school have had an enormous influence on the development of self psychology, a school of analysis originated by the late Hans Kohut. It is in the writings of the self psychologists that the concept of self becomes most prominent in the area of psychoanalysis.

In his early writings (especially, his 1971), Kohut develops a theory about one kind of clinical problem, narcissistic personality disorder, that allegedly has a different etiology from the typical psychoneuroses, the so-called "transference neuroses." He agrees that the latter exist, and that their central psychopathology concerns structural conflicts over libidinal and aggressive striving, as Freud had claimed. Kohut holds, however, that the central psychopathology of the narcissistic personality disorders concerns the self and what he calls "archaic narcissistic objects" (page 19).

One way of distinguishing the two sorts of disorders is in terms of symptomatology. Patients with narcissistic personality disorders, in contrast with those suffering from transference neurosis, tend to display the following characteristics. Their symptoms are initially ill defined, and the patients are not able to focus on the essential aspects of their problem (although they recognize secondary problems such as work inhibitions or trends toward perverse sexual activities). As the analysis progresses, however, the most significant symptomatic features can usually be discerned with clarity. Patients will describe pervasive feelings of emptiness and depression; they will let the analyst know, especially when the transference has been disrupted, that their emotions are dulled, or that they feel as if they were not fully real, or that they work without zest.

Although the above symptoms do occur frequently in cases of narcissistic personality disturbance, Kohut holds (page 23) that the crucial diagnostic criterion is to be based not on symptomatology but on the analysis of the transference.

There are three kinds of transference that occur in the analysis of narcissistic personality disorders: a mirroring, idealizing, and twinship transference. Each of these reflects a different kind of "selfobject" need of childhood.

There is some confusion about what this crucial term "selfobject" refers to, and even how to spell it; Kohut (1971) hyphenates the term, other self psychologists do not. Some writers use the term to refer to people, especially the parents, who are important in the child's development. What makes them "selfobjects" is that they are not clearly differentiated by the child from its self (see Lynch, 1991: 18). Kohut himself sometimes uses "selfobject" to refer to persons, as do other self psychologists. For example, one writer says that the fragmenting self is "caused by the unresponsiveness of childhood selfobjects," which suggests that a selfobject is a person (Nicholson, 1991: 31).

Yet Kohut also talks (1971: 32) as if a selfobject is not a person but the mental representation of one, as when he equates the narcissistic object with the idealized parent imago (that is, image). Other writers define "selfobject" not as a person or an image but as a *relationship* between a self and another person (White and Weiner, 1986: 13). So, a selfobject could be a person, a relationship, or a mental representation of a parent or some other person of significance to the child. However, to make sense of what Kohut is saying in many contexts, "selfobjects" should be interpreted to refer to mental representations, especially images.

To return to the different types of transference postulated by Kohut, each one reflects experience of a lack of satisfactory response by a parent or other to a different type of need of the child. These needs correspond to three different sectors of the self: the grandiose, idealizing, and twinship sectors. As to the first, the child has a need of "mirroring" responses from others; that is, ones that seem to confirm the child's sense of his or her own greatness. Second, the child has a need of others whom it can see as infallible or perfect, or in some respect ideal. Third, the child needs to experience others who resemble it, who act as its "twin."

The failure to satisfy one of these needs will be reflected in one of the several types of transference. In the mirroring transference, the therapist is experienced as part of the patient's grandiose self. The patient is likely to have an inflated view of himself, and will often express rage and disappointment with the therapist's perceived shortcomings. In the idealized transference, the therapist, in contrast, is seen as all-knowing and impotent – in short, as a reflection of the idealized parent. In the twinship transference, the patient will see the therapist and himself as if they were very much alike, sharing the same values and beliefs.

If the transference neuroses are essentially the result of unconscious psychic conflicts, the key problem with those with narcissistic personality disorders, according to self psychologists, is one of self-deficit: the failure to develop an intact self. In early infancy, the child is thought to have a nuclear self, but beginning at about 18 months a tripolar self develops. If the needs of one or more poles of this tripolar self are unmet, then the individual develops a fragmented self.

What are the signs of a fragmented self? Someone with a "healthy narcissism," as one self psychologist puts it, exhibits self-confidence and self-esteem, and is able to develop stable and growth-producing relationships, whereas the pathologically narcissistic individual, the person with the fragmented self, has grandiose fantasies of self-importance, a sense of entitlement, and an inability to see others as anything but need-gratifying objects (Nicholson, 1991: 27–8).

Self psychologists disagree somewhat about which elements of their treatment cure, but it is generally agreed that interpretation of the transference is but one factor, and not necessarily the most important. Other elements include the use of empathy, the therapist's placing himself imaginatively in the center of the patient's inner world (Ornstein and Ornstein, 1984: 4), acceptance, and understanding on the part of the therapist.

Finally, if self psychology is a theory of treatment and etiology of one type of clinical disorder, pathological narcissism, then it may be merely an important addition to psychoanalysis, as some of Kohut's colleagues claim (for example, Basch, 1989: 20). However, in his later writings, Kohut applies his ideas to far more than one type of clinical disorder. In any event, he does not speak for all self psychologists, some of whom claim that *all* psychological difficulties are disorders of the self (Nicholson, 1991: 30). Conceived in this much broader fashion, self psychology constitutes a clear rival to traditional Freudian theory and therapy. Whether it should be classified as non-Freudian psychoanalysis or not a version of psychoanalysis at all is harder to decide.

The views of at least one other influential psychoanalytic theorist of the self warrant mention. The American analyst Otto Kernberg embraces some of the ideas of the object-relations school, but applies them within the traditional Freudian framework of the dynamic unconscious, the sexual and aggressive drives, and the id–ego–superego mental apparatus; for a comparison with the views of Kohut, see Akhtar (1989). When the analysis of defense mechanisms permits the emergence of the previously repressed into consciousness, Kohut notes, what we observe are not simply drive derivatives but repressed internalized object relations. The repressed unconscious, he continues, is constituted by real or fantasied repressed internalized relationships of the patient with parental objects under the influence of sexual and aggressive drives. We never observe pure drives in clinical practice, but only drive-invested object relations (Kernberg, 1987: 4).

Employing this idea of infantile experience of parental objects, Kernberg sketches an account of how the self originates. Very roughly, the self is said to develop out of the infant's unconscious experience of early objects. It is a structure, according to Kernberg, that emerges within the original ego/id, and later the ego, which gradually evolves into a central position within the intrapsychic world and the total personality (Kernberg, 1987: 19–21).

Discussion Some of the most important issues about the various psychoanalytic theories are empirical and, in a broad sense, "epistemological"; some of these are taken up in Chapter 7. Here, I want to raise a conceptual issue: What is meant by the term "self" in psychoanalysis? As has already been suggested, there is more than one answer. I began by noting that Freud sometimes used the term to refer to a person and at other times to part of a person (that is, the ego).

Later analysts introduced still other uses of the concept of self. For example, in an influential paper on the psychoanalytic theory of the ego, Heinz Hartmann (1950: 84) notes that in analysis, a clear distinction is not always made between the terms "ego," "self," and "personality." Assuming that he is correct, but that analysts are not merely guilty of conceptual confusion, a third sense of "self" needs to be added to our list: in some psychoanalytic writings, the term means "personality." In the works of other analysts, the self is identified with the entire mental apparatus, namely, the combination of id-ego-superego.

In the writings of some of the object-relations theorists, the self, or at least the "true self," is said to be not the entire personality but rather the "core" of it (Winnicott, 1960: 590).

Self psychologists use the term "self" in still other senses. For example, Kernberg (1987: 18) uses it to refer to what he calls "self-representations." In his early work, Kohut apparently means the same thing when he talks of the self as "a content of the mental apparatus" (1971: xv). He also says explicitly that the self is not one of the agencies of the mind (see 1971: xv). In his later writings, however, when he talks of a "superordinate self," he writes as if it were an agent within the person with its own drives and/or defenses (Kohut, 1977: 97; Kohut and Wolf, 1978: 414).

Other writers on self psychology also write as if the self is an inner agent. For example, the nuclear self, which the child is believed to have at birth, is said to develop, under favorable conditions, into an adult cohesive self which will "guide the higher forms of narcissism" and participate in the fulfillment of sexual and assertive needs (White and Weiner, 1986: xix–xx).

The above list is incomplete. Some analysts talk of different kinds of self, such as the real self, the nuclear self, the bi-polar self, the fragmented self, and so on. However, we already have a rather large list of uses of the term "self," enough to raise the points that I want to address. The list includes the use of the term to refer to: (1) a person, (2) the ego, (3) the mental apparatus, (4) a personality, (5) the core of one's personality, (6) a set of self representations, and (7) an inner agent.

The first, and most obvious, point to make about these uses is that when different analysts propound theories of the self, they are often talking about very different sorts of things. It would not be unfair, in fact, to refer to the collection of psychoanalytic writings about the self as a conceptual mess. In saying this, I am not suggesting that merely because of the various, often unexplained, uses of the term "self" there is irremediable unclarity. We could in principle complete the job that I began; we could move through all of the writings of Freud and his successors, and for each passage in which "self" appears, clarify the sense in which the term is used.

A more substantive point is that even after the proper distinctions are made, unclarity remains concerning *some* of the psychoanalytic uses of the concept of self. Some philosophers and psychologists, primarily eliminative materialists and some behaviorists, would find all of the above concepts of self mysterious in so far as they presuppose the existence of something mental. Putting such general anti-mentalistic concerns aside, however, it is primarily uses (2) and (7) that raise deep metaphysical questions.

If the self is conceived of as an agent, as in sense (7), as it often is in self psychology and (perhaps less often) in object-relations theory, if it is said to be something with its own drives, desires, and defenses, then traditional metaphysical questions may well be asked. What sort of thing are we talking about? Are we postulating an entity of some sort? Is it supposed to be part of the brain, or something irreducibly mental? How, if at all, is it related to an individual's self–identity?

Metaphysical issues need not arise if we use "self" in sense (2) – that is, if we identify the self with the ego; whether they do or not depends on how the ego, in turn, is conceived. Some leading ego psychologists distinguish self and ego, but go on to treat the ego itself as an agent, as something who decides and acts. For example, one influential ego psychologist, Heinz Hartmann (1950: 75), says of the ego that it organizes and controls motility and perception, that it tests reality, and that one of its functions is action. Another analyst says explicitly that the ego is an agent, also that it is an organizer, balancer, and central regulator, something that perceives, thinks, and acts (Hamilton, 1988: 21–2). If this is how we think of the ego, then the traditional metaphysical questions about the self will arise concerning it, regardless of whether we identify the self with the ego or distinguish between the two.

When the self is thought of as inner agent, an entity who thinks and decides, the thing that is postulated is sometimes referred to as a

"Cartesian self" because this is how Descartes conceptualized the self. However, Descartes also believed that the self survives when the body dies, but not everyone who believes in a self as inner agent agrees with this thesis. So, it needs to be understood that to believe in a Cartesian self is not necessarily to share all of Descartes' beliefs about the self.

Even analysts who define "self" reductively sometimes use it in a non-reductive fashion, to postulate something of apparent metaphysical interest. As I noted earlier, Kohut first used the term to refer to mental representations, but later used it to refer to something with its own drives and defenses. Kernberg, too, equates the self with a set of mental representations, but also writes of the self *and* self-representations (as if they were different), and talks of "the self as postulated by philosophers" as coming into full existence (1987: 19, 11). Although he does not specify the philosophers he has in mind, I assume that Kernberg does not mean the postulation of mental representations. Furthermore, he links his study of the self to philosophic issues concerning the mind-body problem, personal identity, and freedom (1987: 3), again suggesting that he has more in mind than a set of mental representations.

Even if some psychoanalytic theories of the self are postulating an inner agent of some sort, are questions about its alleged nature relevant to psychotherapy? Of course one can practice psychotherapy without serious concern about metaphysics. Yet some of the theories in question are influential, and do purport to explain the development of psychopathology in terms of the origin and, in some cases, the splitting of, or lack of cohesion of, the self. These theories, in turn, provide the rationale for doing therapy in one way rather than another. For these reasons, it is relevant to ask: What are they talking about when they postulate a self?

Some analysts appear to be unconcerned about this question because the self, they say, is just a construct. This view, however, is incorrect. The *term* "self" may be a construct, just as "neutrino" or "virus" may be said to be constructs, but what the terms allegedly refer to are not themselves constructs. Nor is the self as postulated by analysts merely an abstraction, as some contend. In order for the theories in question to be correct, the self must enter in some way into causal relations. It needs to be explained how an abstraction could do that.

I will return to questions about the nature of the self in the second part of this chapter. Before doing that, I want to look briefly at how the concept of self is used in other psychotherapeutic research traditions besides psychoanalysis.

Humanistic Psychotherapy

It is not clear that the expression "humanistic psychotherapy" picks out a distinct paradigm or school of thought in the field of psychotherapy. The term "humanistic psychologist" was used in the 1950's and 1960's to refer to a diverse group including client-centered therapists, phenomenological and existential psychologists, and indeed virtually any psychologist who was not a psychoanalyst or behaviorist. Later, however, the use of the term was widened to include some psychoanalysts, cognitivists, and even behaviorists. Consequently, it would be difficult today to say precisely what distinguishes humanists from non-humanists. In any event, I will not attempt to draw such a distinction here. However, within what was called the "humanistic" camp, there is a clearly identifiable school of psychotherapy, that of client-centered therapy (now more commonly referred to as 'person-centred therapy), whose founder, Carl Rogers, has been one of the most influential of all psychotherapists in the twentieth century. It is his views of the self that I want to consider.

In a large number of books and articles, Rogers lays out a clear vision of what ought to be done in psychotherapy. It is not, he holds, the training or technical skill of the therapist that determines therapeutic success; what is crucial, instead, is the therapist's holding of certain attitudes and communicating them to the client. In his early writings (for example, Rogers, 1951), he stresses the therapist's belief in the worth and dignity of the individual, and the capacity to provide a relationship of safety and freedom in accord with his basic respect for the client. In his later writings, he specifies exactly three attitudes that, if communicated by the therapist and perceived by the client, are necessary and sufficient for therapeutic success (Rogers, 1989b: 10). These are: congruence or genuineness, unconditional positive regard, and a sensitively accurate empathetic understanding.

The first of these, Rogers holds, is the most basic of the three. People who play a role, who say things they do not feel, are said to be exhibiting "incongruence." They are not being "genuine." The genuine person presents himself or herself transparently or openly, exactly as he or she really is. "Genuineness in therapy," Rogers writes (1989b: 11–12), "means that the therapist is his actual self during his encounter with his client."

Genuineness, or congruence, is required for the activation of the other two conditions which are also necessary for therapeutic success. The second condition, that of unconditional positive regard, requires the therapist to communicate a deep and genuine caring *uncontaminated by evaluations of the client's thoughts, feelings, or behavior.* (Rogers does mention one class of exceptions to this rule about being non-judgmental: clients who are either extremely immature or regressed. He mentions (1989b: 14) in particular certain chronic and unmotivated schizophrenic clients.) This communication of unconditional positive regard, Rogers notes (1989b: 14), provides the non-threatening context in which "the client can explore and experience the most deeply shrouded elements of his inner self."

If there is anything that constitutes the "work" of the therapist, it is his or her satisfaction of the third condition: The therapist must perceive accurately the feelings and experiences of the client. The focus of the therapist should be on, what Rogers calls (1989b: 22), the "immediate phenomenal world" of the client. He must sense the client's fear, confusion, anger, or rage as if it were his own, and then communicate this understanding to the client, allowing the client more clearly to sense and formulate his own fear, rage, and so on.

Although the concept of self is used in some of Rogers' early work, it becomes more important in his later writings in his description of therapy. The data of therapy, he notes (1989b: 23), made it seem imperative that more attention be paid to the "place of the self" in the client's experience of personality disorganization, and subsequent change and reintegration. He writes (1989b: 24, quoting himself):

> Yet so much of the verbal interchange of therapy had to do with the self that attention was forcibly turned in this direction. The client felt that he was not being his real self, often felt he did not know what his real self was, and felt satisfaction when he had become more truly himself.

One other idea about the self that Rogers makes important use of is that of "self-actualization," a concept that he credits to Kurt Goldstein. The concept is central to what Rogers calls the "growth hypothesis": in most, if not all, individuals, there are growth forces, tendencies toward self-actualization, that may act as the sole motivation for therapy.

These tendencies, if not impeded, lead a person to develop a number of characteristics, including the following. In someone moving toward self-actualization, there will be a decrease in the number of defensive barriers that prevent the natural movement toward greater rationality. Once self-actualization occurs, the only control necessary is the natural and internal balancing of one need against another. The experience of extreme satisfaction of one need (say, for sex) is greatly decreased. The individual is able to participate in the vastly complex self-regulatory activities of his organism so as to live in increasing harmony with himself and others. Clients who have moved significantly in therapy toward self-actualization, Rogers points out, live more intimately with their feelings of pain but also experience more vividly their feelings of ecstasy; their anger is more clearly felt but so also is love; and although they know fear more deeply, they also better know their courage (Rogers, 1989b: 28).

Discussion As with other kinds of psychotherapy, the claims of client-centered therapists raise important issues that are straightforwardly empirical rather than philosophic. I will mention one here. Rogers' claim about what is necessary and sufficient for successful psychotherapy constitutes quite a strong empirical thesis. It logically implies, first, that if one takes the totality of successful cases, whether the therapist was a Skinnerian, a psychoanalyst, a cognitivist, or eclectic, the therapist in every single case had the characteristics of congruence, unconditional positive regard, and empathetic understanding. Second, it implies that in every case of therapeutic success, the therapist communicated these attitudes to the client. Third, the thesis implies that even in cases typically difficult to treat with psychotherapy, such as schizophrenia, the possession and communication of these attitudes will suffice for therapeutic success. I will not try to demonstrate this, but I think that the outcome record for psychotherapy will refute every one of these three propositions. If that were demonstrated, then, I assume, the convinced believer in Rogerian therapy would weaken Rogers' claim considerably, and would be content to specify under what therapeutic conditions the communication of the basic three therapeutic attitudes will help and in what way. I have no idea, however, of how this weakened thesis is likely to look. I turn now to Rogers' discussion of the self.

As many analysts do, Rogers uses the term "self" in more than one sense. Sometimes he means "person," but when he uses "self" as an explanatory concept, he typically means something different. In many of his writings, Rogers uses "self" in pretty much the way Kohut uses it in his early writings: He uses it to mean *self-conception*, or the set of self-attitudes that a person has. However, in developing his theory of personality (1951, chap. 11: 498), he defines "self" differently; he says that the term refers to the *awareness of being*. Moreover, in some of his works, where he talks about the real self, he talks as if it were an inner agent. For example, he writes of the self as the "internal locus of evaluation" (1961: 119); he also speaks of getting in touch with this "real self underlying all my surface behavior" (page 108), of "the unknown elements of self," and the discovery of "the stranger who has been living behind these masks" (pages 123–4). It is possible that Rogers intends here to be speaking metaphorically, but many readers, I suspect, will read him as saying that not only do we have a conception of self but we also have something that the conception is of: our real, underlying inner self that we discover when we strip aside the façades that we have defensively erected.

Cognitive-Behavior Therapy

Talk of the self moves in a very different direction in the work of Albert Bandura, probably the most influential theorist among cognitive-behavior therapists. Bandura's key theoretical concept is that of a "self-efficacy belief," roughly one's belief in one's capacity for organizing and executing certain plans of action. In contrast to a Freudian view, it is these self-efficacy beliefs and expectations, rather than unconscious drives, that are the key to explaining much of an individual's behavior; in contrast to an operant conditioning viewpoint, it is not the contingencies of reinforcement by themselves, but how we process information about them, that is crucial in determining how humans act.

To date, there have been more than 900 research studies of self-efficacy factors, many of them tightly controlled. Many of these studies deal with the origin of self-efficacy beliefs and how they interact with other causal factors to determine human action.

As to the origin of beliefs in self-efficacy, Bandura (1995) holds that there are four main sources. The first, and most effective, way to develop such beliefs is through "mastery experiences." People do things that convince themselves that they have the capacity to succeed at a certain task. Second, agents acquire beliefs in self-efficacy through "vicarious experiences." They see people similar to themselves succeed by persistent efforts, thereby creating the expectation in themselves that they too can master comparable tasks. A third source is that of "social persuasion." People can often be persuaded through argumentation or other verbal means that they are capable of succeeding. Finally, people can alter their efficacy beliefs by enhancing their physical status, reducing stress and negative emotional reactions, and correcting misinterpretations of bodily states.

Possessing beliefs in self-efficacy is, on Bandura's view, no guarantee that an individual will act on them. Instead, beliefs in self-efficacy affect behavior through four major processes: cognitive, motivational, affective, and selection processes. Much of the research of Bandura and his colleagues is designed to pinpoint precisely how beliefs in self-efficacy interact with these four processes to determine how the individual acts. In the psychotherapeutic area, for example, researchers have tried to gauge the effects of self-efficacy beliefs, in combination with these other factors, on a wide variety of clinical problems and their treatments, including phobic reactions (Biran and Wilson, 1981), anxiety (Bandura, 1991), depression (Alloy and Abramson, 1988), alcoholism (Annis and Davis, 1988), and drug use (Ellickson et al., 1993).

Discussion B.F. Skinner and other behaviorists have often complained that appealing to the inner man within us, the self, to explain behavior is a theoretical dead end; for such an appeal immediately generates the question of what causes the inner man to act. Bandura, however, explicitly disavows talk of an inner agent (Bandura, 1982: 12). When he speaks of the self or of the agent, he means the person, not an agent within the person. Even if no inner agent is postulated, Skinner has another complaint: that postulating beliefs or other cognitive states to explain behavior leaves unresolved the issues of where they originate and how they affect behavior. As I suggested earlier, however, the research program originated by Bandura and executed by many of his colleagues and himself is designed to answer both of these questions.

In some of his writings, Bandura has raised issues about how ideas about self-efficacy, and what he calls "reciprocal determinism," bear on traditional philosophic questions about free choice and action. Apart from questions about freedom, however, the issues raised about the self in the writings of Bandura and his colleagues are primarily empirical. No inner agent is postulated; consequently, metaphysical questions about the self are not generated. That does not mean, of course, that such questions cannot be raised. If persons are essentially inner selves or a combination of physical bodies and inner selves, then in not speaking about the inner agent, self-efficacy theory is leaving out something important. Whether something of metaphysical importance is left out is a question I address later.

Behaviorism

Given their anti-mentalistic stance, most behaviorists have no inclination to use the concept of self. Hence, little discussion is needed here of their use of the concept. A few points, however, might be mentioned.

Although logical behaviorism, the view that mentalistic sentences can be given behavioral translations, appears to have little impact today in psychotherapy, there may still be a few adherents of the view working in the area of applied behavior analysis (see Chapter 5). If there are, they can tolerate the use of the concept of self *provided* that it is ultimately eliminable by behavioristic translations. Furthermore, some who describe themselves as "behaviorists," such as Hans Eysenck (see Chapter 6), are willing to employ cognitive concepts, even if their main emphasis is on conditioning factors. They could in principle make use of the concept of self in explaining behavior. Finally, it should be obvious that in asking whether a behaviorist can consistently employ a concept of self, we need to specify not only the kind of behaviorist we have in mind, but also the sense in which we are using the term "self." If, for example, we mean "person" or "organism," then clearly some behaviorists would have no objection to speaking of selves. However, if we have something in mind of more metaphysical interest, such as the real self that lies within the person, which can be discovered by undergoing psychotherapy, or the inner agent or ego, then most if not all behaviorists will object. Whether they are right to object is an issue discussed in the next section.

Conclusion

Because the term "self" is used in the psychotherapy literature in so many different ways, it is not possible to identify just one sort of thing that it allegedly refers to. As I noted in discussing psychoanalytic theories, the term is used to refer to (among other things): (1) a person, (2) the ego, (3) the mental apparatus, (4) a personality, (5) the core of one's personality, (6) a set of self representations, and (7) an inner agent. Not all of these uses raise metaphysical questions. It is primarily uses (2) and (7) that invite such questions, and even then only if "ego" is used, as Hartmann (1950) and others use it, to refer to something within us that thinks, or decides, or tests reality, and so on.

If one moves beyond the mainstream literature, one can find numerous other uses of "self" to refer to some inner entity with agent-like qualities. However, even in these other works, it is not always clear whether the author really is postulating an inner self, or is merely speaking metaphorically, or perhaps is just writing carelessly. Here are some comments of two well-known psychotherapists who work in what is called "the recovered memory movement" (see Crews, 1995). They are talking about what is called "the inner child":

> Many survivors have a difficult time with the concept of the child within, even though forgiving that child is an essential part of healing. . . . You may feel split, caught in a real schism. There is the "you" that's out in the "real" world, and then there's the child inside you who is still a frightened victim: "I felt like all my successes had been one big fake, because I ignored the little child who never got over it, and who lives her life in humiliation and pain because of it." (Bass and Davis, 1994: 122)

Are the authors postulating an inner child who can be discovered in the process of undergoing psychotherapy? I think they are, but I am uncertain. One test to apply in such cases is this: If the theory is interpreted non-realistically – that is, as *not* postulating an inner agent – does it lose its explanatory power *even if it is true*? Using that test, many theories both within and beyond mainstream psychotherapy really are postulating a self conceived of as inner agent of some kind or other. (See, for example, some of the papers on the use of self in therapy in Baldwin and Satir, 1987.)

PHILOSOPHIC THEORIES OF THE SELF

Experiencing the Self

Who or what am I? What is the real me? I close my eyes and think of what is essential to my being me. Clearly, even if I mark my identity in terms of my job, or possessions, or family relationships, they are not essential to what I am. I might lose them and yet still be me. Just as obviously, I would still be me if I lost certain parts of my body. I might lose my feet, say, or my esophagus, or an ear, and yet I would continue to exist. It seems as if, at least sometimes, that what is essential, the real me, is somehow lodged in my head behind my eyes. If that were true, then the one body part I could not do without is my head. Where my head goes, I go. Yet even my head seems expendable, at least in principle. What of those people who have near death experiences and witness their entire body on the operating table, as they themselves float in space? It is unlikely that such events really do occur, but are they not at least conceivable? If they are, then it is at least logically possible, is it not, that I can exist with no body at all? If that is possible, not physically but logically possible, then does it not follow that I am not my body?

Descartes used an argument very similar to the above one to show that the self, the real me, is not physical, but instead is a non-extended thinking substance that at least in principle can survive the destruction of the body. Many psychotherapists who think of the self in a Cartesian way might question the stress on being a *thinking* thing; they might add that the self also has affective states, such as fear, anguish, anger, and so on. Some will also disagree with Descartes about our prospects for surviving bodily death, and some will add that much of the self is unconscious. Yet what many find agreeable is the idea that the self is an inner agent, that thinks, decides, and feels; one that can divide or fracture because of early childhood experiences such as child abuse or even just inadequate mothering; one that can be discovered in the course of psychotherapy.

Despite the natural attractions of this view of the self, it is well known that the view is also problematic. Suppose that Descartes is right in saying that I am not just my body, is there any good reason to think that what I really am is an immaterial self, or that such a self exists at all? I know that there is more to me than my body; I know that I have a mind, at least in the sense of possessing not an entity but a collection of mental states. I feel pain and have emotions, and through introspection I can be aware of my thinking, but how do I know that I have a self?

There is a widely quoted passage from David Hume, where he addresses this question. He notes that when he reflects, he never encounters his self: "For my part, when I enter most intimately into what I call *myself*, I always stumble on some particular perception or other, of heat or cold, love or hatred, pain or pleasure." The philosopher Dan Dennett expresses a similar point using modern neurobiological terminology:

> Searching for the self can be somewhat like [the following]. You enter the brain through the eye, march up the optic nerve, round and round in the cortex, looking behind every neuron, and then, before you know it, you emerge into daylight on the spike of a motor nerve impulse, scratching your head and wondering where the self is. (1991: 355)

Defenders of Descartes are unlikely to be convinced by either of the above-quoted remarks. For one thing, Hume's own theory of the self, one that reduces it to a "bundle" of perceptions, also seems problematic. The standard objection to this theory is that Hume cannot explain why any particular set of sensations or perceptions should be associated with my self, unless he tacitly appeals to *my* sensations and perceptions, thus making his account circular.

Although Dennett was not trying to prove in one brief passage the non-existence of the self, it is still worth remarking that if we took the tour he talks of, we would also not notice any feelings of sorrow or despair, any thinking or sensation. Yet, unless we are eliminative materialists (philosophers who deny the existence of all mental states), we are not likely to conclude that such things do not exist. So, more needs to be said. Yet the point that Hume and Dennett raise is still profoundly troubling. If no one has ever observed a self — that is, one conceived of as an inner agent — what reason do we have for thinking that it exists?

Most contemporary philosophers contend that there is no such reason, but not everyone agrees. A few still take the position that the self *can* be observed, not with our eyes, but through introspection, despite Hume's denial.

One prominent philosopher, Roderick Chisholm, argues that philosophers as diverse as the logical empiricist Rudolph Carnap and the existentialist Jean-Paul Sartre have denied the observability of the self because they have been misled by Hume's errors. One of these mistakes is to treat our idea of something, such as a peach, to take one of Hume's examples, as the idea of a collection of qualities. Thus, Hume claims that our idea of a peach is an idea of a particular taste, color, size, and so on. This is wrong, Chisholm points out (1994); our idea of a peach is an idea of an individual X such that *it* is sweet, round, and fuzzy.

An analogous thought holds of the self. Our idea of the self is not the idea of particular perceptions of love, hate, or warmth, but of an individual thing that loves, or hates, or feels warm, and so forth.

Hume's second mistake, according to Chisholm, has to do with the interpretation of certain introspective data. Hume says that when he reflects ("when I enter most intimately into what I call *myself*"), he always stumbles on some particular perception of heat or cold, or love, or hatred, and so on. However, what the data actually show is that *someone*, namely himself, stumbles on these things.

Finally, there is a third mistake, which Chisholm attributes to both Kant and Sartre: Even if there is a subject who thinks and feels, and so forth, we have no acquaintance with it, they say; we know only its manifestations. This is muddled thinking, according to Chisholm. Manifestation is the converse of acquaintance. Something manifests itself to you if and only if you are acquainted with it. So, if the self manifests itself to me, then I am acquainted with it.

This last point seems right. If a client walks into the office, and I see his face, the way he is dressed, and the odd way he walks, I should not say: I am acquainted only with his manifestations. By meeting him, and noticing certain things about him, I become acquainted with *him*.

Chisholm's first point, that our idea of a peach or self is not the idea of particular characteristics, seems right as well. It is his second claim that is dubious. Do the data of introspection reveal, or provide evidence, of a self? Chisholm says that in reporting his data, Hume must say such things as "*I* stumble on heat or cold," thereby implying the existence of a self. He would be wrong to say merely "Heat or cold are found." There is, however, another obvious third alternative. Hume can say "I stumble on heat or cold," but the I who does this is a person, someone who has a body and mental states. As far as the data of introspection show, it is not a self who does the stumbling or finding. Chisholm could, of course, say that by "self" he means "person," not an inner agent, but that would reduce his position to something too obvious to require defense; none of the philosophers he refers to denies that we can observe persons. I conclude that Chisholm has given us no reason to think that when someone introspects, he or she observes a self.

Another philosopher, John Foster (1991), provides a series of arguments designed to discredit current forms of materialism. However, an important distinction should be noticed here: between refuting materialism and establishing the existence of an immaterial self. Many philosophers writing today (exactly how many is unknown) reject materialism, or what is also called "physicalism" (see, for example, the papers in Robinson, 1993); they adopt the position that mental states and events have properties that are irreducibly mental. What almost all reject, however, is the existence of a self or a mind that is an immaterial substance.

So, refuting materialism is not enough to demonstrate that the self as an inner agent or immaterial substance exists; another argument is needed. Foster also tries to provide this additional argument.

He begins with two stipulative definitions (1991: 203). The first applies to a "mental subject." Something is a *mental subject* if and only if it has mental states or engages in mental activities. Second, there is the concept "basic mental subject." Something is a *basic mental subject* if and only if it is a mental subject and is represented as such in the conceptually fundamental account of the metaphysically fundamental reality.

A materialist who believes that the mind is the brain, or at least is reducible to something physical, will deny that mental subjects are basic. However, Foster takes himself to have refuted reductive materialism, and indeed all forms of materialism. Whether he has in fact done this is itself controversial, but assuming that he has, he concludes that all basic subjects are non-physical. On Foster's view, then, the thing that has mental states or engages in mental activities is an immaterial self.

Apart from being non-physical, what is this self like? To that question, Foster replies, it has an attribute that each of us is aware of, or can be aware of, in introspection, but which no more can be conveyed to someone else than can the character of visual experience be conveyed to someone who is congenitally blind. Here a question will naturally arise. Whether or not the character of visual experience can be conveyed to someone blind from birth, those of us who can see are typically aware of our having this experience. How many of us, however, are aware of the attribute that Foster speaks of, that which characterizes the immaterial self. I am not aware of any such attribute, and Foster gives us no reason to believe that he or anyone else is either. So, he has not made the case for saying that through introspection we are aware of an immaterial self.

Suppose that there is no such thing as an immaterial self. What, then, is the mental subject, that is, the thing that has mental states? Foster considers the possibility that a corporeal object, namely, our body has mental states, but rejects that possibility partly on the grounds that this would disqualify the subject of mental states from being basic. If I understand him, however, I fail to see that he rules out a more obvious possibility: The thing that has mental states, the thing that feels pain or that thinks, is neither a body nor an incorporeal self but is rather a person. If we say that, then we may be forced to say that there are no "basic" mental subjects (in Foster's stipulated sense), but I fail to see why saying this would be problematic. His argument, then, depends on an unsupported premise: that there are, in his technical sense, "basic mental subjects."

I conclude that, as far as I can see, Foster has given us no good reason to say that an immaterial self can be observed in introspection, or for saying that it exists at all (it is possible, however, that I have misconstrued his argument; so, I refer the reader to his 1991 work, especially chapter 7).

Although more needs to be said about this issue, let us assume from now on that the self, conceived of as an inner agent, is not observed in introspection. Contrary to what Hume suggests, it does not immediately follow that we have no reason to believe in its existence. The self might be like a molecule or a black hole, something which needs to be postulated in order to explain known phenomena. After all, psychoanalysts who speak of the self as an inner agent do not generally cite introspective evidence to support their claims. Rather, they more often than not postulate the self to explain certain clinical phenomena. I turn next to an examination of some of these phenomena.

Clinical Phenomena and the Self

(a) Multiple Personality Disorders   There is now a body of philosophic work on what used to be called, at least in the United States, "Multiple Personality Disorder," but is now called "Dissociative Identity Disorder" in DSM-IV (American Psychiatric Association, 1994). For an excellent brief piece on the subject by a philosopher and psychologist, see Humphrey and Dennett (1989); for more extended philosophic treatments, see Braude (1991) and Hacking (1995).

Let us assume that there are "multiples," as they are called, at least in the sense that some people meet the criteria for having a dissociative identity disorder that are laid down in DSM-IV. If one accepts that assumption, one might reason as follows. Individuals who meet the criteria have multiple, distinct selves, each of whom at various times decides, plans, and chooses, and in consequence determines how the individual acts. Yet these selves cannot be identified with the physical body of the individual; for there are multiple selves and only one body. So, the existence of so-called "multiples" proves the existence of inner selves.

How cogent is the above argument? It assumes the very thing that it purports to prove: that the individual with the disorder in question has a self, and in fact has more than one. The argument, consequently, is worthless. Those who are skeptical about the existence of the self will reject the initial premise. However, instead of relying on it, why not appeal directly to the DSM-IV criteria, one of which requires that the individual have two or more distinct identities or personalities or personality states? If someone meets this criterion, does it not follow that he or she has multiple selves? It does not; in order to meet this particular criterion, it is sufficient that the individual have at least two or more distinct *personality states*. It is not required that there be different persons or selves within the single individual.

It could be replied that "self" in this discussion just means "personality"; so, if multiples are conceded to have more than one of the latter, they must also have multiple selves. To say this, however, would be to trivialize the position concerning the existence of the self. If we are trying to prove only that each of us has a personality, we need not appeal to cases of multiple personality to prove what no one disputes.

Even if meeting the DSM-IV criteria does not by itself guarantee the existence of multiple selves, perhaps there are other known facts about multiples that require the postulation of more than one self. The challenge then would be to say what these facts are. Even if multiples have at least two stable and distinct personalities (something that is not beyond dispute), what facts require us to say that besides having more than one personality, they also have more than one self? Although Hacking (1995, chapter 16) and Humphrey and Dennett (1989) deny that there are any such facts, Braude (1991) disagrees. He argues that the different "alters" (that is, alternate personalities) are distinct selves, but underlying this multiplicity is a unified self, or as he also puts it a "transcendental ego" (page 187). Establishing even one of these claims is sufficient to establish that a self exists.

In arguing for the first claim, Braude appeals to certain alleged facts, and then argues that they are best explained by postulating distinct selves. For example, alters claim to be distinct persons "and not merely personalities" (page 67); there is often a visible struggle between alters for executive control of the body (page 67); there is the phenomenon of attempted "internal homicide," where some alters try to kill others (page 68); and some alters come to know the mental states of others in ways that are different from the ways one knows one's own mental states. However, Braude presents no credible evidence that any of these alleged facts really are facts. If we observe someone meeting the DSM-IV criteria, we do not observe different personalities (alters) claiming to be different people. What we observe is one person, under the guise of first one personality and then another, making certain claims. (Once we allow that a personality states something, believes something, knows something, and so on, we are already close to treating it as a person.)

We likewise do not observe different alters struggling to take control; rather, we observe but one person acting as if there were different people inside of him or her. No one has witnessed internal homicide, or even attempted internal homicide. We, once more, observe a person who sometimes displays one personality and then another; later one of these personalities is no longer on display. None of these facts justifies the postulation of distinct selves.

Whether or not there are distinct selves, Braude has a separate argument to show that there is a unified self (or what he calls a "transcendental ego") underlying the various personalities. He claims (1991: 170) that there is an "overlapping" of alters that is extensive enough to strengthen the case for explanations in terms of a single synthesizing ego. To take his example, suppose that an alternate personality has the function of shopping for groceries. In carrying out that function, it must have skills that the other alters will also have, such as being able to read a shopping list, to interact with other shoppers, to be able to pay a cashier. How does any of this, however, constitute evidence of a single self or synthesizing ego? We observe, say, a female client who shops, and who later cruises bars, but who has no memory of the latter activity when she displays one sort of personality. Given that, as far as we can tell by observation, there is only one person, we hardly need to postulate a synthesizing ego to explain the "overlapping" abilities, to explain how the woman who shops and bar hops can both read and walk. What needs to be explained, rather, is the partial memory lapses. We do that in terms of her clinical disorder (I leave it open how satisfactory the explanation is), but postulating a synthesizing ego is not necessary, and Braude does not claim that it is, to explain the memory lapses.

(b) Narcissistic Personality Disturbances Self psychologists postulate a fragmented self to explain the symptoms of narcissistic personality disorders, although the therapeutic goal is often said to be more than merely symptom relief. As one writer puts it, "Rather, the goal is to rehabilitate the self structure to a new level of health and maturity" (Lynch, 1991: 25). As I noted in the first part of this chapter, some self psychologists try to explain *all* psychological problems as disorders of the self (Nicholson, 1991: 30). Whether one makes the more modest or more ambitious claim, the same question can be asked: Do the observable clinical phenomena justify the postulation of a self, whether intact or fragmented?

I have no reason to question the claim of self psychologists that certain patients exhibit certain behavior patterns. For example, those who are said to have an "unhealthy narcissism" are said to exhibit grandiose fantasies of importance and an inability to see others as anything but need gratifying objects (Nicholson, 1991: 27–8). Or, as Kohut notes in one of his early works (1971), his patients expressed feelings of emptiness or said that they felt as if they were not real. It is not out of place to ask, however, what the argument is for postulating a fragmented self to explain such symptoms.

As I noted in the first part of this chapter, in his early writings, Kohut, in talking about the self, was apparently not talking about an unobservable, inner entity, but rather was talking about the person's representations of himself or herself. However, in his later writings, when he talks of the "grandiose self," Kohut does appear to be postulating an inner entity. As Eagle (1984: 66) notes, Kohut and his followers, when they speak of "a fragmented self," often talk as if they were referring to actual cracks in a substantive structural entity. If these were just examples of metaphor or careless writing, then no issue of substance would arise. However, in many writings of self psychologists, the theories offered would lose their explanatory power, even if they are true, if "self" were taken to refer either to a person or a person's theory about himself rather than to an inner agent of some kind. Furthermore, it is quite clear that some ego psychologists (such as Hartmann, 1950: 75) and object-relations theorists, as I noted in the first part of the chapter, do intend to refer to an inner agent when they postulate an ego, a true self, or the real self, and so on. Although, once again, I am not questioning the reality of the clinical phenomena, I fail to find any cogent argument that these phenomena justify belief in the self as an inner agent. (Some analysts will no doubt appeal not to the patient's symptoms, but to the analysis of the transference; but this appeal works no better. See Erwin, 1996: chapter 7.)

(c) Self Deception   Self deception is not a distinctively clinical phenomenon in the way that, say, depression and schizophrenia are. Most of us deceive ourselves at sometime or other but few would seek psychotherapeutic help for that problem alone. Yet self deception is a form of irrationality of some interest to psychotherapists, and has been widely discussed in both the philosophic and psychotherapy literatures (for some of the philosophic references, see the papers in McLaughlin and Rorty, 1988).

Philosophers have been drawn to the subject in recent years largely because the phenomenon of self deception seems so puzzling. If I believe that my best friend's wife is *not* having a love affair, I am innocent of deception if I try to convince him of her loyalty *even if* I am mistaken. Furthermore, even if I know about the affair, I am not being deceptive when I inadvertently get him to believe in his wife's fidelity. I inadvertently provide her with an alibi, for example, when I tell my friend that she came to my party the night he was in a different city. What appears to be required for my deceiving someone is that I *intentionally* try to convince the person to believe something that I myself believe is false. How, then, can I be guilty of deceiving myself? Suppose that it is my wife that I suspect of having an affair. If I truly believe that she is, how can I intentionally get someone to believe otherwise when that someone is me? The person that I intend to confuse, to deceive, to hold a false belief, will catch on to what I am trying to do; for after all, I am he and he is me.

Some psychoanalytic accounts of self deception explain the phenomenon in a mechanical fashion (see some of the cases discussed in Erwin, 1988a). Why, for example, did Richard Nixon tape himself and, consequently, put his presidency at risk? One theory is that the taping provided a defense against his masochistic self-voyeurism (Rothenberg, 1976). If the theory is true, then Nixon was deceived about his real motives; so, he was guilty of self deception. However, if the infantile wishes that are postulated worked mechanically, and the defense was unconscious, we need not speak of a deceiver who intentionally was trying to deceive someone. The theory may be false, but if it were true there would appear to be nothing paradoxical going on. Some philosophers are likely to object, however, that the case, as described, is not one of "full-blown" self deception. In the psychoanalytic case, someone makes a mistake about his own motives; so, he is deceived about himself. Yet he is not intentionally trying to deceive anyone. Consequently, it might be said, it is not "deception" in the sense in which one person is said to deceive another. Whether this reply is right or not, let us put aside such examples as the Nixon case, and talk only about "full-blown" cases of self deception, cases where the deceiving is intentional.

One way of handling such cases is to postulate two selves in a single body, one who does the deceiving and one who is deceived. Another is to speak of splits in the self, somewhat the way self psychologists do. One part of the self has its own plans, beliefs, desires, and intentions; another part has its own ideas, dreams, intentions, and so on (see, for example, White, 1991: 193). When things go wrong, the one part may deceive the other.

Some philosophers and cognitive scientists who speak of the self being subdivided are not postulating an immaterial inner agent; so, their theories are not directly relevant to the present discussion. However, the single point I wish to make may have implications for the grounds for their theories. The point is this. Some philosophers who write on self deception engage in unwarranted a priori theorizing about empirical matters. They reason as follows. Self deception obviously occurs. In order for it to be truly "deception," and be truly deception of the "self," such and such must be true of the self. There must be a divided self, or perhaps multiple selves in the same body. I say that this reasoning is mistaken.

Let's distinguish two senses of "self deception." In the first, the "full-blown" sense, self deception requires an intention to deceive and that something else be true about the self (such as that there be two selves or one split self). In the second sense, self deception requires that a mistake be made about one's self, but the mistake need not be intentional. It does not matter to my point whether the first or the second (or neither) is the ordinary sense of "self deception." My point is that by analyzing the full-blown sense of "self deception" we may be able to figure out a priori that *if* self deception occurs in that very sense, then such and such must be true about the self. For example, there must be multiple selves or a split self. What we cannot figure out a priori, however, is that self deception occurs in that sense. To find out if it does occur, we first have to find out if the such and such really does exist. We first have to find out if, for example, there really are two selves or split selves. That, however, requires empirical evidence. We cannot move from the proposition that self deception occurs *in some sense or other* to the proposition that it occurs in the sense that requires that there be a self at all, let alone a split self or multiple selves.

It is hopeless, then, to try to prove that the self exists (in the sense of an inner agent) by analyzing some concept of self deception, whether it be the ordinary one, if there be such a thing, or some philosopher's invention. If, in some sense of "self deception," saying that self deception occurs logically entails the existence of a Cartesian self, then in order to get evidence that it ever occurs we first have to get evidence that the self exists.

I am not saying that we could not in principle get empirical evidence that the self exists by arguing that its postulation is required to explain some behavioral data. What I am objecting to are a priori arguments that appeal to analysis of some concept of the self to prove what, in fact, requires empirical evidence.

Conclusion: I have not examined all of the empirical arguments that have been offered in the last several centuries that purport to establish the existence of the self as an inner agent. I have focussed only on recent attempts by philosophers to show that the self is discoverable through introspection, or its nature established by conceptual analysis, and by attempts to appeal to clinical data to demonstrate either of these two things. So, it is possible that there is somewhere a cogent argument for the existence of the self. I, however, am not aware of any such argument.

If there is no such argument, then, as far as we know, neither cognitivists nor behaviorists are leaving out anything of explanatory importance, when they talk of organisms or persons, but omit all references to a self (unless "self" is used to mean "person"). Still, many psychotherapists will object that some important things *are* left out when we drop all talk of the self. One way to see what these things might be is to ask about the sorts of things that we tend to associate with the development of a self.

The Virtual Self

The first, and perhaps most fundamental thing, that motivates talk of a self is reflection on the subjectivity possessed by certain kinds of entities. As the philosopher Thomas Nagel once expressed the point: There is something that it is like to be me. I have certain subjective experiences of taste, pain, love, dread, despair, anguish, and so on, and these experiences are mine alone. Rocks and mountains, in contrast, and probably computers and robots, do not have them.

As Nagel (1974) also points out, however, there is also something that it is like to be a bat. Bats, too, have subjective experiences, as do newborn human infants. If we say that human infants develop a self only after a certain period, and that bats never do, then more than subjectivity is required for possession of a self. A second thing that at least appears to be required is a kind of reflexivity: I am not only aware of my environment to some degree, I am also aware of my being aware. Included as part of this reflexivity is a third thing: the possession of a theory, or rather a collection of theories, that I have and that are about me (what some therapists refer to as my "self-concept").

A fourth thing associated with the concept of self is a sense of identity. I am not merely aware of my being aware; I am also aware that it is *I* who am aware and that I am a particular person and no other. Fifth, I have a sense of continuity, a sense of persisting as time passes: I sense that a certain individual who yesterday left a certain house, went to a certain job, and ate certain food is *me*. That child who left my mother's womb many years ago sometimes seems unrelated to the present me, but in fact I am that person. Finally, there is a sixth thing: a sense of privacy, a sense that no matter how self-deceived I might be, and no matter how much I might reveal to my therapist, there is an enormous fund of information about me that I have acquired in a way that is different from the way that others have come to know me. Much of this information will never be known by anyone except me.

There are, then, certain characteristics that we associate with having a self, including subjectivity, privacy, reflexivity, a self-concept, a sense of identity, and a sense of continuity. I will say that an individual who has all of these things has a "virtual self." Aha! So, now another kind of self is added to the list of real selves, true selves, core selves, nuclear selves, fractured selves, and so on. No. I am not adding to but subtracting from the list, in fact, recommending its abolition. I use the term "virtual self," as one might readily guess, to suggest something that is not real at all. Still, there are reasons why we think of ourselves and others as having a self. I am not referring here to the various arguments developed by philosophers, but rather to certain phenomena that we typically associate with having a self. If we make no reference to such phenomena, as most behaviorist theories do not, we leave out something important to psychotherapy; if we try to unify them by postulating a self, an inner agent, then we wind up with a ghost-like object that is within us, but because it is not a physical object cannot be within us. The phenomena are important; the postulation of the entity is not.

Can we reduce a self, then, to a virtual self, by translating talk about selves into talk about the features that I mentioned? I doubt it. In any event, I am not suggesting that the concept of self can be analyzed in terms of these features. Some of them may not even be necessary for having a virtual self. For example, a very disturbed individual might still have a self (that is, a seeming self, a virtual self) but lose his or her sense of continuing to exist through time. I am saying, however, that the phenomena in question are often associated with having a self; that they are, of course, real; and they may be very important to the theory and practice of psychotherapy.

Analysts may be right when they say, for example, that the important thing is not the behavior of the client, but his or her private, subjective world. (Whether this is so or not raises empirical and evaluative questions that I am not addressing here.) Others may be right in contending, as Carl

Rogers does, that the therapist needs to enter the phenomenal world of the client, to see how the person sees his or her self, and environment. In certain cases, the feeling of a lack of identity may cause other psychological problems. In other cases, a client may report that he feels as if he is not real, or as if his self is split, or that another self within him has taken control. The reports are clinically important, or at least they may be; the metaphysics is expendable. We can describe and explain the clinical phenomena, but to do that we need postulate no inner self. My objection, then, to psychotherapeutic theories that postulate a self as an inner agent is not that they are metaphysical; it is rather that concerning the thing they talk about, we have no reason of any kind to think that it exists. Talk of persons and a virtual self – that is, of subjectivity, reflexivity, privacy, a sense of identity, and so on – is all that is needed.

4

Postmodernist Clinical Epistemology: a Critique

More than 40 years ago, a leading logical empiricist was asked why he had consulted a psychoanalyst, given that his philosophy should make him skeptical of Freud's science and therapy. He allegedly replied: "When in the jungle, see the witch doctor." His point, obviously, was that besides psychoanalysis, there was little else available for his psychological problems. Today, however, that same philosopher would have the choice of hundreds of different types of psychotherapies, in addition to somatic treatments. Not all of these psychotherapies are used to treat the same sorts of problems, but many are in direct competition with one another.

When we inquire about the origin and maintenance of clinical problems, we find that here too Freud has many competitors. Not only are there non-Freudian psychoanalytic theories, such as those discussed in the previous chapter, but also a variety of behaviorist and cognitivist theories. Not all purport to explain exactly the same clinical phenomena, but many *are* incompatible rivals.

On what basis can we choose between these competing therapies and theories? The obvious answer is this: We let the empirical evidence decide. The evidence by itself, however, is silent; it needs to be interpreted and evaluated. What are the standards for doing this? If we disagree about this issue, we can both be competent, non-ideological, and intellectually honest, look at exactly the same evidence, and reach very different conclusions. Yet there is little agreement today among psychotherapists about the proper epistemic standards for evaluating evidence. Some philosophers and psychologists, furthermore, have abandoned the entire project of trying to find objective, defensible epistemological standards.

One consequence of the growing skepticism about discovering objective epistemological standards is a turn toward "post-modernist epistemology." The term refers to a loosely connected set of ideas that developed largely in response to the perceived failures of logical empiricism. The postmodernists have had little time to work out their ideas compared to the time allotted traditional epistemologists. Some postmodernist theories having currency today will, no doubt, be discarded as time goes on. The whole movement is nowhere near assuming any final shape, but it is beginning to have an impact on the field of psychotherapy, and its influence is likely to increase. One writer claims that its growth in the discipline has been "exponential" (Held, 1995). Another writes of a "sea change" that is occurring in the way many psychotherapists conceive of their work, as those in a psychotherapeutic avant-garde who have become disenchanted with traditional positivist and realist assumptions now prefer to think of their activities on the analogy of poetry, art, or rhetoric (Sass, 1992: 166).

Because of their potential significance for the field, postmodernist epistemologies warrant at least a preliminary evaluation. I provide one in the first part of this chapter; in the second part, I try to develop an alternative.

I

Some writers use the term "postmodernist epistemology" to refer to "constructivist" epistemological doctrines; others use it more broadly to include constructivism *plus* other anti-objectivist views. I will begin with constructivism.

What is constructivism? One key doctrine is that reality is created by us (Mahoney, 1989: 145), although different writers put this point differently. For example, some constructivists say that our experience *constitutes* the world (von Glaserfield, 1984: 24), or that we *invent* our environment (von Foerster, 1984: 42), or, more cautiously, that "facts" are at least *in part constructed* by the perceiver (Houts, 1989: 67).

This doctrine (or family of closely related doctrines) looks more like an ontological than an epistemological thesis, but when combined with other assumptions, it may have implications for the validation of knowledge claims. For example, if reality does not exist independently of our constructions, it may be pointless to try to validate knowledge claims by appeal to empirical evidence.

Postmodernist epistemologies are not applicable to psychotherapy alone; they are intended to cover all of psychology and psychiatry, and indeed all of science. However, there have been a few attempts to extract special lessons for psychotherapy in particular.

Neimeyer (1993), for example, tries to draw connections between constructivism and cognitive therapy. There is mounting evidence, he claims (page 222), that challenges the objectivist equation of mental health with the accuracy, rationality, or "positivity" of one's cognitions. This, in turn, has challenged the foundations of the cognitive therapies, Neimeyer contends. Constructivists reject the correspondence theory of truth and its corollary assumption that beliefs that fail to correspond to objective reality are, by definition, dysfunctional. They hold, instead, that the viability of any given construction is a function of its consequences, as well as its overall coherence with a larger system of personally or socially held beliefs into which it is incorporated (page 222).

Postmodernist ideas have also had an impact on the practice of psychoanalysis, as Sass (1992) notes, encouraging the tendency to view psychoanalytic interpretations not as something allegedly corresponding to actual occurrences in the client's history but as "creations," and client memories as "inventions." On this view, the analyst should give up on the traditional task of finding out what brought about the client's difficulties, and should understand psychoanalytic interpretations as having only an "artistic truth" (Spence, 1982: 269–70). As Sass points out (1992: 167), some analysts now claim that the psychoanalytic enterprise should become a branch of literature.

An Assessment

If we ask, "Which of the postmodernist epistemological theses are true?" or "Which are supported by good argument?," we might be accused of presupposing the very doctrines that postmodernists are attacking. For that reason, I will begin with a different question: So far, of what use have these ideas been?

If we ask about their clinical utility, there is good reason to be skeptical. Take, first, the "mounting evidence" that Neimeyer refers to (1993: 222) about the rationality or accuracy of one's cognitions. The evidence cited shows, at best, that under certain limited conditions, it may be useful to hold false or irrational beliefs, hardly a novel finding. There is no evidence cited that one is *generally* better off being wrong or irrational. Moreover, the experiments that are cited in no way presuppose or support any constructivist epistemological doctrine.

As to the correspondence theory of truth, it does not have as a corollary, contrary to what Neimeyer asserts (1993: 222), that beliefs that fail to correspond to objective reality are by definition dysfunctional. Is the holding of a false belief sometimes or always dysfunctional? That is an empirical question to which the correspondence theory of truth provides no answer. Finally, as to the constructivist alternative, that the *viability* of any given construction is a function of its consequences, this looks like either an obvious falsehood or an empty tautology. It is false if "viable" means *true*; for false beliefs can have useful consequences. It is empty if "viable" means "useful"; for Neimeyer would be saying no more than this: Whether a belief is useful depends on whether its consequences are useful.

In brief, there are important empirical questions that still need to be addressed about the causal role of false beliefs and faulty reasoning in the etiology of depression, and about the clinical value of eliminating false beliefs through cognitive therapy (see Chapter 6). It remains to be demonstrated, however, that constructivist epistemology is of any use in answering these questions, or any other interesting question about cognitive therapy.

A similar skeptical verdict is warranted about the contribution of postmodernist epistemology to discussions of psychoanalysis. It may very well be, as some psychoanalysts now claim, that it is generally impossible to verify psychoanalytic interpretations about a client's past life. That could be because the relevant part of Freudian theory is false, or because client memories about early childhood are too unreliable, or for some other reason. It may also be true, as some psychoanalysts claim, that mythical interpretations can have as much therapeutic value as correct ones. These claims, however, raise primarily empirical questions. It is unclear how postmodernist epistemology can contribute anything of interest towards answering any of them. I do not deny, however, what I take to be Sass' (1992) point: that some psychoanalysts have been persuaded to give up on the idea that psychoanalytic interpretations need be true partly because of their acceptance of postmodernist ideas.

It is not surprising that an epistemology would have no direct, useful implications for the practice of psychotherapy. I have discussed the issue only because of claims made by constructionists, such as Neimeyer (1993) and others, about the clinical implications of postmodernism. These claims, at least the ones just discussed, are unfounded. Still, postmodernist ideas may be useful (whether or not they are true) in discussing *epistemological* issues of relevance to psychotherapy. So, they may still be relevant in an indirect but important way. I turn next to this issue.

Neimeyer (1993: 222) presents a table with the heading "Philosophical Contrasts between Objectivist and Constructivist Epistemologies." This table deserves scrutiny if, as Neimeyer suggests, it reflects the view of many, not necessarily all, constructivist epistemologists. One section concerns contrasting views of validation (I have supplied the numbers):

Objectivism		Constructivism	
	Criteria for Validation of Knowledge		
(1a)	Validation of knowledge provided by the real world through the senses	(1b)	Validation of knowledge through internal consistency with existing knowledge structures and social consensus among observers
(2a)	Identical matching or correspondence of representation with reality	(2b)	Fitting and viability (i.e., accuracy of predictions according to that interpretative framework)
(3a)	Only one true meaning (i.e., *the* truth)	(3b)	Diversity of possible meanings and alternative interpretations

Item (3b) is acceptable, and would, in fact, be accepted by most objectivists. This client is male, British, depressed, hostile, oral dependent, easily conditioned, and so forth. If the descriptions are logically consistent with one another, they may all be true; or they may all be false. The idea that there are multiple meanings, if this means merely that there is more than one correct way to describe the universe, is a platitude. Can all of these multiple meanings ultimately be reduced to one final, true description of the universe? That seems hardly likely, and possibly incoherent. It would be difficult to find a single objectivist epistemologist who would disagree. In any event, to say there are multiple meanings is not yet to offer any criterion, good or bad, for validating knowledge claims. The other two criteria are supposed to serve that purpose.

The first (1b) is: the validation of knowledge through internal consistency with existing knowledge structures and social consensus among observers. How will this work? Suppose that I claim that alcoholism is always due to faulty conditioning. I check, and find that my hypothesis is consistent with current classical conditioning theory. Furthermore, my behaviorist friends all agree with me. Is that sufficient for validation? Suppose that current classical conditioning theory is basically mistaken. Why would consistency with a false theory plus a social consensus provide any good reason whatsoever for thinking my hypothesis to be correct?

We could say: In order to qualify as a knowledge structure, a theory has to be more than accepted; it has to be supported by good evidence. Of what use, then, would be Neimeyer's first criterion? To apply it, we would first have to figure out if the existing knowledge structure (in my example, classical conditioning theory) were validated. How would we decide that unless we had some other criterion of validation that was sufficient? In that case, it would not be clear why we would need Neimeyer's criterion.

Neimeyer could also say that his criterion has not been met in my example. Behaviorists might agree with my hypothesis about alcoholism, but cognitivists and psychoanalysts would disagree. Consequently, there would be no social consensus. However, if all schools of psychotherapy have to agree, then in discussing most of the debated questions in the field, Neimeyer's criterion would be useless. The question of which epistemic standards to use arises primarily because, on so many of the major issues, there is no social consensus. If postmodernist epistemology could be brought on stage only after consensus arrives, it would have no useful epistemological role to play.

I conclude that Neimeyer's first criterion is hopeless. One does not need a social consensus to validate a knowledge claim; nor is the forging of a consensus (which is not easy in the field of psychotherapy) sufficient. Consistency with currently held theories is also not necessary, unless they in turn are supported by good evidence, which we can determine only by going beyond Neimeyer's criterion. Even if we were to stipulate that the existing knowledge structure must have independent empirical support, consistency with it is, at most, necessary (and even this needs qualification) but is not sufficient for validation. Most psychotherapeutic hypotheses are consistent with current quantum theory, but by itself this confirms none of them.

Neimeyer's other criterion (2b) is an improvement: Fitting and viability (that is, accuracy of predictions according to that interpretative framework). At least, this criterion suggests an appeal to empirical testing. However, as will be argued in the second section (see Differentialness), although accuracy of predictions is important, it is not sufficient for validation. Other equally plausible but competing explanations of the phenomena need to be discounted. To illustrate: I predict, on the basis of my clinical theory, that after three years of psychoanalysis, my client's depression will take a turn for the better, but a spontaneous remission hypothesis will predict the same thing. Why would the accuracy of my prediction support my theory over the rival account? It would not; again, see the second section of this chapter.

Mere accuracy of prediction is not sufficient for validation, but there is a deeper problem here for constructivism. Many take the position that theory so infects observation that there are no theory neutral observations for choosing between competing theories. If that were true, then there would be a problem in even applying Neimeyer's criterion in cases where theorists disagree. I predict that a behavioral treatment of a child's enuresis will result in the appearance of a new and probably worse symptom. Two days after a successful treatment, the child becomes quite angry when scolded by his parent. Did my prediction turn out to be accurate? I see Oedipal rage (at least, I think I do), but the behaviorist sees merely a child responding to a scolding. If the theory-ladenness of observation prevents us from deciding who is right, then we cannot even apply Neimeyer's final criterion: We cannot decide whether our predictions are accurate.

Neimeyer could reject the idea that observations are so infected with theory that appeal to them is useless in deciding between rival theories. However, this would constitute an abandonment of one of the main constructivist reasons for rejecting an objectivist epistemology. So, even if it is not a problem for Neimeyer, it is a problem for other constructivists.

There is, finally, an even more serious problem with Neimeyer's last criterion. What does it mean on a constructivist view to say that a prediction is "accurate"? Suppose we say that my prediction about the child developing a new symptom was accurate. Does this mean that what I said was true? Neimeyer might say "no, accuracy does not require truth." In that case, it is not clear what his final criterion even says. I say: "The prediction was quite accurate; it just was not true." What would this mean?

Neimeyer might say that for a prediction to be accurate, it must be true. What would *he* mean, however, in saying that my prediction about the child was true? He could not consistently say that my prediction corresponded with what actually occurred. To interpret "true" in this way would be to rely on the correspondence theory of truth, which is rejected by most constructivists, including Neimeyer (see the left side of his table, 1993: 223).

Constructivists, however, still have two alternatives: rely on a different theory of truth *or* find a substitute for truth. Let us start with the first option.

Some constructivists appear to accept a pragmatic account: A proposition is true exactly if believing it works. However, as Neimeyer himself suggests, sometimes it is useful to have a false belief. So, the fact that a belief works, if this means "useful," is no guarantee that it is true. A pragmatist can always say: Well, that is not what I mean by "works." The problem then becomes one of explaining this crucial notion in a satisfactory fashion. I would simply ask: Can one point to any place in the philosophic literature where this has been done?

Many constructivists, however, do not support a rival theory of truth; rather, they recommend a substitute for truth. For example, Polkinghorne points out (1992: 151) that on a postmodern view, one does not ask whether a knowledge claim is true but rather whether it produces successful results. Mahoney (1989) makes essentially the same point. He notes that modern constructivists are essentially asserting that *viability* is a much more adequate and heuristic schema for epistemic inquiry than is *validity* and ontological correspondence.

Let us see how this is supposed to work. Take first the report that constructivists want to substitute viability for truth. Is this report true? We are not supposed to ask that question. We should inquire only about viability. Yet if it is not true that constructivists want to do without truth, then this is not even their position. What, then, are we debating?

Take next the issue of what viability is. I theorize that all neuroses are due to faulty conditioning. This theory works for me in that I use it to guide my therapeutic interventions, and I think that I get good results. But, how am I supposed to determine that I do? I could inquire as to whether it is true that my clients tend to improve. However, I am not permitted to ask that question. To ask it would be to bring back the concept of truth. Do not ask if my belief that I get good results is true; ask only if the belief is *viable*. However, so far there is nothing to the idea that my etiological theory is viable; given what has been said so far, there are no good results that we know of.

Perhaps my belief that I get good results, although quite possibly not true, is itself viable: It helps quash some nagging doubts about my clinical work. I ask again: Is it true that this result obtains? Perhaps my doubts have increased. Unless my belief that I get good results is true, I have made no progress at all in explaining how my etiological theory is viable.

In brief, if it is not true that holding a theory leads to some useful result, then what does it mean to say that the theory is "viable"? If it does have to be true, then truth is required in order for viability to obtain. In saying, then, that a belief is viable, we are tacitly presupposing that something is true – namely, that useful results obtain. In fact, we have to presuppose a great deal more than that about truth. If there are useful results, what is the relationship between the belief and those results? Is it logical, as when we derive a true prediction from our theory? Or, is it causal? On either option, more truth is required. For my belief to be viable, it is not enough that by coincidence good fortune follows: it also has to be true that the right sort of connection holds between my holding the belief and some sort of useful result.

The same sorts of problems arise if we substitute "generative capacity" for *viability*. Kenneth Gergen (1994) suggests that rather than ask if a theory is true or false, ask about its generative capacity, its capacity to challenge the guiding assumptions of the culture, to raise fundamental questions regarding social life, to foster reconsideration of that which is taken for granted, and thus generate fresh alternatives for social action. Empirical research can still continue, Gergen notes, but only to provide *rhetorical* support for a theory.

Having a good deal of generative capacity may be a good feature for a theory to possess, but it is no guarantee or even evidence of truth (something that Gergen does not deny). A false, empirically unsupported theory can have generative power. Gergen can agree to that, but a more serious, in fact fatal, problem is that a theory can have generative power only if certain things are true. It must be true that the results that Gergen speaks of can obtain: that the prevailing assumptions can be challenged, that new approaches are possible, and so on. Furthermore, there must be some sort of connection between the theory (or acceptance of it) and the successful challenges or the production of alternatives. Finally, why care whether a theory has generative power unless the currently held theories are false, or at least it is true that challenging them would produce some good result, which in turn requires that something else be true? Generative power, like viability, may be one criterion for judging theories; it does not, however, provide a workable general substitute for truth.

In sum, the attempt to explain how we can dispense altogether with the concept of truth by talking about viability or generative power is a total failure. That means that Neimeyer's final criterion, which talks of accuracy of predictions, is also a failure, although it fails for many other reasons as well. Where, then, does this leave the constructivist criteria for validating knowledge claims? They are of no use whatsoever. I have spent time on these criteria not because they are Neimeyer's, but because I believe that he is correct in saying that these are validational criteria generally accepted by constructivists. That does not mean that they are universally accepted, but where are there better proposals in the post-modernist literature? It is not enough to reject the correspondence theory of truth and the appeal to empirical observations on the grounds that they are theory-laden. Unless one is simply urging a total skepticism, one needs some substitute. The substitutes proposed by postmodernists so far, including those of Mahoney (1989), Polkinghorne (1992), and Gergen (1994), whether they are wrong or right, are not useful in validating knowledge claims.

There would be little point in inquiring further about the truth as opposed to the utility of the doctrines just examined. Arguing for their falsity would involve repeating many of the arguments given above. Consider, for example, Neimeyer's three criteria of validation. As already argued, checking the consistency of a hypothesis with existing knowledge structures and seeing whether there is a social consensus is neither necessary nor sufficient for validation, or confirmation to any degree. "Fitting and Viability," which Neimeyer explains in terms of accuracy of predictions, is a trivial necessary condition of validation. It amounts to no more than the trivial logical point that a true hypothesis cannot imply a false proposition. Taken as a sufficient condition, the criterion is wrong (see Differentialness in section II of this chapter). Neimeyer's third "criterion," that there is (and perhaps ought to be) a diversity of interpretations, is not a criterion of validation at all. It is not needed where the diverse interpretations are not in conflict, and it is of no help where they are.

As to viability and generative power, it is false, for reasons given earlier, to say that they are adequate substitute criteria for truth. Their very application requires that certain propositions – for example, about a theory's consequences – be true and that others be false. In any event, whether they are true or false, the positive epistemic theses of post-modernism are of little or no help in determining which psychotherapies are effective for certain problems, or which underlying clinical theories are at least on the right track.

Before turning to a rival approach, it may be useful to comment on the main reasons that typically drive postmodernists to reject an objectivist epistemology. They concern: (1) the rejection of the correspondence theory of truth; (2) the alleged theory-ladenness of all observations; (3) anti-foundationalism; and (4) the alleged relativity of epistemic standards. There is an extensive philosophic literature on each of these topics, the upshot of which is to undermine the postmodernist claims. Rather than try to demonstrate this last point here in detail, I will merely sketch how the argument would go.

(a) Rejection of the Correspondence Theory of Truth

(a) *Rejection of the Correspondence Theory of Truth*   Partly due to the influence of the philosopher Richard Rorty (1979), constructivists and other postmodernists tend to reject the correspondence theory of truth. What, however, are they rejecting? There are different versions of the correspondence theory. On what is sometimes called "an inflationary" version, the world is said to contain facts and propositions. Truth is said to consist of a correspondence between them. So, a proposition is true when and only when it corresponds to the fact that it purports to state. The standard objection is that there is no illuminating way to explain the concept of a fact or the correspondence relation. Some philosophers also have doubts about saying that facts are entities that exist in the world.

There are, however, "deflationary" versions of the correspondence theory that do not have metaphysical implications. On one version, for example, a proposition is true if it says what is the case, and is false otherwise. Such "theories" (really definitions) are not very illuminating, but it is not clear that having an objectivist epistemology requires an illuminating (inflationary) theory of truth. One possibility is to explain truth in terms of what is called "disquotation." For example, Freud says that there is a mental apparatus. What is necessary and sufficient for this being true (not for our knowing it to be true, but merely for its being true)? The answer is given by the following: "There is a mental apparatus" is true if and only if: There is a mental apparatus. In general, we provide truth conditions for a sentence or proposition by substituting in the following schema: "*P* is true" if and only if *P*. (For a good discussion of this sort of account of truth, see Horwich, 1990.)

Although postmodernists may not yet have noticed this, Rorty has now changed his mind about truth. In a recent paper (1995), he points out that pragmatists such as himself tend to swing back and forth between trying to reduce truth to something like warranted assertability and accepting a minimalist – that is, a deflationary – account of truth. Sooner or later, he points out, any reductionist account always falls victim to the objection that the conditions of the account might be met by a belief that is not true. There may still be, as Rorty suggests, something more to be discovered about truth than is provided by deflationary accounts. John Searle (1995: 200–21) suggests one possibility: Use a disquotational criterion to explain the ideas of "fact" and "correspondence," and thereby make more illuminating the traditional correspondence theory of truth. However, the key point is that, as far as anyone has shown, an objectivist epistemology has no need of anything more; a deflationary account is sufficient for its purposes.

(b) Anti-Foundationalism   "Foundationalism" is the name of the theory that says, roughly, our non-basic beliefs are ultimately justified by so-called "basic beliefs," and these in turn are either self-justifying or are in no need of justification. One of the main reasons given for the turn to a postmodernist epistemology is that all foundationalist theories are said to have failed.

The problem with this reason is that objectivist epistemology does not presuppose a solution to the problem that motivated traditional foundationalism; see Haack's incisive reply to Rorty on this point (1993: 182–94). Suppose that all current solutions to the problem are wrong; it does not follow that there is no objective supporting evidence for any belief at all, or even that we cannot articulate general objective epistemological standards. I will discuss some objective standards in the next section that are relevant to debates about psychotherapy. None of these presupposes a solution to the problems concerning foundations.

It should also be mentioned that there are different versions of foundationalism. Although this has not clearly happened yet, one of them may eventually be worked out in a satisfactory manner.

Finally, on the issue of ultimate support for our beliefs, foundationalism is not the only game in town. A traditional rival is coherentism, interpreted not as a theory of truth but of justification (for the best-developed version, see Bonjour, 1985). Another rival is called "Foundherentism" (Haack, 1993, especially chapter 4).

(c) The Impurity of Observation   A third favorite thesis of postmodernists is the idea that there are no "pure" observations. Observations are said to be tainted by or laden with theories, and this is supposed to make it difficult or impossible to choose between competing theories by appeal to empirical observation.

Are all observations theory-laden? That depends on what is meant. Sometimes all that is meant is that we do not see pure sense data. Take my example of the psychoanalyst and behavior therapist who disagree about whether the purely symptomatic treatment of a bed-wetting child will soon be followed by the appearance of a new symptom, one that is caused by an unresolved unconscious conflict. They both observe the child soon after he is "cured" and watch him as he screams angrily at his mother. Neither sees merely the appearance of a child nor a child-like sense datum; rather, they see a child, one who is screaming at his parent. Virtually no philosopher writing today would disagree with this. If all that is meant by the slogan "There are no pure observations" is that we generally see physical objects and events, as opposed to sense data, then so-called "objectivist" epistemologists agree. What they would challenge is the claim that this relatively trivial thesis supports relativism, or poses any threat to the objective empirical warranting of hypotheses. Where is the cogent argument that will take us straight from "We do not see sense data" to skepticism, relativism, or anything similar?

There are other ways to interpret the slogan that all observations are theory-laden (see Erwin, 1988b), but on none of them is the thesis both simultaneously plausible and supportive of any interesting postmodernist epistemological doctrine. Barbara von Eckardt (1981) puts the key point nicely: To obtain *objective* data evidentially relevant to a theory T, it is sufficient that the data can be collected by someone whether or not he or she believes T, or even whether or not he or she has any knowledge of T. There is no reason to believe that the "impurity of observations" makes such a collection of data having probative worth impossible.

(d) Relativism   A fourth plank in the postmodernist program is epistemological relativism. As Kuhn suggests (1977), different paradigms have different standards for evaluating evidence. The relativist contends that evidence is always evaluated relative to these different standards, but

the standards themselves, it is alleged, cannot be evaluated in a paradigm-neutral manner.

This thesis should be distinguished from an empirical proposition about the history of science which says that in some paradigm disputes each side was relying on different epistemic standards, but neither side made a rational case for its respective standards. For example, Dalton and the pre-Daltonian chemists might have begged the question against each other by relying on their respective *unsupported* standards (see Doppelt, 1988). This empirical thesis might be true of some disputes in the history of science, but it does not imply the relativistic thesis that, even in principle, no further rational considerations could have settled the disputes.

One obvious question for the relativist is this: If a paradigm assesses evidence by appeal to a certain standard which is neither obviously true nor well supported, why would satisfying *that* standard count as warranting a proposition? In Bachrach et al. (1991), a sub-committee of the American Psychoanalytic Association appeals to Kuhn's views to justify their use of specifically psychoanalytic standards to assess the psychoanalytic outcome evidence. Even if all psychoanalysts were to endorse these standards, would meeting them be any guarantee that the data in question are confirmatory? The standards might be far too weak to suffice for confirmation, as in fact they are (see Erwin, 1996: chapter 6).

Some explanation is needed, then, as to why acceptance of just any old standards by a paradigm guarantees that meeting them is sufficient for warranting a hypothesis. Assuming that members of a paradigm are fallible, perhaps they are all in error in choosing their evidential standards.

Suppose, furthermore, that it were true that we could justify any proposition just by selecting evidential standards that gave it a passing grade *even though* there was no reason to think that the standards were correct. In that case, the relativist would have another serious problem: by my standards, relativism is false. So, it logically follows, on the supposition in question, that we are warranted in believing that relativism is false. The truth of relativism will be warranted relative to the relativist's own standards, if he chooses wisely, but that does not change the fact that, according to the relativist's own theory, there is good reason to believe that the doctrine is false. Even if my reason is checkmated by the relativist's appeal to his own standards, there is just as good a reason to believe that relativism is false as to believe that it is true – see Erwin (1988b), and Siegel (1988) for further discussion of these points and other objections to relativism.

I am not trying to prove, incidentally, that relativism is false; I am arguing for the weaker claim that we have no reason to think it true. One could reply that in arguing that relativism is unwarranted, I take for granted a certain view of logic that is challenged by radical behaviorism. Follette and Houts (1992: 253) make this charge against me, and refer the reader to Houts and Haddock (1992) for a defense of their behaviorist view of logic. I take up their defense when I discuss radical behaviorism in Chapter 5, but I will say now that this view of logic lends no support to relativism.

Some relativists concede that their doctrine is unwarranted. For example, Gergen (1985: 272) says that, although constructivism casts doubt on objective warranting, accounts of social construction cannot themselves be warranted empirically. I assume that Gergen is not making the erroneous point that constructionism can be warranted a priori; he is clearly suggesting that *any* kind of warranting is challenged by constructivism. If, however, constructivist epistemological doctrines in general, or relativism in particular, are completely unwarranted, then any argument that depends on them lacks cogency. We have no reason, then, to think that any of these theses are true.

Gergen contends in the preface to the second edition (1994: ix) of his 1982 book that his arguments place in jeopardy traditional assumptions of objectivity, rationality, and truth (among other things); that they are still cogent; and that they have not been answered. My reply is this: His main arguments have now been answered in so far as they rely on the postmodernist epistemological doctrines that I have examined. His arguments are *not* cogent, and they pose no threat to reasonable, traditional assumptions about either objectivity, rationality, or truth. I have said nothing, however, about much of what Gergen has argued about other matters. To take one example, his idea that psychologists are wrong to search for general laws is interesting, provocative, and possibly correct. However, this claim entails nothing about truth, objectivity, or rationality. On the contrary, we would be rational in believing it to be true only if we had objective empirical evidence to support Gergen's hypothesis.

There is one remaining thesis to consider, one that lies at the very foundation of constructivism, although it is not an epistemological claim: that reality is constructed by us. It is quite remarkable how often this claim has been repeated without any attempt to make clear what it means. Gergen, however, is an exception. Under the heading "The Scientific Creation of Reality," he writes:

> In the act of description scientists establish an essential inventory of "what there is." In this sense, such terms as "repression," "socioeconomic class," "schizophrenia," "learned helplessness," "midlife crisis," "dissonance reduction," and so on are not the results of keen observation. Rather they operate as lenses supplied by the theorist to colleagues and society alike. *The world is not so constituted until the lens is employed.* (Gergen, 1994: 23; 1982; my italics)

What I have italicized is deeply mistaken. Not only does it not follow from the preceding, but it is patently false. Even now there may not be any such thing as repression, at least in a Freudian sense (see Erwin, 1996), but if it does occur, it most likely occurred before Freud ever wrote. Schizophrenia, to take another example, used to be called "dementia praecox," but there were schizophrenics before the term "schizophrenia" was coined. The proposition that there were schizophrenics in the nineteenth century does not logically entail that the term "schizophrenic" was in use at that time. People had the HIV virus before it was given a name. We did not create the HIV virus by naming it; it was there, one of the constituents of reality, before we invented the term. If the "lens" is a particular concept C, what C designates may exist before anyone ever employs C. The world, contrary to Gergen, *is* "so constituted" before the lens is employed.

One could say, however, that *part* of reality is created by us. Someone coined the expression "learned helplessness"; someone else invented the expression "schizophrenia," and so forth. This is quite true but one does not get the Nobel Prize for cloaking such banalities in philosophic jargon. Somebody created the expressions, but saying that is very different from saying that the realities they refer to — namely, learned helplessness and schizophrenia — were created by us.

So-called "social realities" may be different in this respect. We not only invent the terms but, unlike the moon and the stars, we also bring the referents into existence. Through various social arrangements, we create such things as marriage and labor unions. Even in these cases, however, it can be seriously misleading to say that the *continued* reality is created by us. If I start a club, then I deserve credit for the creation of one social reality. Once it is created, however, its existence does not depend on my belief that it exists; it can continue to exist even after I lose interest in it. Moreover, if I make empirical claims about the consequences of joining my club, they require objective warranting like any other empirical proposition. There may be things to be said of real philosophic interest about the creation of social realities, such as marriage, the parliament, the church, and so on — see Searle (1995) for such a discussion — but the fact that they are created lends no support to the radical thesis that all of reality is created by us.

Some constructivists say that it is not reality but our knowledge of it that is socially constructed. This is quite a different thesis, but it, too, on further examination, turns out to be trivial or false. Sometimes what is meant is that what is constructed is the terms in which knowledge claims are phrased. We now know that schizophrenia is at least partly biologically caused, but we would not know that if someone had not invented the term "schizophrenia." This is true but platitudinous. If it is also added that our warrant for our belief about the etiology of schizophrenia is just made up or is just a matter of satisfying certain social conventions, there is no argument for either claim beyond what I have already considered. Those arguments all lack cogency.

More could be said about the constructivist thesis that the world does not exist independently of our constructions, but on these issues, I refer the reader to Searle's excellent discussion (1995: 149–76). There is no interesting version of it that is true.

Conclusion: Based on what has been produced so far, the verdict on postmodernist epistemology must be that its positive proposals about validation are both useless and false; the negative arguments against an objectivist epistemology given by postmodernists are completely lacking in cogency. There are serious problems that threaten the psychotherapeutic enterprise (see Chapter 8), but the turn toward postmodernism will only make matters worse. I turn next to a different approach: one that tries to develop an objectivist epistemology.

II

An Objectivist Epistemology

By an objectivist epistemology, I mean, in part, a set of epistemic standards the truth of which is independent of what any human believes. Some may be peculiar to a particular paradigm, or to an intellectual community, but their truth or falsity is not dependent upon their acceptance or rejection by any individual or group.

Standards that are objective in this sense may, of course, still be either quite trivial or unwarranted. The goal here, however, is to find some warranted objective standards that will be useful in evaluating psychotherapeutic evidence. Although only a few such standards are discussed, they were chosen because they either have already played an important role in evaluating psychotherapeutic evidence or they have that potential.

Causal Relevance Most psychotherapeutic theories talk about causal factors that are not claimed to be either necessary or sufficient for the occurrence of an event; at best, they are causally relevant, that is, they make a difference of some kind or other. By what standards do we evaluate claims of causal relevance? The work of the philosopher Wesley Salmon is of help here (see as well Grünbaum, 1993: 163).

Salmon (1984: 185) makes the point that to test the hypothesis that a factor is generally causally relevant to the production of some effect, we need to find evidence in the form of a statistically relevant relationship. For example, suppose that I hypothesize that a certain genetic abnormality is causally relevant to the development of alcoholism in men over the age of 50. Call this genetic factor G. First, we need to develop what Salmon calls "a reference class." This is the class of things in which the effect is being postulated. The reference class in this case is the class of males over the age of 50. Call this class C. The next step is to divide C into two subclasses: those males with G and those without it. To test our hypothesis, we need to do a statistical comparison to find out if the frequency of alcoholism is greater in the G class than in the non-G class. If the incidence of alcoholism is greater when G is absent, that is evidence that the genetic factor is not making a difference to the development of alcoholism in men over 50. Suppose that we were to find just the reverse: that there is more alcoholism among men over 50 with the G factor than without it. Finding that out would generally be necessary for confirming the hypothesis, but it would not by itself be sufficient. At the very least, the differential condition (see below) would also have to be met.

Although Salmon's principle needs some minor modifications which I will not go into here (see Erwin, 1996: 76–84), it is important for assessing claims that certain factors are *generally* causally relevant to the occurrence of some event or condition. It is also indirectly applicable to the assessment of singular causal claims. I say that the client's relationship with his mother determined his homosexuality. I am talking about only one case, but one way to get evidence that the relationship made an important difference is to determine whether these types of relationships generally (not necessarily always) are causally relevant in determining sexual orientation.

Differentialness I suggested above that confirmation of the causal hypothesis about alcoholism would require more than the finding that the rate of alcoholism goes up when the *G* factor is present. That is true partly (but not only) because a rival theory might provide an equally good, or even better, explanation of this finding. We might have reason to believe that the greater incidence of alcoholism is just a coincidence.

More generally, whenever a theory predicts a certain result, we need to check whether an equally plausible incompatible theory explains the result just as well, all things considered. Suppose I predict that if I pray for someone's well-being over a period of three weeks, then his affliction will vanish. If his problem is merely a common cold, the truth of the prediction is hardly sufficient to confirm the claim that prayer made the difference. Even if no one thought to bring in a spontaneous remission hypothesis before the "cure," it can be appealed to now. It provides, given what we know about the longevity of colds, as good an (in fact a better) explanation as the prayer hypothesis.

This case suggests the following general condition for confirmation: Data confirm a hypothesis only if they do so *differentially*. This means the following: For any body of data *D* and hypothesis *H*, *D* confirms *H* only if *D* provides some reason for believing that *H* is true, and does not provide equal (or better) reason for believing some incompatible rival that is just as plausible.

The differential principle nicely explains why there is no confirmation in the prayer case, but that one case is insufficient reason to accept it. There is, however, a more general argument. Suppose that two hypotheses *A* and *B* are logically incompatible, and certain evidence *E* is neutral between them. Given our total evidence, *E* gives us no more reason to believe *A* rather than *B*, or conversely. If we were to say that *E* nevertheless supports *A*, there would be no reason to deny support to *B*, and to the same degree. However, if *E* supports *B*, it just as well supports the denial of *A*; for *B* entails not-*A*. So, if *E* were to support *A*, it would equally well support not-*A*. That means it does not support *A* at all.

Suppose that I say that my evidence supports the hypothesis that all mental health problems, including psychoses, are due to faulty conditioning. However, I then concede that my so-called evidence provides just as much reason to believe that my hypothesis is *false*. Should I not concede that because my evidence is neutral between the truth and falsity of my hypothesis, it really fails to support it? Evidence that gives us just as much reason to deny a proposition as to affirm it does not give us any good reason to affirm it. (For further discussion of the differential standard, see Erwin and Siegel, 1989; Erwin, 1996: 44–54.)

If the differential standard is correct (as a necessary but not sufficient condition of confirmation), it is especially important in the field of psychotherapy. It quite frequently happens that a psychotherapist will claim support for a proposition without making any attempt at all to discount obvious rival hypotheses that appear to be just as plausible. Unless greater effort is made to insure that the differential standard is satisfied, controversy will continue in this field and progress will be stifled.

Inference to the Best Explanation Many psychotherapeutic theories talk about unobservable events or states such as repressed wishes or unconscious phantasies. If we ban all references to unobservables, as some behaviorists demand, then we rule out in advance of empirical inquiry causal hypotheses that might be crucial for an understanding of clinical phenomena. If we are willing to entertain such hypotheses, however, then we face the problem of how we establish their truth. The standard philosophic solution is to rely on the rule of inference called "inference to the best explanation" (or IBE).

Roughly the idea, which is ancient, even if the name is relatively new, is that we postulate certain unobservables in order to explain observable phenomena. We postulate, say, events that go through an infant's mind shortly after birth on the grounds that the postulation best explains the observations that the therapist makes during the transference. If the explanation really is the best one, then, it is claimed, we have at least some grounds for accepting our hypothesis, for thinking it is true.

At least two sorts of questions need to be answered about IBE. First, how do we determine what is the "best" of the available explanations? Some philosophers say that in addition to appealing to relevant empirical evidence, we can also rely on so-called "pragmatic" criteria, such as simplicity, parsimony, and explanatory power. My own view is that plausibility is all that matters from an epistemological point of view, and that is determined solely by logical considerations (such as the internal consistency of the theory) and the empirical data. Of course, well confirmed theories might be appealed to as well, but their being well confirmed ultimately depends on the observational data. On this view, which is probably not the standard one among philosophers, simplicity and other pragmatic considerations play no independent epistemic role, although in a certain domain, we may have empirical evidence that the simpler of two theories is more likely to be true. My reasons for holding this view are discussed in Erwin, 1996: 54–60.

Whatever position one takes on the aforementioned issue, another must be faced. However one decides what is the best available explanation of certain data, does the fact that it is the best one anyone can think of suffice for having grounds for thinking the hypothesis is true, or at least approximately true? In other words, does IBE take the following form: "H (if true) explains *D* better than any competing explanation that is available; consequently, we have some evidence (it could be rather weak) that H is true"?

If we read the psychotherapy literature, we will find that reliance on this very rule, although not stated in the same words, is very common. Quite often, a psychotherapist will give an interpretation of the client's behavior or will embrace some general etiological theory, and will offer no more grounds than: This is the best explanation of the phenomena that anyone has thought of. When stated in the above form, however, IBE provides much too low a standard for judging hypotheses. Use of the rule would guarantee support for any hypothesis with the capacity to explain certain data merely because no one could think of a rival. We could use it to support hypotheses not merely about such things as neutrinos or black holes, but also about such things as alien kidnapings and religious miracles. That will not appear objectionable to those who find the latter sort of postulations credible, but there are independent reasons to reject IBE *if* stated in the above form (see van Fraassen, 1989; Erwin, 1996: chapter 3).

How to state IBE in a form that is simultaneously plausible and non-trivial is an unsolved philosophic problem. So, I will not try to state a new version here; see Erwin (1996: chapter 3) for further discussion of this issue. I will simply comment that we need not go as far as those behaviorists who reject a priori all explanatory hypotheses that talk about unobservables, but neither should we adopt a standard for their confirmation that is absurdly low.

A Science of Psychotherapy? Some postmodernists have metaphysical objections to the idea that psychotherapy can be an applied science. Human beings, it is argued, are free and autonomous, or at least can be made so through the use of psychotherapy, and this fact is said to be incompatible with determinism, and perhaps any causation of human action. My reply in Chapter 1 was: (1) the compatibility of a strict determinism with human freedom of the sort required for moral responsibility is still a live option; and (2) the sort of autonomy that we clearly do have and which psychotherapists seek to enhance is obviously compatible with there being causal explanations of human action.

Another metaphysical objection is that the mental is (allegedly) irreducible to the physical. This objection is a bit tricky: There may be some sort of connection between mind–body dualism and the possibility of a psychotherapeutic science. However, as long as there are causal connections between mental events and behavior, these relationships can be studied scientifically regardless of the ultimate metaphysical status of the mental.

A third metaphysical objection is that there are no psychotherapeutic laws awaiting discovery. This may well be true if we are talking about the sorts of natural laws discovered in physics and chemistry, although only empirical inquiry can settle this question. For a science of psychotherapy to exist, however, there need not be such laws. It is enough that there be clinically significant true generalizations stating causal relationships between certain causally relevant factors and certain effects. In other words, such generalizations need not be of the form "All B-type events are caused by A-type events." Instead, they may be of the sort "Under certain initial conditions, *C*, A-type events generally make an important causal difference to the occurrence of B-type events." For example, it might be true that a certain sort of treatment, under such and such conditions, can help relieve a certain type of depression for a certain type of client in a certain percentage of cases.

It may also be true, as Gergen argues (1994), that the causal relationships discovered today will be inapplicable later. This need not be because the original generalizations were false, but because the initial conditions no longer hold. A certain cognitive therapy may help in treating depression provided that certain initial conditions hold, but 50 years from now, they may no longer hold. So, it may be unrealistic to expect true, interesting *timeless* generalizations, if this means ones that postulate initial conditions that hold for all time. A science of psychotherapy does not need such generalizations.

Some psychotherapists, however, object to any sort of psychotherapeutic generalization. Held (1995: 18) makes the point that the importation of postmodern ideas has meant, for some therapists, that each client must be viewed as a unique individual, with his or her own history or set of experiences, and that, consequently, predetermined diagnostic categories, such as "depression," no longer apply to the therapeutic enterprise.

Although she is generally skeptical about postmodernism, Held herself says (1995: 19) that no two "schizophrenics" are alike for *all* therapeutic purposes. I agree with this rather obvious point, but not with certain inferences that are sometimes drawn. Why does the uniqueness of each individual prevent informative generalization in psychotherapy but not in other disciplines that study people, such as physical medicine?

Yes, each client is different in many respects, but all have some characteristics in common (in fact, an infinite number), and some share properties of causal significance. Clearly, all clients are clients; all are male or female; all will live and die; and so on. A sub-set of these clients are schizophrenic or depressed, and that has causal significance. One need not say that all schizophrenics are alike for all treatment purposes in order to say, truly, that most having a certain type of schizophrenia will respond in such and such a way to a certain type of psychotropic drug under certain conditions.

In short, the perfectly sober point that diagnostic categories such as "depression" have a limited significance, because depressed people may differ in causally significant ways, does not support the extravagant doctrine that no interesting generalizations are possible. All clients are different, but all are also alike. Neither platitude makes a science of psychotherapy impossible.

Finally, there is the claim of those analysts who hold that therapeutic interpretations are stories which should be judged by aesthetic or poetic criteria. This claim entails nothing about the possibility of a psychotherapeutic science. Such stories may be poetic or not, but we can still ask: Do they accurately portray what caused the client's problems? Answering that question requires empirical information. Some analysts will respond that there is no need to ask that question; what matters clinically is not whether such stories are true, but whether telling them helps the client. Assuming that one does not care about theory, that, too, may be true; it may be the credibility rather than the truth of such stories that matter from a therapeutic point of view. However, asking whether the telling of such stories helps any clients, and if so, which ones, is to ask a causal question. This is a question that can and should be addressed in a scientific manner.

In sum, the main impediments to the development of a psychotherapeutic science are epistemological rather than metaphysical, but they too present no obstacles that are impossible to overcome. There is an appalling lack of clarity and rigor in the writings of many psychotherapists; there is often no expressed need to bolster grand conjectures by any empirical evidence; the little evidence that is cited often falls below minimum epistemological standards. None of these failings, however, reflects any difficulty in principle. There is nothing about psychotherapeutic phenomena that guarantees a low level of argument, or a failure to do experiments, or a tendency to pay no attention to experimental findings. The proof of this is the high level of argument and the well-designed experiments that have been provided in certain areas of psychotherapy, and not just by cognitivists and behavior therapists, but by some psychodynamic theorists and therapists as well.

Some postmodernists make a different point, not that a psychotherapeutic science is impossible but that it is undesirable. Given the nature of the phenomena, it is argued, the field is and ought to remain one of the humanities. My reply is that the field needs better clinical theories, outcome measures, diagnostic categories, and most of all more effective therapies. To say this is seriously to understate the problems, despite all that has been accomplished (see Chapter 8). How are these problems to be solved without developing causal generalizations of some sort and testing them empirically (in many cases, experimentally)? If one agrees that there is no reasonable alternative, but insists that the field should still be one of the humanities, then the difference between us is merely verbal.

If, however, one argues that clarity, precision, rigorous empirical testing and the like are unnecessary, what is being rejected is not merely the need for more and better science, but also a firm basis *of any kind* for believing psychotherapeutic claims. The inevitable result of that approach will be continued confusion and sterility.

Part II
Psychotherapeutic Paradigms

5

Behavior Modification and the New Behaviorism

In the second half of this book, I follow the practice of many writers on psychotherapy in organizing the field into paradigms. However, my divisions and use of the term "paradigm" require a brief explanation.

As I use the term, a "paradigm" in the field of psychotherapy includes several elements. First, it includes what Kuhn (1977) calls an "exemplar," except that I broaden the notion to include an apparently successful therapeutic strategy *or* a research strategy, whereas Kuhn, with physics in mind, includes only the latter. Watson's conditioning of Little Albert in order to demonstrate the conditioning basis of neurosis is an example of an influential research strategy, whereas Mary Cover Jones' (1924) use of Watson's ideas in treating a small animal phobia is an example of a therapeutic strategy; namely, counter-conditioning. Both count as "exemplars," that is, as important examples that were influential in the development of behavior modification.

Second, psychotherapeutic paradigms include one or more forms of psychotherapy (using this term to include any kind of psychological therapy) and one or more empirical theories, usually about how clinical problems originate or how therapies work, or both.

Third, such paradigms include various assumptions about methodology, values, philosophy, or all three.

The use of the concept of a paradigm is helpful in organizing theories, therapies, and more, but it can also mislead. Many psychotherapists are eclectic in their orientation, and so would not accept the tenets of any of the major paradigms. That is, they would not accept *all* of them, but most borrow something or other from the leading paradigms. (It would be hard to reject all such paradigm doctrines and still do psychotherapy.) In many cases, what eclectic psychotherapists appropriate, they often leave unexamined and sometimes unarticulated. They are guided by key ideas of, say Freud, or Skinner, or Carl Rogers without ever having evaluated or even marked out clearly what these ideas are. Consequently, despite the prevalence of eclecticism, it is still useful to try to lay out some of the foundational assumptions of the main paradigms and expose them to rational discussion.

Even within a paradigm, there is often considerable disagreement. Consequently, when I identify an assumption of a paradigm, I am not implying, unless I say so, that most or all within the paradigm accept the assumption.

Finally, I reject the epistemological relativism adopted by many who speak of paradigms. One reason is that, as I argued in the last chapter, relativism when applied to itself undermines its own warrant. Therefore, there is no good reason to believe it. Second, the epistemic standards that I defended in the last chapter apply across paradigms. They can be used to challenge standards that are internal to a paradigm, if they need challenging. Consequently, we need not restrict the inquiry to a description of the standards of various paradigms. We can also say: Yes, they are the commonly accepted standards of such and such a paradigm, but are they *right?*

The Old Behavior Therapy Paradigm

In the 1960's and 1970's, it was common to talk about a single behavior therapy paradigm, or, as it was also called, a "behavior modification" paradigm. (I will initially follow the practice of this period and use the terms "behavior therapy" and "behavior modification" interchangeably.) The original paradigm was heavily influenced by various kinds of behaviorist doctrines. Furthermore, most of those who founded the paradigm described themselves as "behaviorists." Finally, "behavior therapy" was commonly defined as *conditioning therapy*, and by that was meant a therapy based on *behavioristic* conditioning principles.

The original behavior therapy paradigm contained a number of elements, although for most of these, there never was unanimity. Some of the more important are the following: (1) a commitment to some form of conditioning theory; (2) an acceptance of certain philosophic doctrines, such as logical behaviorism, operationism, or methodological behaviorism; and (3) a rejection of the medical model; for definitions of these doctrines, see Erwin (1978: chapters 2 and 4).

The above doctrines were most crucial to the old behavior therapy paradigm, but there were others as well. For example, most agreed to the idea that human behavior is lawfully determined, a view sometimes called "macrodeterminism." Behavior therapists also tended to be empiricists in so far as they agreed that all non-definitional claims could be warranted only by empirical observations. However, these other philosophic theses were also acceptable to many Freudians and cognitivists as well.

With a few exceptions, it is difficult to discern any distinctive set of values among behavior therapists of this period. The first exception is a tendency to value therapeutic outcomes that involve behavioral change. Second, there also seems to have been a good deal of agreement that the client rather than the therapist should determine the therapeutic goals. Many non-behaviorists, however, shared this value. (A few other examples of the values of behavior therapists are discussed in the next chapter.)

By the late 1970's, the cognitive revolution in behavior therapy had taken root. Today, behaviorists are probably in the minority among those identifying themselves as "behavior therapists," at least in the United States. In a poll of its membership, the Association for the Advancement of Behavior Therapy found that 75 per cent said they were "cognitivists" and only 25 per cent called themselves "behaviorists."

The consensus about the old paradigm may have crumbled for multiple reasons, some of which are sociological and psychological. I think that most historians of the behavior therapy movement will agree that a number of works made a difference, but that the writings of Albert Bandura and Michael Mahoney were especially influential. What follows is a summary of an argument of my own that I believe tells against the old behavior therapy–behavior modificationist paradigm. I make no claim, however, about its historical influence.

In Erwin (1978), I argued that the conditioning claims of the old paradigm seemed to be on firm ground only because they were systematically shielded from the force of counter-evidence by a web of interlocking philosophic ideas. Reject the bad philosophy, I argued, and the evidence for the behavioristic conditioning foundations of behavior therapy will be shown to be too weak to be supportive. The argument runs as follows.

If one defines "behavior therapy" as therapy based on conditioning principles, then of course it follows that behavior therapy is based on conditioning principles. However, it then becomes an empirical question as to whether most of what are commonly called "behavior therapy techniques" really qualify as behavior therapy. As a preliminary to investigating that question, I proposed a theory neutral account of what behavior therapy is.

The account was formulated in terms of seven principles (Erwin, 1978: 40–4). An oversimplified statement is that behavior therapy is a non-biological form of therapy that developed largely out of learning theory research and that is normally applied directly, incrementally, and experimentally in the treatment of specific maladaptive behavior patterns.

Behaviorists could have tried to rest their case solely on empirical considerations, but most did not do that. Instead, they relied partly on one or more of the philosophic doctrines mentioned earlier. For example, those who accepted logical behaviorism did not deny that mental imagery, for example, played an important role in the most heavily researched of all behavior therapy techniques: systematic desensitization. Instead, they replied that references to "mental imagery" were merely shorthand for talk about behavior. So, it was concluded, systematic desensitization, contrary to appearances, is really purely behavioristic.

Operationism played a similar strategic, protective role. For example, Bandura and his colleagues provided compelling experimental evidence that cognitive factors and *not* counter-conditioning explains how systematic desensitization works (Bandura and Adams, 1977). However, Bandura's views were dismissed by those who appealed to operationism (see, for example, Gerwirtz, 1971: 303).

Of even more importance than the reliance on logical behaviorism and operationism were the various arguments of the methodological behaviorists who tried to rule out all cognitivist explanations on a priori grounds. Cognitions, it was said, were unobservable, or private, or their reports were unreliable, or they could not be manipulated, and so forth. In Erwin (1978: 66–74), I examine 12 such arguments and explain how each one fails. That these arguments should prove worthless is not surprising. It is an empirical question as to what causes what. One cannot decide by armchair philosophic reflection whether nature has allowed only for the sorts of causes that behaviorists like to talk about, ones that are public, observable, manipulable, and so on. If empirical inquiry shows that human behavior is determined partly by cognitive causes, then to ban them from psychotherapy is to guarantee in advance that the discipline will remain explanatorily sterile.

Some behaviorists will no doubt respond that they are not interested in explaining behavior; their only scientific goals are the ones set by John Watson (1913): the prediction and control of behavior. Someone who takes this position, however, must in all consistency abandon the attempt to explain the workings of behavior therapy in terms of conditioning factors.

In addition to criticizing all of the extant arguments for methodological behaviorism, I also argued in Erwin (1978) against the remaining behaviorist doctrines, including operationism and logical behaviorism, although many of my objections were not new. My conclusion was (1978: 82) this: Although behaviorism once served a useful heuristic purpose in developing behavior therapy, it is false, and for that reason should be rejected; it is time, I noted, to get behaviorism out of behavior therapy. Here, I was clearly referring to a set of philosophic doctrines. One could give up on these doctrines, and still try to uphold a behavioristic conditioning foundation for behavior therapy. In principle, such a foundation could survive on its own, but in fact, it does not.

Once the seemingly protective philosophic doctrines are stripped away, the empirical evidence quite clearly does not support conditioning principles that make no room for cognitive causes and yet are of sufficiently wide scope to ground behavior therapy principles.

Start with the question: Exactly what is the evidence that would lead one to believe that all behavior is a function of its consequences, or, as Skinner puts it, that the causes of all human behavior lie in the environment? It is not enough to point to experiments where we seemingly condition people by systematically manipulating rewards or punishments. The differential principle of confirmation (see Chapter 3) requires that we do more than this; we also need to discount credible rival explanations. The main rival explanation in most conditioning experiments of non-retarded, non-psychotic humans is a cognitive one, and it is generally ignored by behaviorists. The main exceptions are the experiments employing a "dissociative" design, in which the experimenter attempts to separate awareness of the subjects from the alleged conditioning process. The results of these experiments, however, overwhelmingly support a cognitive explanation; see Brewer's (1974) review, and the discussion in Erwin (1978: 110–13).

Beidel and Turner (1986: 181) respond to the dissociative design experiments that the subject's conscious hypotheses about the consequences of their behavior are, in fact, descriptions of the contingencies which govern behavior. However, this is clearly false. The proposition that the subject believes that a certain response will be followed by a reward is not equivalent to the proposition that the reward is contingent upon the response. The second proposition could be true and yet the subject might be unaware of the contingency; hence, the proposition attributing a certain belief to him or her might be false.

Beidel and Turner also try a different tack, one that presupposes that a thought or belief is separate from the contingency that it is about. They point out that as a result of publicity campaigns people have become aware that "Seat belts save lives." Yet despite the thought that this is so, the percentage of drivers wearing seat belts remained quite low until the introduction of the "contingency" that those not doing so would be fined. Beidel and Turner conclude that "this example provides evidence that the contingency and not just the thought, is responsible for behavior change" (1986: 181).

Does this example provide such evidence? Does the proposition that thinking has causal consequences logically imply the further proposition that just *any* thought will affect behavior under just *any* conditions, no matter what the person's other beliefs and motivation? Of course, it does not. But, then, how is it counter-evidence to the first proposition to find a case where a belief had no effect? Incidentally, although my point does not depend on what the answer is to the following question, we might ask: How do Beidel and Turner know that the reason that the publicity campaign failed was not that most people had another belief – namely, that they themselves were not likely to be in an accident?

Beidel and Turner's example provides no evidence whatsoever for what they claim, but it does illustrate the implausibility of their view. Suppose that the fines had been introduced but the public had not been told of this contingency. How likely is it that the fines would have had the same effect even if the public generally continued to think that they would not be fined whether or not they wore their seat belts?

In addition to the data from the dissociative experiments, there was a great deal of other evidence even in 1978 supporting claims of cognitive causation, and telling against a behavioristic conditioning explanation of the workings of behavior therapy; see Erwin, 1978: chapter 3. As American psychology has become more and more cognitivist in its orientation, and as the a priori restriction on the appeal to cognitivist explanations has been largely abandoned, evidential support for the purely behavioristic conditioning position has eroded further.

What, however, of the status of such operant conditioning principles as the law of effect? Have they been falsified by the observational evidence? Not necessarily. It depends on how they are formulated.

Biglan attempts to convey "how powerful" principles of behavior analysis can be. One of these, apparently the main one, is this: "Both positive and negative reinforcement *increase* the subsequent probability of behavior" (1993: 254, his emphasis). This is a statement of the traditional law of effect. It is not based on any empirical evidence; it is not powerful at all; it has never been falsified because it is in fact a trivial tautology. Why do I say these things? The reason is because just prior to stating the principle, Biglan defines "reinforcement" as consisting of the events that, when made contingent on a behavior, increase the likelihood of that behavior in situations similar to the one in which reinforcement initially occurred (1993: 254). Given this definition, anything that fails to increase the subsequent probability of behavior is, by definition, not reinforcing. So, of course, the tautology that reinforcement (that is, whatever increases the probability of a response) increases the probability of a response has not been falsified. Empty tautologies hold true no matter what the world is like, but for that reason they are useless in either predicting or controlling behavior.

It is possible that in stating his principle about positive and negative reinforcement, Biglan did not intend to give an example of these allegedly "powerful" principles of behavior analysis. If not, then my objection does not apply to his discussion, but a reading of the literature will show that many other supporters of Skinner's views have claimed that the tautological version of the Law of Effect is a fundamental principle of behavior change. There are non-tautological versions of the principle and of other behavioristic conditioning principles, but they all have other fatal problems; see Erwin, 1978: chapter 3.

The main conclusion of Erwin (1978) was: There are no well-confirmed behavioristic conditioning principles of sufficiently wide scope to serve as a foundation for behavior therapy or behavior modification. Many writers continue to talk as if there were such principles, but they generally cite the discredited law of effect – see the objections in Erwin, 1978: chapter 3 – or make no attempt to say what these principles are. For example, Beidel and Turner (1986: 179) contend that a cognition can be viewed as simply another behavior subject to the same laws of acquisition as other behaviors. What, however, are these same laws of acquisition? There are no such laws, at least none that have been confirmed.

What has been the verdict of behavior therapists on the above set of arguments? Eysenck (1979a) agrees that the arguments tell against the Skinnerian position, but argues that they fail to undermine his newer version of a classical-type conditioning theory (Eysenck, 1987a). Eysenck is right about this. Although he has sometimes appealed to logical behaviorism, his "conditioning" theory in no way depends on that unacceptable doctrine. Furthermore, the empirical evidence that I cited in support of cognitive causation is neutral with respect to Eysenck's theory; for his theory allows for cognitive causes. So, the arguments of Erwin (1978) do not eliminate the possibility that some or even most behavior therapy techniques can be explained by so-called "conditioning" factors. I will consider Eysenck's view in the next chapter, but I will point out now that the target in Erwin (1978) was various philosophical behaviorisms and the empirical claim that behavior therapy was based on *behavioristic* conditioning principles – namely, principles that assigned no causal role to cognitive factors. Eysenck's theory is not behavioristic in this sense, whether or not it is aptly called a "conditioning" theory (see my remarks in the next chapter).

On what was my subject, the alleged behavioristic foundations of behavior therapy, one leading behavior therapist writes the following: "Erwin (1978) was the first to demonstrate clearly that, contrary to its stated position, behavior therapy was not really behavioristic in a formal sense" (Rotgers, 1988).

If Rotgers is right, then why is behaviorism still flourishing – see Friman et al. (1993)? Even if it is no longer the dominant position within the field of behavior therapy, there clearly are a number of behaviorists who still practice behavior modification; they are typically referred to as "applied behavior analysts," or more simply as "behavior analysts." One reason that their research takes the form that it does is that a new behaviorism has developed. I turn now to this new development.

THE NEW BEHAVIORISM

The "new" behaviorism is not entirely new. What is new is the mix of various ideas including radical behaviorism and contextualism.

Radical behaviorism comes from Skinner, although it has been developed by others as well – for example, Day (1976). Contextualism originates in the work of the philosopher Stephen Pepper (1942).

Pepper's work has long been familiar to philosophers. It is mainly associated with the idea that there are exactly four "world hypotheses," each associated with what Pepper calls a "root metaphor." The four hypotheses are: formism, mechanism, organicism, and contextualism. The root metaphor for mechanism is, not surprisingly, a machine. Those who hold this world theory (it is a collection of hypotheses rather than just one) see the world as one gigantic machine. It is more difficult to say exactly what the root metaphor is for contextualism, but an approximation, Pepper suggests (1942: 232), is the historic event. By this, he means the historic event as it continues into the present, but not an act conceived of alone; it is an act in its setting – that is, its context. The whole universe, according to the contextualist, is this event, Pepper notes (1942: 235).

There is much in Pepper's discussion of contextualism that is unclear. For example, he continually shifts without notice from talking about the meaning of a sentence and its words to talking about the meaning of the *event* of writing the sentence. Pepper's whole discussion, moreover, moves at such a high level of abstraction, with so few examples, that it is often difficult to discern his intended meaning. For example, what could he mean by saying that the universe, according to the contextualist, consists of a single event (1942: 235)? Given the obscurity of Pepper's discussion, it is not surprising that when psychologists become "contextualists," they take the view to mean various things that are not consistent with one another; see, for example, the papers in Hayes et al. (1993).

The problems inherent in interpreting Pepper, however, need not prevent us from moving forward. What is mainly relevant here is what "contextualism" has come to mean to contemporary behavior analysts. Here we are helped by a lucid discussion, as lucid as the subject permits, by Hayes et al. (1988) on the implications of Pepper's views for behavior analysis.

One thing the authors do is to draw parallels between concepts of behavior analysis and contextualist concepts. For example, they compare the idea of an operant class, which has no fixed boundaries, with that of the contextualistic conception of similarity. Another comparison is this. Radical behaviorists, such as Skinner (1974: 235), adopt the same criterion of truth as contextualists: Truth is successful working. (Pepper does say that although contextualists start with this criterion, they move to what he calls "qualitative confirmation"; see his 1942: 268–79. However, this point makes no difference in the present discussion.)

Hayes et al. (1988) make use of another of Pepper's ideas, one concerning criticisms of world theories. They point out (1988: 97) that behavior analysis has always had conflicts with other psychological perspectives, and at their most fundamental level, these conflicts are often philosophical. They then argue that the fundamental disagreements between cognitivists and behavior analysts are pseudo-conflicts among world views. The behavior analysts are contextualists and the cognitivists tend to be mechanists, although some, such as Chomsky, may be viewed either as organicists or as formists. What can be done to resolve these conflicts, or rather pseudo-conflicts? Nothing. Here the authors follow

Pepper, claiming (1988: 98) that it is illegitimate and inherently useless to use the categories of one world view to criticize another.

If Hayes et al. are right, then we are forced back to a kind of epistemic relativism. Psychoanalysts, cognitivists, and behavior analysts ultimately base their respective theories on one of Pepper's world theories, and none of these in turn can be criticized from the vantage point of a rival world theory. What, however, of someone who does not share any of the four views? Is it legitimate for that person to provide criticism? Pepper might deny that there is such a person. He does say (1942: 2) that we all have and use world hypotheses. That might be true if all that is meant is that we all have some basic ways of looking at the world, but if he means that we are all formists, organicists, mechanists, or contextualists, then we might ask how he knows this. Although some contemporary philosophers might be classified as "mechanists," I know of no evidence that very many, if any, accept any of the other theories, either consciously or unconsciously.

Pepper might reply that the terms he has coined are just names for commonly held philosophic views. For example, formism is just realism – he apparently means "Platonic realism" (1942: 42); contextualism is commonly called "pragmatism," and so on (1942: 42). The difficulty, however, is that Pepper has so added to these views that they are no longer identical with the original positions. So, there are philosophers writing today who, in some sense or other, are pragmatists, but is it quite unclear that they would accept most of the basic tenets of contextualism. It appears that Pepper has stitched together a patchwork of views and given each a technical name, but has neglected to check whether the views are widely held.

Doubts could also be raised about the claims of Hayes et al. concerning cognitivist psychologists. Chomsky, for example, might accept a proposition here and there from either organicism or formism (see Hayes et al., 1988: 108) but that does not mean he accepts the rest of either position.

Why, then, cannot psychoanalysts or cognitivists who reject all four of Pepper's world views criticize contextualism without relying on any distinctive or question-begging tenet of one of the three rival views? They can, but there remains a serious epistemic problem. Suppose that I argue that much of what is said by contextualist-behavior analysts is *unjustified*, or that some of their arguments are *illogical*, or that some of their key doctrines are not *true*. Even if I do not argue any of this from the vantage point of a rival world view, the opposition can still reply that my criteria for justification, logical validity, and truth are not theirs. The fact is that they do hold distinctive views on all three of these things, and that gives them a way of blunting criticism. As I noted in the previous chapter, for example, Follette and Houts (1992: 253) accuse me of begging the question in Erwin (1988b) in that I assume the norms of elementary logic; for a different view, they refer the reader to the radical behaviorist approach to logic. Other contextualists, such as Hayes et al., would undoubtedly fall back at some point on their criterion of truth, and others on a radical behaviorist view of justification (see Leigland, 1993).

Where the disagreements are so deep that the very ideas of truth, logic, and justification are at issue, can anything be said that does not simply beg the question? If not, then we have an ultimate standoff: behavior analysts can render their position invulnerable, but so too can cognitivists and psychoanalysts, which is exactly the point made by Hayes et al. (1988). This is not a benign result for the field of psychotherapy. We have not just these three paradigms, it should be kept in mind, but rather many different points of view, and we would be left with no rational way to choose between them. The only way out of this black hole is to challenge the radical behaviorist-contextualist theories about truth, justification, and logic.

Truth

Many contextualists adopt some form of a pragmatic criterion of truth. Steven Hayes, for example, explains the idea in terms of "successful working," as do other contextualists. To be a useful criterion, Hayes points out (1993: 16), "successful working" must help us sort verbal statements into true and false categories. However, he adds a further criterion that guarantees that this will not happen. To be counted as a truth criterion, he notes (1993: 16), successful working first requires a goal, *and that goal must be stated verbally* (Hayes' emphasis). This will not work. Many of the true beliefs that I have are not associated with any goal at all, and certainly no articulated goal. To take two trivial examples, I believe that 7 is a prime number, and that it is greater than 5. If one prefers not to talk about beliefs, I will state both propositions, and both of my statements will be true, but neither is associated with any goal.

Even if the above argument could be answered, there are other problems with utility-based criteria of truth, as detailed in the previous chapter. One is that in the very application of a utility-based account, a different concept of truth needs to be presupposed. Let us suppose that my goal is shaping the bar-pressing behavior of an autistic child, and that I do shape the behavior in the desired manner. Is it true that I have reached my goal? On the "successful working" criterion, it is not enough that the behavior is shaped in the way I wanted; to say it is enough is to use a different criterion of truth, a correspondence criterion. The statement that I have reached my goal is true, on the "successful working" criterion, only if it in turn is useful in reaching another goal. However, I have not yet done that. Consequently, my statement that I have been successful is not true; consequently, neither is my original statement. We can wait until I have stated a goal for my second statement, and then achieved it, but we will have to be extremely patient. For the same problem will arise again when we claim that the next goal has been achieved; that claim may be true in the correspondence sense but not in the "successful working" sense unless it is true that the new claim also is useful in meeting some goal (see the previous chapter for further details).

In practice, most contextualists would count the successful shaping of the child's behavior as meeting my goal. However, in doing so, they are abandoning the "successful working" criterion if they agree that it is true that I have been successful even though *this* statement has not yet engendered any success. This is apparently why Linda Hayes (1993: 41) initially objects to the "successful working" criterion on the grounds that its application requires the use of a correspondence criterion.

Finally, even if none of the above mattered, the "successful working" theory fails for the very reason that Richard Rorty (1995) was forced to admit defeat for all pragmatic theories: false beliefs sometimes work just as true ones do. So, if, as S. Hayes suggests (1993), a "successful working" criterion of truth must be able to sort the true and the false if it is to be a useful criterion, then it is not useful (or correct); for it fails to do that.

Despite her initial objection, Linda Hayes (1993) nevertheless argues for the adoption of a utility (namely, "successful working") criterion on the following grounds. On the basis of her objection to several theories of truth, she concludes (1993: 44) that truth as identified by philosophers is "illusory" regardless of the criterion that is adopted. In short, she concludes, it makes no difference which criterion is adopted. The adoption of any particular criterion is a matter of convention, and the convention for contextualists is to employ a utility criterion.

This argument does not work at all. One problem is that Hayes does not consider all of the traditional theories of truth; she fails to consider disquotational accounts (see Chapter 4 this volume p. 68), which are immune to her criticisms. Even if she were to refute every single theory of truth, it would not follow that truth itself is illusory. What would follow is that we have no adequate theory of truth. Furthermore, no other argument could establish the proposition in question. Let R be the proposition that truth is illusory. R is either true or false. If it is true, it is false (for there would be at least one truth), and if it is false, it is false. So, it is false that truth is illusory. We could make an exception for R, and say that except for it, truth is illusory. However, an argument very similar to the one just given will show that that cannot be true either. If S is the proposition that R is true, then R is true only if S is true. But, then, there would have to be two truths, and that would falsify R.

Finally, it does make a difference if one adopts a wrong criterion of truth. For example, a behavior analyst might believe that a certain technique is effective when, in fact, spontaneous remission explains all of her so-called "results." If she adopts a "successful working" criterion, she may well hold that her belief is true; for it does direct her to a certain desired outcome. So, she may persist in using an ineffective behavioral strategy. More generally, utility-based criteria of truth function the way logical behaviorism and operationism did for the old behaviorism; such criteria serve to protect the new behaviorism from rational criticism. Or rather, they seem to; to say that adopting them really is a successful defensive strategy is to subscribe to an illusion.

I conclude that attempts to work out an adequate "successful working" criterion of truth have failed. There is good reason to think that future efforts will fail as well. The basic problem that cannot be circumvented is that false beliefs, given the right context, can sometimes be just as useful as true ones. Consequently, a "successful working" criterion does not correctly sort verbal statements into "true" and "false" categories.

Justification

From the viewpoint of a behavior analyst, how is one to justify a scientific hypothesis? One could say: We provide some good reason for believing it. The reason might consist of empirical evidence or some sort of supporting argument. However, some, such as Skinner (1957), regard this idea of justification as too mentalistic, and look for an alternative.

Leigland (1993) provides a nice formulation of the radical behaviorist alternative, although it is not clear whether he means to endorse it or not. He points out (1993: 31) that the case made by some behavior analysts for not justifying scientific goals concerns "rationalistic" justification, but does not exclude justification of another sort. Suppose, for example, that a behavioral scientist makes the following recommendation to a school administrator: (1) "Your school *should*, or *ought*, to adopt such-and-such educational practices in teaching your students." This statement, Leigland claims (page 32), might be formulated in terms of contingencies as follows: (2) "*If* your professional behavior is reinforced by documented evidence in your students of broadly based and generalized academic skills X, Y, Z, (etc.), *then* your behavior will be more effectively reinforced if you adopt such-and-such educational practices, since we have the following empirically based *evidence* that these practices *produce* such educational results with students . . . (etc.)."

Leigland suggests that (2) is a reformulation of (1); elsewhere (1993: 31), he refers to similar "reformulations" as "translations." In fact, they are neither. Statement (1) says that certain educational practices should be adopted; (2) says nothing about this. Instead, (2) speaks of the reinforcement of the professional behavior of an administrator if certain conditions are met. Proposition (2) might well be true and (1) false, or conversely; so, the two statements cannot possibly be identical. To illustrate, introduction of the practices in question might improve student performance on a particular test, and consequently the administrator's professional behavior might be reinforced, but the overall effects on the students might be harmful. Because that is possible, (2) also fails to provide a justification for (1).

Is it unfair to complain about the lack of justification or translational equivalence? After all, radical behaviorists want to do without such mentalistic notions. When they speak of a "translation" of evaluative statements into the technical vocabulary of contingencies of reinforcement (Leigland, 1993: 30), do they really mean that the technical statement will mean the same as the original? I believe that, in fact, this is what they do mean (see Leigland's discussion, page 31). Suppose, however, that they were to deny this. What they might have in mind, instead, is the functional-analytic interpretation of the verbal behavior of scientists and others who make value statements.

As Skinner suggests (1957: 29), one of the ultimate achievements of a science of verbal behavior may be an empirical logic, or a descriptive and analytic scientific epistemology. What he means by this is that the verbal practices of logical and scientific thought may be explained in terms of contingencies of reinforcement. But what will the justification of these explanatory hypotheses look like? Suppose that we were to ask if there is any reason at all to think that such hypotheses are true? Will behavior analysts provide further functional analyses of why we ask such questions? Suppose that they were to do that. That would only invite the question: Why believe the additional functional analyses? In the absence of acceptable translations, the whole approach goes nowhere. To propose a causal explanation of why logicians or scientists make such and such statements is not to offer an alternative account of justification, nor is it to provide an empirical logic or scientific epistemology.

Logic

In a reply to a paper of mine, Follette and Houts (1992: 253) accuse me of begging the question by taking for granted the norms of elementary logic. They counter that if such norms can be seen as having normative import in virtue of being socially accepted, then logic will be subsumed within a social and behavioral science analysis of verbal behavior. They refer the reader to Houts and Haddock (1992) for details.

Houts and Haddock provide a radical behaviorist account of logic, one they credit to Skinner. The basic idea is that principles of logic are to be treated as verbal behavior to be analyzed in terms of the external variables that control them. They function as discriminative stimuli that people provide for themselves as occasions for performing behaviors that get reinforced by environmental consequences, including the social consequences provided by logicians and philosophers.

One obvious problem with this sort of account concerns the possibility of its validation. If its correctness undermines the normative force of elementary logic, then what of the normative force of the arguments allegedly supporting this point of view? The principles governing these arguments will lose their normative force as well. If it is replied that the account is meant only to explain, not to undermine, the normative force of logic, then what becomes of the charge of begging the question? If the standard principles of elementary logic retain their full normative force after they are explained in radical behaviorist terms, then it is unclear why anyone would be begging the question in taking their validity for granted, as I did.

In fact, even if the radical behaviorist account of our verbal behavior concerning logic were demonstrably correct, that would do nothing either to undermine or to explain the normative force of logical principles. To say that an argument form is "valid" implies nothing about the social reinforcement of the utterance of the sentence expressing the applicable logical principle. It is to say instead that the argument form is *truth preserving*: Any argument of that form will necessarily have a true conclusion if each premise is true. What verbal utterances are reinforced or punished makes no difference to whether an argument has this truth-preserving property.

Consider, for example, the fundamental logical principle *Modus Ponens* expressed as a statement: If P is true, and if P then Q is true, then Q is true. The principle has normative force at least in this sense: If I say that an argument has the logical form of Modus Ponens, I imply that it is logically valid. Now, suppose that someone gives a correct causal explanation of why some people, such as logicians, utter Modus Ponens, and why other people say that arguments having its form are valid. Contrary to what Follette and Houts claim, this would do nothing to show that Modus Ponens has normative import, as they put it, "in virtue of being socially accepted and enforced." Even if its utterance were never socially accepted or enforced, it would still be true that arguments of the Modus Ponens form are logically valid.

Conclusion: Many behavior analysts still claim that there are no cognitive causes, and that all behavior is a function of its consequences. As I argued in Erwin (1978), there never was any firm supporting empirical evidence for either of these propositions. There is no such evidence today. The case for these theses now rests on philosophic claims of the new behaviorism. These include a combination of contextualist-radical behaviorist propositions about truth, justification, logic, and other matters. Each of these philosophic theses fails to survive a critical examination. They are either false or unwarranted, and for that reason provide no support for any behavior analyst doctrine.

THEORETICAL AND THERAPEUTIC ASSESSMENT

My main concern has been to challenge the philosophical underpinnings of applied behavior analysis, but this challenge has implications for their clinical theories and, to a lesser degree, therapeutic practices.

Once the philosophy of radical behaviorism and contextualism are swept away, then the empirical evidence tells heavily against the behaviorist doctrine that there are no cognitive causes. The result is that any clinical theory that presupposes this doctrine – one that says, for example, that all or most behavior is just a function of its consequences, or that all behavior is environmentally caused – is undermined by the available evidence.

Can a radical behaviorist or contextualist of the sort discussed earlier now accept cognitive causation, but make accommodations for it within operant conditioning theory? In an excellent discussion of issues about cognitive causation, Overskeid (1994) argues persuasively that radical behaviorists, who generally allow that there are "private events" (such as thinking), should also agree that there are cognitive causes. He also raises the possibility that this would allow for a possible rapprochement between behaviorism and cognitivism. In one sense it would, but only in the sense that behaviorists would thereby abandon behaviorism and become cognitivists. As a leading radical behaviorist notes: "the major behaviorist argument has been against causal . . . mentalism" (Catania, 1973: 441, quoted by Overskeid, 1994: 36).

Furthermore, accepting cognitive causation would do far more than eliminate the key element of behaviorism. If behavior analysts agree that there is cognitive causation, what remains of operant conditioning theory? Suppose that I say that certain behavior of schizophrenics in a token economy program was reinforced by the presentation of tokens contingent on their performance, but I agree that this means something like the following. The subjects were given tokens immediately after performing in a certain way. They realized, perhaps because the staff told them, that a repetition of the behavior would result in their being given more tokens. They also believed that they could cash the tokens in for things they valued, and that repeating the behavior was worth the effort. As a causal consequence of their beliefs and desires, they decided to repeat the behavior that the staff wanted repeated.

A behaviorist who makes this sort of concession should take one further step, and concede that operant conditioning "theory" is mainly empty verbiage. Talk of reinforcing and punishing events would become just an inflated way of talking about beliefs and other mental events and states, and their causal connections to behavior. The acceptance of cognitive causation, it is true, does not logically entail going quite this far; so, one might be able to salvage important elements of operant conditioning theory. Still, it is worth asking anyone who wishes to combine cognitive causation and operant theory: Exactly how do you propose to do this?

I turn next to behavior modification techniques.

Even one who is skeptical about the underlying philosophy and clinical theory can agree that behavior analysts have fashioned a number of techniques that are useful in treating certain populations with certain problems. Furthermore, it is not true that they can be used only with schizophrenics, autistic children, and retarded adults and children. Behavior modification has been applied in the last two decades to a variety of populations, including "normal" pre-school children, married couples, delinquents, and head-injured individuals. Not all of these techniques would be recognized as "therapies," but many of them would be.

The research literature on these techniques is so vast that not even a large volume could do justice to them. For reviews of some of the recent literature, see Bellack and Hersen (1993). Rather than attempt any overall description, I want to take up one issue. In the design and application of conditioning techniques, including aversive therapies based on Pavlovian ideas and operant strategies based on Skinnerian ideas, not enough attention is paid to cognitive factors, or, in the case of operant techniques, to emotional, motivational, or physiological factors. This is hardly surprising, of course, given the extreme environmentalism of most applied behavior analysts, and the stress on conditioning placed by followers of Pavlov. However, if they are wrong, if not all causes of behavior lie in the environment or are non-cognitive, then the neglect of non-environmental causes, especially cognitive causes, is likely to have adverse effects. In fact, that has often happened.

Consider first an illustration concerning classical rather than operant conditioning. Pavlovian theory inspired a number of techniques that were used in the 1960's and 1970's to treat sexual deviations, alcoholism, obesity, and cigarette smoking. Because of Pavlov's influence, many clients were treated by simply pairing repeatedly some unwanted behavior with an aversive stimulus. In the United States, centers were set up for profit, where clients would bring food or cigarettes, and would be subjected to electric shock or nausea-producing drugs while eating or smoking.

In their classic discussion of the subject, Rachman and Teasdale (1969) were guardedly optimistic about the utility of such techniques, but they noted the insufficient attention paid to cognitive variables by those using them. They also noted (page xii) that there was what they called a "major puzzle." Why, they asked, do patients treated with aversion therapy refrain from engaging in the deviant behavior after they leave the hospital? For example, a transvestite treated by aversion therapy *knows* that if he cross-dresses in the safety of his home, he will not receive a shock. Yet, Rachman and Teasdale point out, for long periods of time, many patients do not carry out their so-called "deviant acts."

From the standpoint of classical conditioning, however, there is no puzzle. Once the conditioning bond is established, the patient's knowledge should make no difference. If relapse were to occur, moreover, it would not be because of the patient's beliefs or knowledge; it would rather be due to an automatic and mechanical response: namely, extinction. It is only when, as Rachman and Teasdale suggest, due weight is given to cognitive factors, that there is any puzzle at all. Why did aversive conditioning work even temporarily if the clients knew that they could avoid punishment after they left the clinic and hospital, assuming that such knowledge of causal connections matters? One possibility is cognitive dissonance; the clients paid their money and were not ready to concede a quick defeat. Another is that they feared going back to the therapist for a booster shot. A third possibility is that they were strongly motivated to modify their behavior, which is why they put up with the shock or nausea-generating drug in the first place. All three of these factors might have been in play.

From a cognitivist point of view, however, it looks dubious from the outset that in adult human beings, shocking them is going to have durable therapeutic effects. As Rachman and Teasdale note, the client can figure out that he can drink, eat, or smoke with no reasonable expectation of further shock; so, if he is really motivated to begin the unwanted behavior again, he is likely to relapse. That, quite generally, is exactly what did happen in very many cases. Aversion techniques for treating weight reduction, alcoholism, sexual problems, and cigarette smoking had many initial successes, but the relapse problem proved fatal. It is a fair comment that none of these aversive techniques today is reasonably considered the treatment of choice for any of the aforementioned problems.

I would agree that the poor track record of certain classical conditioning techniques has no direct implications for the use of operant techniques, but the same sort of problem has arisen in the practice of behavior analysts when cognitive and emotional factors have been ignored. Many token economy programs, for example, seemed effective at first. In fact, as Lowe et al. point out (1987: 156), work on token economies has often been cited as evidence for the effectiveness of operant contingencies with humans. This is a mistake, although not one made by Lowe et al. Even if token economies worked perfectly, their success would be neutral between an operant explanation and one that appealed partly to cognitive factors.

Token economy programs, in any event, have encountered serious problems, and are not used nearly as widely as they once were. As Glynn (1990) points out in her review of the token economy literature, although they have not disappeared altogether, they have generally fallen into disfavor. There is more than one reason for this decline, but one very serious problem was the failure of many psychotic patients to continue performing after the tokens were withdrawn, or after they were moved to a new setting. Many of these patients could figure out the causal connections between their receiving tokens and their obeying certain rules. Their behavior was not the automatic and mechanical response to contingent consequences that was postulated by behaviorists. From a cognitivist point of view, it was predictable that as their calculations or motivations changed, the patients would once again engage in the unacceptable behavior. It was misleading to characterize the problem as a failure of response or stimulus generalization, suggesting that the relapse problems could be repaired without paying attention to the clients' cognitions or motivation.

Higson and his colleagues take up a closely related issue. Higson reports running a token economy program with long-stay patients in a psychiatric hospital (Higson et al., 1985; Woods et al., 1984), where a detailed analysis showed that verbal control was an integral part of the program. He and his colleagues (Lowe et al., 1987: 157) note that it might be argued that a good behaviorist should minimize verbal instructions, and concentrate instead on getting right the response–reinforcer relationship. They cite evidence, however, that this would be a recipe for failure. There is no reason, however, why behaviorists cannot agree with this. After all, verbal behavior occurs in the environment, and can be accommodated within an operant conditioning framework. Suppose, however, that we take the next step, and ask why verbal instructions were important in token economy programs, and why the failure to utilize them properly led to the "contingency insensitivity" reported in token economy programs (Lowe et al., 1987: 158).

Ayllon and Azrin (1964), for example, found that providing a tangible "reinforcer" to modify the meal-time behavior of psychiatric patients had no effect unless it was accompanied by instructions that specified the reinforcing contingency, although the instructions without the "reinforcement" also did not work. Is it not likely that the instructions were needed because without them the patients did not *understand* the relationship between their performance and their obtaining tokens? Suppose that in cases where instructions are needed, we present them intelligibly to some patients, and garble them, or present them in a heavy unintelligible accent, to others. Do we really need an experiment to know that the latter group will respond differently? Assuming that they would, would there be the slightest plausibility to the idea that their reinforcement histories, if only we knew them, could be invoked to explain the results? Would it not be far more likely that their failure to understand the instructions, and consequent failure to form the right belief about the response contingency, would account for the different responses of the two groups.

In short, I agree with Lowe et al. (1987) that the evidence shows that the failure of those running token economy programs to pay attention to verbal instructions has often led to failure. As they point out (page 158), once humans acquire language, they often respond to contingencies differently from other animals: they reflect; they consider various possibilities, and so on. However, to admit this is to agree that the verbal behavior is but one element in the causal chain. What also matters is whether the client understands the instructions, what he or she comes to believe as a result of reflecting, imagining other possibilities, and so forth. In general, it was not merely the inattention to verbal instructions that led to "contingency insensitivity"; it was also the failure to pay attention to the beliefs and motivation of the clients.

6

Cognitive Therapy and Behavior Therapy

Some writers group together cognitive therapy and behavior therapy, and refer to them both as "behavior therapy," or, alternatively, as "cognitive-behavior therapy." Others distinguish the two. Without taking any position on this classification issue, I will discuss separately the two leading cognitive therapies, those of Aaron Beck and Albert Ellis, and then turn to the behavior therapies.

Even if cognitive therapists are excluded from a behavior therapy paradigm, they might still share many of the philosophical and evaluative views held by their behavior therapy colleagues. I believe that, in fact, the similarities are great enough that it would be largely redundant to lay out such views twice, first for Beck and Ellis, and then for behavior therapists. For that reason, I will postpone the discussion of philosophy and values until I discuss behavior therapy.

COGNITIVE THERAPY

Beck's Cognitive Therapy

Aaron Beck (1967), the originator of one sort of cognitive therapy (CT), theorizes that false beliefs and faulty logic play an important causal role in the origin and maintenance of depression. In recent years, Beck and his colleagues have extended the theory and treatment to cover other clinical problems, such as phobias and anxiety disorders (Beck et al., 1985), but the bulk of the research has been done on depression, and for that reason I will focus on this problem.

Depressed individuals, according to Beck and his colleagues, tend to have unwarranted negative beliefs about themselves, their present state, and their future. The main therapeutic strategy is to identify, challenge, and then correct these faulty cognitions and defective reasoning, and what CT theorists refer to as the underlying "dysfunctional schemata."

Although they focus on cognitions for treatment purposes, cognitive therapists agree that behavior and biochemistry are also important causal factors in depression. They also agree that typically one cannot eliminate the causally relevant cognitions merely by presenting a cogent counter-argument. There is, consequently, much emphasis on what is sometimes called "behavioral components," such as providing homework assignments, and scheduling the use of self-reliance techniques, cognitive rehearsal, and role playing.

As CT has been used in recent years (see Young et al., 1993), symptom reduction is typically the goal in the first phase of the therapy. The therapist begins with an assessment of the client's problems, and a joint determination of goals for the therapy. After explaining the rationale for the therapy, an attempt is made to elicit from the client "automatic thoughts." An automatic thought is one that intervenes, often unnoticed, between outside events and an individual's emotional reactions to them.

One method for eliciting automatic thoughts is to ask patients what went through their minds in response to particular events. Another technique is to ask them to close their eyes and imagine themselves in distressing situations. They are then asked about what they are thinking as they imagine the event.

Once a key automatic thought is identified, the therapist and client treat it as a hypothesis to be tested. The client is asked to list the evidence both for and against it. If the available evidence is not decisive, the client is asked to design an experiment to yield new evidence, which may or may not disconfirm the hypothesis. The goal here is not merely to help patients see that certain automatic thoughts are wrong, but also to help them learn the process of rational thinking. In addition to the testing of automatic thoughts, behavioral techniques, as noted earlier, are also used to change the patient's cognitions.

In recent years, a second phase has been added to the treatment, the "schema-focused phase." The reason for this addition is to prevent relapse. The therapist and client jointly try to identify and modify underlying "schemata." What precisely schemata are is somewhat unclear. Some of them are said to be *perceptions*, such as the perception of instability or unreliability of those available for support (see the table on page 243 of Young et al., 1993). Others include *expectations* (such as the expectation that one's desire for emotional support will not be met), *fears*, *beliefs*, and *emotional involvement*. Not all of these things are propositional in form. For example, fears and emotional involvement, unlike beliefs, are not either true or false. For that reason, it is unclear as to how one could test them in the way that one tests a hypothesis. What might be meant is that there is a hypothesis associated with, say, a fear or emotional involvement, and it is the hypothesis that is tested. For example, if the client fears something, he or she believes that that thing is threatening.

Beck and his colleagues now theorize that some of the patient's "core" schemata develop in childhood and persist beneath the level of consciousness, making him or her vulnerable to recurring bouts of depression. The therapist tries to identify these schemata by reviewing the patient's history, using the Schema Questionnaire, and by triggering a schema through the use of experiential means.

Assessment The development of cognitive therapy for depression, and the execution by its proponents of a serious research program to test theoretical and outcome hypotheses, are, in my view, among the most exciting developments in the field of psychotherapy (although not everyone agrees with this assessment; see Wolpe, 1993). Yet, as Beck and his colleagues would agree, some important questions still need to be answered; and ongoing research inevitably generates new ones. I turn now to some of the unanswered questions.

One question is this: How reliable are the cognitive therapist's methods for identifying automatic thoughts? Often we can figure out what a person believes by asking. Do you believe in God, or in the Republican party, or whether this therapy is likely to help, and so on? Non-verbal behavior often furnishes further reliable evidence. Automatic thoughts, however, are often beneath the threshold of consciousness. Something may come to mind *now* when thinking about certain events or when certain questions are posed, but how does the therapist know whether the client had the beliefs before entering therapy? In asking clients to introspect and identify beliefs that they did not know that they had, we are, in effect, asking them to theorize about what they formerly believed or believe now. Research in cognitive psychology questions the accuracy of much of this sort of theorizing (Nisbett and Ross, 1980).

The epistemic problems multiply when the therapist tries to identify underlying schemata and to establish that some of them developed in childhood. Now, the patient and therapist must theorize about the distant past, utilizing apparent memories that may be distorted or fabricated. The problems here are somewhat analogous, although not nearly as difficult, as those that Freudians face when they try to uncover repressed wishes said to have originated in childhood.

A further epistemic burden is taken on when the therapist tries to establish not only that the client possesses certain automatic thoughts and schemata, but also that they play a certain causal role in maintaining the depression. In some cases common-sense psychology may suffice as support of the hypothesis, but where it does not, how does the therapist know that of all the patient's many beliefs, fears, and expectations, a certain sub-set contains the culprits that maintain the depression? One could appeal to research on the theory of cognitive therapy, but that will not be enough *if* the research also utilizes what may be unreliable methods for identifying automatic thoughts and underlying schemata.

In short, although the existing evidence may provide some support for Beck's theory about the role cognitive factors play in the etiology and maintenance of depression, as long as questions persist about the reliability of the methods for identifying automatic beliefs and schemata, it is premature to say that the theory has been established. The evidence concerning the efficacy of the therapy, in contrast, is generally believed to be more impressive. I turn now to that evidence.

CT is one of the best researched of all the psychotherapies. After Beck developed his version of it in the 1960's, he and his colleagues began a series of controlled experiments that have generally had positive findings. In one recent review of the literature, Dobson (1989) found 28 studies employing Beck's cognitive therapy and a common outcome measure of depression. Using meta-analysis to average the results, Dobson found a greater degree of change for CT compared with a waiting list or no treatment control, pharmacotherapy, behavior therapy, and other psychotherapies.

On the basis of such findings, most commentators have concluded that CT has been shown to be an effective treatment for clinical depression, even if not every single client is helped by it (Robins and Hayes, 1993: 208). Arnkoff and Glass (1992: 663) conclude that CT has been shown to be at least as effective as tricyclic pharmacotherapy and sometimes is more effective. Despite this consensus, I believe there is reason to be more cautious.

One question to ask is this: Even if CT is effective in treating depression, is it generally more effective than a simple, inexpensive placebo, such as a sugar pill plus minimal therapist attention? The early studies did not answer this question; for they failed to include a placebo control. That omission was remedied when the National Institute of Mental Health developed the Collaborative Research Project to test the effectiveness of CT along with another psychotherapy (interpersonal psychotherapy), a drug treatment (Imipramine) and a pill-placebo. The ensuing study, conducted with 250 depressed patients at three different research sites, is generally considered the best, and one of the most expensive, outcome studies of psychotherapy ever conducted. As the years passed, preliminary results were announced in the press and for both psychotherapies were quite favorable. However, when the final results were tabulated, it was found that overall, the cognitive therapy was unable to outperform the placebo, a sugar pill plus minimal clinical management (Elkin et al., 1989). Although some differences did emerge, the other two therapies also did roughly the same as the placebo, except that the drug did best with the most severely depressed patients.

One response to these disappointing findings (Hollen et al., 1991: 92) is to explain the poor showing of the cognitive therapy in terms of its being implemented improperly. This is a possibility: the therapists were relatively inexperienced at the outset in using cognitive therapy. However, the most that can be inferred from this fact is that CT was not shown by the NIMH study to lack the capacity to outperform a credible placebo; it does nothing to answer the charge that as of now there is no evidence that CT has that capacity.

Even if it is conceded that the superiority of CT to a credible placebo has not yet been demonstrated, few would agree that it has not been shown to be effective at all. After all, in numerous controlled studies, CT has been compared not merely to no treatment, but also to a drug treatment antecedently known to be effective. In most such studies, CT has done as well as or better than the drug treatment. Despite these seemingly impressive results, however, there are problems in interpreting the data.

To begin with, how effective are the standard drug treatments for treating depression? Greenberg and Fisher (1989: 7) conclude on the basis of their review of the controlled studies of drug treatments that in two-thirds of all cases, depressed subjects will do as well as or better with a placebo than they would if treated with an active medication. As they also note, this may be too optimistic an assessment of drug effectiveness. The evidence that drugs are superior to an equally credible placebo in treating non-psychotic depression is in fact mixed. In 30 to 40 per cent of the early studies, no difference was found in response to drugs and placebos (Smith et al., 1980). In 16 newer studies discussed by Greenberg and Fisher (1989: 19), the majority (62 per cent) show no difference in the percentage of patients benefiting from an active drug as compared to a placebo.

Given the variability in how depressed people respond to drug treatment, it is also reasonable to ask if those in a particular sample were helped by the drug treatment. As Hollen et al. (1991) point out, in the absence of a placebo control or a demonstration that the drug was effective with the particular sample being studied, there is no way to rule out the possibility that the cognitive and drug treatments were both ineffective in the non-placebo studies.

Another question to ask is whether the conditions for the optimal use of the drug treatments were met in the cognitive therapy–drug comparisons. Meterissian and Bradwejn (1989) argue that five such conditions must be met, but in their review of the psychotherapy–pharmacotherapy comparison literature, they conclude that all five conditions were met in *none* of the studies, and that few studies met more than two of the conditions.

Because of these difficulties, Steven Hollen, who had earlier concluded that CT is effective, now argues, following Klein (1989), that the evidence of effectiveness can be considered only "suggestive" at the present time (Hollen et al., 1991). In other words, CT has not yet been shown to be an effective treatment for depression.

There is a further complication, which Hollen does not consider, due to the fact that many people can tell when they are in the placebo group because of the absence of side effects. In studies that have controlled for this factor, the drug only rarely beat the placebo. For this reason, the power of a placebo may have been underestimated. This issue is taken up in Chapter 7, but it is relevant to the assessment of cognitive therapy: Trying one of the standard drug treatments for depression looks a lot less impressive if that drug is no better than a pill placebo.

Conclusion: Cognitive therapy remains a promising treatment for depression, one that may be superior to a credible placebo. (Although that was not the finding in the NIMH study, more than one study is needed to show that CT can generally do no better than a placebo.) Nevertheless, despite all of the research findings, two skeptical verdicts are warranted. First, until we obtain new evidence, it is premature to conclude now that CT is generally more effective than a credible placebo in treating depression. Second, because of the absence of a placebo comparison in almost all studies of CT, there is reason to question whether its effectiveness in treating depression has been established. This is a bit weaker than saying flatly that the evidence is inconclusive; but it does imply that not all reasonable doubts have been answered.

Rational Emotive Therapy

Albert Ellis, the originator of rational emotive therapy (RET; now more commonly referred to as "Rational Emotive Behavior Therapy"), is generally considered one of the most influential of all psychotherapists (Smith, 1982; Warner, 1991). He developed his theory and treatment in the 1950's, but has modified both in recent years. I begin with some of his early formulations.

A crucial assumption in the beginning (Ellis, 1962), and one that is still maintained, is the so-called "ABC theory of human disturbance." On this view, people experience undesirable activating events (A); they have rational and irrational beliefs (B) about these stimuli; and they create either appropriate emotional and behavioral consequences with their rational beliefs, or inappropriate and dysfunctional consequences with their irrational beliefs (C) (Ellis, 1993). In brief, emotional disturbances are not caused by unfortunate life events themselves, but by the unrealistic and illogical beliefs we form about these events.

To eliminate the irrational beliefs, Ellis has advocated that the RET therapist actively dispute the beliefs, while also teaching clients the use of hypothetical-deductive reasoning so that they can dispute their own irrational beliefs. As in Beck's cognitive therapy, RET employs homework assignments and other behavioral techniques, but there are also some important differences between the two approaches. Whereas Beck favors a more gentle, Socratic questioning, where both client and therapist work in a spirit of "collaborative empiricism," Ellis supports a more direct and disputatious challenge to the client's irrational beliefs. In addition, RET places less emphasis on developing skills for challenging irrational beliefs compared to the disputing of what Ellis calls "absolutistic musts" (Kendall et al., 1995: 170).

In his early writings, Ellis identified a short list of irrational beliefs (11 of them) said to be commonly encountered in clinical practice. One example is the proposition that it is a dire necessity to be loved or approved of by virtually every other significant person; another is the idea that human unhappiness is externally controlled, and that people have no ability to control their unhappiness. Over time, the list grew to include hundreds of beliefs (Kendall et al., 1995: 172). In recent years, attempts have been made to reduce the number by subsuming particular irrational beliefs under more general categories.

An even more important change concerns the very definition of RET. Ellis now distinguishes general RET, which he sees as synonymous with general cognitive-behavior therapy, and "preferential" RET, which he sees as a unique form of cognitive-behavior therapy (Ellis, 1993: 199). In his conversation with Windy Dryden (Dryden, 1991), Ellis explains preferential RET in terms of the following eight principles. All page references are to Dryden (1991); for a slightly different formulation, see Ellis (1993).

First, by and large, human beings are "constructivists." Although they take over standards, goals, values, and preferences from others, they are unique individuals, and, consequently, have some choice in deciding what standards to accept, and how to apply them. People partly construct their preferences, and frequently their beliefs about these preferences (Dryden, 1991: 24–5).

Second, RET is mainly concerned with what people are doing right now to make themselves disturbed – in other words, how they perpetuate their disturbance rather than how they acquired it (page 27).

Third, RET distinguishes between self-acceptance and self-esteem. The latter, according to RET, involves measurement of the self, and, because of its global character, is invariably inaccurate. Instead of saying, "What I did was wrong" (a statement not necessarily objectionable on RET principles), people are prone to say such things as "*I* am a bad person." They rate their entire self or being, and their ratings are always, or almost always, wrong. Self-acceptance, however, is different. It need not depend on any sort of self-evaluation. RET holds that you should accept yourself no matter how badly you behave (pages 27–8).

Fourth, cognition, emotion, and behavior all interact with one another (see my earlier statement of the ABC theory of human disturbance). Our beliefs affect how we feel, including our desires, which in turn affect what we believe, which affects how we behave, and so on (page 23).

Fifth, people do not get upset from conditions, circumstances, and their early childhood, but, instead, most are born with a strong tendency to upset themselves, and to blame their "upsetness" on their parents and their environment (page 11).

Sixth, the "principle of the must": humans have many irrational beliefs, but it is mainly a sub-set of them that is linked with disturbance and irrationality. The key ones are about absolutist, dogmatic shoulds, oughts, and musts. According to RET, if humans would act on their simple preferences, they would not, by and large, get into emotional trouble. The problems arise when they "transmute" them into "absolute musts." My preference for X becomes "Because I like X very much, I *absolutely must* have it." I want you to love me, but that desire becomes deformed, and becomes "Because I want you to love me, I *absolutely must* win your love." In addition, most of our judgments about what is intolerable derive from these largely unconscious beliefs about what must be so. Because I believe that I absolutely must have your love, which in fact I cannot have, I infer that life is just awful and that I cannot bear my situation (page 15).

Seventh, the philosophy of unconditional musts is generally held unconsciously. That is, people are generally unaware that they hold these beliefs (see above) about what must occur in their lives. When they are confronted with them, they often do either of two things: deny that they have such beliefs, or hold that they are true (pages 22–3).

Eighth, the two main sources of just about all neurosis are ego anxiety (or "self-drowning") and discomfort anxiety (or low frustration anxiety). People exhibit the first when they judge themselves unworthy and unlovable because of their misdeeds, and then infer, "It's horrible not to be loved because I am not going to be cared for as I *must* be." They exhibit the second (low frustration anxiety) when they make themselves depressed, and then infer, "My depression is *too* uncomfortable! I *shouldn't* be that uncomfortable." According to RET, ego anxiety and discomfort anxiety generally interact with each other (page 28).

Assessment   I will focus mainly on Ellis' preferential RET theory as expressed by the above eight principles, but a few preliminary questions should be asked about the earlier theory. After all, Ellis does not speak for all influenced by his ideas; some presumably still utilize some of the earlier formulations.

One question is this: What criteria do RET therapists use to separate irrational from rational beliefs? One example on Ellis' original list is "The idea that certain people are bad, wicked, or villainous and that they should be severely punished and blamed for their villainy." Supposed that I believed this about some of the most notorious tyrants and serial killers of the twentieth century. Is it impossible that my belief be supported by good reasons? Why must it be irrational?

One could say that it is not the absence of supporting reasons but, rather, the effect of holding the belief that makes it irrational. Thus, Ellis and Bernard say (1986: 7) that "rational thoughts are defined in RET as those thoughts that help people live longer and happier." Presumably, irrational thoughts on this proposal are those that have the opposite effect. However, as Haaga and Davison (1993) point out in an excellent discussion of this issue, this renders tautologous the claim that holding irrational beliefs leads to unhappiness. It should also be added that on the Ellis and Bernard definition, a therapist cannot identify a belief as being irrational merely by examining its content or lack of evidential support. The therapist would have to establish first that for this particular individual the retention of the belief causes unhappiness or shortness of life.

There are other proposals in the RET literature for identifying irrational beliefs, but as far as I can tell, none is satisfactory. One possible way out is to adopt some criterion such as the following. A belief is irrational if it is supported by no good evidence or rational argument whatsoever, and in addition, the believer insists that it is likely that the proposition in question is true despite the lack of evidence. On this criterion, if someone believes in God but concedes that there is no evidence to back up the belief, the belief need not be irrational. Irrationality comes in only when the believer adds that it is certain or at least very probable that the belief is correct. However, there are problems with my proposal as well. For example, what do we say when the person thinks that the belief is supported by at least some good evidence but is mistaken about this?

Another way out is to give up on the idea of identifying irrational beliefs, especially if one adopts Ellis' preferential theory. Pick out the relevant beliefs by examining their content. The relevant ones are those about what "must" happen and "should" happen (see principle 6 above, the principle of the must). After these beliefs are identified, we can do empirical inquiry to determine whether they play the causal role that RET theory assigns to them.

A second question concerning early RET theory is how Ellis knew that the 11 beliefs that he identified (or some sub-set of them) really were held by most of the clients he encountered? After all, the clients were generally not aware of them when they entered therapy. They may have agreed later that they held them, but did they hold them before they met Ellis, or did he badger them into believing that they held them? How do we tell? This issue is relevant to the current theory as well; so I will say more about it shortly.

Suppose that we do have some reliable way of both identifying irrational beliefs and establishing that clients had them *before* entering therapy. A third problem remains: How do we establish that the irrational beliefs are playing a crucial causal role in maintaining the neurosis (or whatever problem is the focus of the therapy)? This problem too arises for the current theory, to which I now turn.

The above eight principles that constitute the preferred RET theory are a mixture of the relatively obvious and the controversial. The last four principles are central, and it is primarily these principles that require empirical support.

Principle 1 says that people are "constructivists," but Ellis does not mean that they hold the philosophical theory that I discussed in Chapter 4 under the heading "constructivism," namely, that all of reality is constructed by us. He means the relatively platitudinous claim that we sometimes construct our preferences and choose our beliefs. Perhaps the idea that we *frequently* choose our beliefs should be challenged, but that depends on how frequently this is supposed to happen. Suppose that I were to believe that the car is coming right at me, that John Kennedy was assassinated, and that life is generally boring. If I were to believe these things, would that be because I chose to believe them, or because a reflection on the evidence makes the belief unavoidable? If you were to ask me, for example, to please try to believe that Kennedy was not assassinated by anyone, I doubt that my attempt would be successful. However, it may be quibbling to challenge principle 1; so I will let it pass.

Principle 2 is in effect autobiographical. Ellis is telling us what he is concerned with, or perhaps what he is stipulating that RET therapy is concerned with, namely, what people are doing now to make themselves disturbed. There is nothing here to question.

Principle 3, which talks about self-esteem and self-acceptance, can be questioned, given that Ellis emphasizes that *any* measurement of the self is inaccurate. Suppose I say that Himmler was a bad person. This does not mean, of course, that he was not kind to animals, or was never good to any of his fellow Nazis. Still all things considered, he was a bad person. Is that judgment necessarily inaccurate? If it is accurate, suppose that Himmler were to characterize himself in this way. Would he be making an inaccurate judgment? What evidence is there that all self appraisals are inaccurate? However, Ellis could say that enough of them are that we make it a rule of thumb to discourage such global ratings.

As to self-acceptance, RET says that one should accept oneself *no matter how badly one behaves*; see Ellis' remarks in Dryden (1991: 28). It is not clear what Ellis means by "self-acceptance"; so, it is possible to interpret this remark to make it come out true. However, on any ordinary interpretation, Himmler should not have engaged in self-acceptance. He should have challenged his beliefs and questioned his actions, and modified them considerably. Serial killers, too, should not accept themselves the way they are, and RET therapists should not encourage them to do so.

An RET therapist might say: Himmler should have accepted himself *if* he wanted to be happy and free from neurosis. However, I deny that. Even if it would have made Himmler extremely happy and neurosis-free, he still should not have engaged in self-acceptance if doing so encouraged him to continue as before. There are other things to consider besides Himmler's happiness and freedom from neurosis.

Principle 4 is partly trivial and partly not. Anyone who is not a behaviorist is likely to agree that, in some way or other, cognitions, emotions, and behavior interact. Do they interact, however, in precisely the way postulated by the ABC theory, which presupposes that emotional disturbances are generally not caused by horrific events in our lives but by the irrational beliefs we form about them?

Principle 5 implies the same thing. It says that we do not get upset about the conditions of our lives, but rather we upset ourselves by reacting in certain ways. Is this generally true? Take the case of people who experience spinal cord injury. There is evidence that in the immediate aftermath, some patients form overly pessimistic beliefs about their life prospects, and that this contributes to their depression (Frank et al., 1987). This fits with what Ellis is saying. Yet is it really plausible to say that what makes them depressed is the beliefs they form? What about the devastating injury? Even quadriplegics who form realistic beliefs about their condition sometimes get extremely depressed. Of course, it is true that if they were entirely indifferent to their condition, they would not become depressed. So, it is not the injury alone that triggers the depression, but that is no reason to say that spinal cord injury victims "upset themselves," or that they do not get upset because of their conditions (Ellis in Dryden, 1991: 11). Their injuries and their cognitive and emotional responses all contribute to their emotional problems.

Without having certain beliefs and desires, people would not get upset when they lose their jobs, or get sick, or lose a loved one, but it is extremely misleading to say that it is not the life events that made them unhappy, that rather they upset themselves.

Is this being unfair to Ellis? Is his position not really more modest: that in a certain percentage of cases, it is the irrational beliefs that people form in response to unpleasant events that make all or at least most of the difference? If that is his position, then it seems plausible, but not so novel. The interesting questions would then be: What is the percentage, and for the cases in which the theory is right, will the elimination of the irrationalities make an important difference to solving the clinical problem?

I turn now to the more serious problems with Ellis' theory.

Principle 6, the principle of the must, is clearly central to his new theory. It explains the origin and maintenance of most emotional problems in terms of a transmutation of simple preferences into "absolute musts." I strongly prefer X, but I then transform that preference by thinking to myself, unconsciously, that I absolutely must have it. It is this sort of transmutation that leads to emotional problems, according to RET.

The first problem that arises is identical with the one that arose in Ellis' earlier theory. How does he know that people who have emotional problems generally have these beliefs about what they absolutely must or should have? Most therapists who do not subscribe to RET do not report the prevalence of such beliefs. Ellis might say: That is because they do not ask the right sort of questions. Suppose that I tell my therapist that I recently obtained my PhD but I have virtually no prospects for obtaining an academic position. As a consequence, my career dreams are not going to be fulfilled, and this is making me very unhappy. Perhaps the therapist should inquire whether I have more than a simple preference here. Do I believe that I *absolutely must* have an academic career? Well, I never thought of it in quite this way, but maybe the therapist is on to something, maybe that is what I do believe. How does the therapist know, however, whether she triggered assent to the proposition, or whether I unconsciously believed it before entering therapy?

In general, because these beliefs about absolute musts are unconscious, according to RET, there is a problem in detecting their presence. It is not necessarily insurmountable, but it renders suspect reports of RET therapists who claim to find these beliefs extremely common among people with emotional problems. These sorts of beliefs were apparently unnoticed in the early days of RET; then it was the 11 beliefs on Ellis' original list that were "detected." This change in what is allegedly detected raises a further question about the reliability of the methods of detection. I am not suggesting, of course, that we can never tell that a client had such "must" beliefs prior to entering therapy; I am questioning, rather, whether we have firm empirical evidence as of now that such beliefs are present in most cases of emotional disturbance.

If a general correlation has not been established yet, then the causal claim made by principle 6 has also not been confirmed. Yet even with an established correlation, something additional would have to be done. To satisfy the epistemic principles that I argued for in Chapter 4, some sort of comparison study would have to be done; it would most likely have to be an experimental study. At present, we have no such experimental study of the right sort. To do such a study, moreover, we would need to work at transforming principle 6 into a testable hypothesis. What sort of emotional problems does the principle talk about? In exactly what percentage of cases are the problems said to be caused by having unconscious beliefs about absolute musts and shoulds? What is the reliable method for determining whether subjects had these beliefs prior to the onset of their problems?

Principle 7 adds nothing of substance to principle 6; it merely highlights the claim that the beliefs about "absolute musts" are generally unconscious. That emotionally disturbed people are generally not aware of having such beliefs is not controversial; the controversial, and unsupported claim, is that they generally have them at all.

Principle 8 implicates ego anxiety (self-downing) and discomfort anxiety (low frustration anxiety) in the etiology of neurosis. The principle raises the same questions as does principle 6. What evidence is there that one or both of these factors are generally correlated with neurosis, and what evidence is there that if there is such a correlation, there is also a causal connection?

Earlier, in discussing principle 4, I suggested that it might be unfair to take Ellis to be saying that in *most* cases we upset ourselves. In stating principle 8, however, Ellis is quite clear that he *is* making a claim about most cases of neurosis: "The last principle is that two main sources of just about all neurosis are, first, ego anxiety or self-downing, and second, discomfort anxiety, discomfort depression, or refusal to accept uncomfortable things in one's life" (Ellis in Dryden, 1991: 28). I turn next to RET therapy.

RET advocates often claim that the effectiveness of the treatment has now been established, and indeed they can point to much empirical data to back up that claim. Lyons and Woods (1991), for example, present a meta-analytic review of 70 outcome studies of RET. They found significant improvement for RET clients over baseline measures and control groups. Although they temper their conclusion because of certain methodological flaws of some of the studies, Lyons and Woods do say (page 368) that the data show RET to be an effective form of therapy, subject to the qualifications they mention. In fact, they go further and suggest that it is perhaps time to stop the "needless and inefficient discussion of the efficacy of this sort of therapy" (page 368). If this comment suggests that for all practical purposes, the efficacy issue has been resolved, I disagree.

I will express some general doubts in Chapter 8 about the uncritical use of meta-analysis in reviewing outcome studies of psychotherapy, but here I will mention several issues that arise with respect to the Lyons and Woods review in particular.

The proposition that the average "effect size" (see Chapter 8) for a group of studies is both positive and large implies nothing about evidence of effectiveness unless additional premises are added. If in many of the studies that are reviewed, it is not established that the putative cause was even present – that is, that the therapy in question was used – then we cannot infer from an average positive effect size that the therapy was effective. In addition, the inference that beneficial effects were generally produced is unwarranted without firm evidence that the outcome measures correlate with such effects. Finally, even if the first two problems are overcome, but reasonable alternative explanations are not ruled out (for example, that the effects were mainly due to placebo factors), then evidence of effectiveness of the therapy is not provided. All three of these problems arise with the studies reviewed by Lyons and Woods. They appear to concede that the first problem is present when they say (1991: 367) that "there is no guarantee the therapy being used was actually RET as practiced and taught by the Institute of Rational-Emotive Therapy." Without such a guarantee, however, there can be no guarantee of evidence of effectiveness, even if, contrary to fact, all other epistemological problems were resolved.

More recently, Gossette and O'Brien (1992) have provided a qualitative review of 75 outcome reports of RET in which they pay more attention to issues of therapist integrity, placebo explanations, and internal validity in general. They conclude (page 20) that the data indicate that RET has little or no practical benefit for either children or adults, normal or troubled. Although I doubt that their data show that the therapy is *ineffective*, the arguments of Gossette and O'Brien present a strong challenge to anyone claiming that there is presently firm evidence for the effectiveness of RET.

It is not clear that Ellis himself would disagree with a skeptical verdict. In a remarkably candid paper about what needs to be done, he and others familiar with RET research make a number of important points, including the following (Kendall et al., 1995): (1) RET therapists, armed with the theoretical expectation that clients will report irrational beliefs, might obtain confirmatory responses from clients on the basis of suggestion (page 176); (2) it would be desirable to re-establish, with newer measures possessing adequate evidence of discriminant validity, that there is indeed a correlation between irrational beliefs and emotional distress (page 174); (3) measurement of the independent variable in RET treatment research, the therapeutic interventions themselves, has not received the attention it deserves (page 177); and (4) randomized clinical trials, with attention to internal validity, are needed to bolster existing therapy outcome reports (page 182).

Conclusion: The idea that irrational beliefs and illogical inferences play some important role in the etiology and maintenance of emotional problems, and the further idea that the disputation of them, in combination with certain behavioral techniques, is effective in eliminating the problems is interesting and not far fetched. Still, the theory needs to be stated with a great deal more precision than has been provided so far. In addition, there are formidable epistemological problems that have to be overcome before we can reasonably conclude either that Ellis' theory (the earlier one or the preferred theory) or the claim that RET is effective has firm empirical support. At present, these problems have not been resolved. The heart of Ellis' preferred theory (principles 5–8), the earlier theory, and the claims of effectiveness are all still mere speculations, not unreasonable if taken as speculations, but also unsupported by hard evidence.

I turn next to a behavior therapy paradigm.

BEHAVIOR THERAPY

In order to be confident about the identification of distinctive assumptions of a particular paradigm, one needs empirical evidence about what its members believe. Despite some useful beginnings (such as Krasner and Houts, 1984), we generally lack empirical studies in this area. One is forced then to rely on indirect and incomplete evidence from the published writings of members of a given scientific community, and perhaps what they say at professional meetings. Because such evidence can mislead, what I am about to say is conjectural to some degree, but I believe that almost all of it is uncontroversial.

Methodology

The people to whom I am referring as "behavior therapists" share a commitment to the scientific study of clinical phenomena. (On this point, and on most of the subsequent philosophical and evaluative points, cognitive therapists agree. So, whether we call them "cognitive-behavior therapists" or not, they share many of the same paradigm beliefs as behavior therapists.) This commitment does not by itself distinguish behavior therapists as a class from other types of psychotherapists who also want to transform the field of psychotherapy into a science. Differences emerge, however, when we begin to say what the commitment to science amounts to. The majority position among psychoanalysts still appears to be that the single case study is the main vehicle for testing outcome and theoretical hypotheses. Many hold that the introduction of experimental techniques distort the phenomena they wish to study, and that experimental studies of psychoanalysis have yielded little of real value so far. In contrast, behavior therapists tend to deride case studies as generally having only heuristic value (there are some exceptions to this generalization), and to insist on experimental evidence for confirming most theoretical and outcome hypotheses.

Another difference is that behavior therapists generally write as if they are still committed to the ideal of the scientist-practitioner. Effective therapists, on this view, should not only be trained in scientific and statistical techniques, but should use them in their clinical practice. They should take base rates, look for behavioral or at least objective measures of outcomes, draw on experimental findings from outside of clinical psychology, and so on.

The two methodological assumptions just noted are also shared by behavior analysts (those I referred to in Chapter 5 as "behavior modificationists"), but they in turn have their own distinctive methodological views. They generally favor the use of single-subject designs in studying outcomes, and, more generally, the use of other methodological strategies associated with the work of B.F. Skinner, such as doing functional analyses of behavioral changes. Behavior therapists do not generally disapprove of single-subject designs, but they are more likely to use group designs and to eschew the use of operant methodological techniques. A second, and more important, difference is that many behavior therapists are willing to postulate unobservables, especially cognitive factors, and to appeal to them in explaining clinical phenomena. Behavior analysts are also willing to talk about what they call "private events" (they mean mental events), but not as causes. Often, but not always, their grounds for excluding cognitive causes are methodological or philosophical (see Skinner – for example, 1963).

Psychoanalysts obviously agree with behavior therapists about the legitimacy of postulating unobservables, but here another important methodological difference emerges. Many behavior therapists believe it important to consider mental events and processes below the level of consciousness, but few place much significance in, and perhaps do not even believe in, a *dynamic* unconscious (see Chapter 7); nor do they accept the claim of the ubiquity of repression. As a consequence, they are much less likely than psychoanalysts (or dynamic therapists generally) to use methods of free association or dream interpretation, or to use projective tests in measuring therapeutic change.

Values

One value difference between analysts and behavior therapists has already been alluded to; it concerns their views about science. Behavior therapists are more likely than analysts to value experimental studies of theories and outcomes, and the use of experimental techniques in the practice of therapy (although some analysts agree on both points). Another difference is that behavior therapists tend to place much more value on the elimination of specific symptoms than analysts do. A third difference is that many or most behavior therapists approve of taking an active, non-neutral stance toward the beliefs and actions of clients. Those who follow Ellis or Beck, if they count as behavior therapists, think it not just permissible but imperative to challenge the belief systems of clients, or at least to help them discover their own mistakes. In contrast, analysts have traditionally embraced a therapeutic neutrality that required them to accept without criticism the attitudes and beliefs of their clients.

Behavior analysts tend to share many values with their behavior therapy colleagues, but there are at least two important differences. Many behavior analysts (how many is unclear) write as if they agree with Skinner that free choice is an illusion. Many behavior therapists do not take this position. So, even though they generally do not stress the enlargement of freedom or autonomy as the main goal of therapy, they presumably would agree that such outcomes can be valuable. Second, because of the position they take on cognitive causation, behavior analysts write as if they value only one kind of therapeutic change: the modification of unwanted behaviors. Some behavior therapists agree with this (see Martin, 1987: 453), but this is not the majority view among behavior therapists. Many value not only positive behavioral changes, but also cognitive and emotional changes as well.

Philosophy

The behavior therapists of the 1960's and 1970's often relied on various philosophic doctrines, such as operationism, logical behaviorism, and methodological behaviorism. As noted in the last chapter, I challenged these doctrines in Erwin (1978), as have other philosophers. None of these positions is widely held today by behavior therapists.

In fact, it is difficult to find any distinctive positive philosophic doctrines that play a key role in the current behavior therapy paradigm, although individual theorists have opted for one philosophic view or another. What is most salient philosophically about the current behavior therapy paradigm (in so far as there is a single paradigm) is the refusal to accept the philosophies of rival paradigms. For example, few behavior therapists have expressed willingness to accept any of the sorts of post-modernist epistemologies discussed in Chapter 3. Nor have they shown any inclination to embrace radical behaviorism, or pragmatic theories of truth, or operant conditioning accounts of justification and logic. Finally, although there are a few exceptions, behavior therapists as a class have not accepted the hermeneutic views agreed to by a number of psychoanalysts (see Chapter 7).

Instead, contemporary behavior therapists have tended to make the case for their theoretical and outcome hypotheses by appealing almost exclusively to empirical evidence, especially experimental evidence. This commitment to empirical inquiry could itself be classified as a "philosophy," but is it really a distinctive one? Some see it as reflecting an outmoded "logical empiricism," but whether this is true or not depends on what one means by that expression. As philosophers use the term, it refers to a distinctive set of philosophic views held by members of the Vienna Circle, including the verifiability criterion of meaning, the rejection of the synthetic a priori, and an emotivist theory of ethics. There is no reason to believe that most contemporary behavior therapists are logical empiricists in this sense, nor do their clinical views logically presuppose distinctive logical empiricist doctrines.

"Logical empiricism" is also applied more loosely to anyone who requires that hypotheses generally be supported by firm empirical evidence. On this usage, contemporary behavior therapists would then qualify, but so too would most physicists, medical doctors, biologists, and sophisticated dog-track gamblers. The claim that empirical evidence is needed to support most non-tautological hypotheses may be philosophical, but it is hardly distinctive of a behavior therapy paradigm.

Clinical Theory

In earlier decades, in discussing the original behavior therapy paradigm, one could point to a widespread acceptance of operant or classical conditioning theory, or some combination of both. Today, there is no single theory distinctive of the successor to that paradigm. There are two very general theoretical claims, however, that I believe would win general, although not universal, assent. First, contrary to what Freudian theory holds, the postulation of either repression or a dynamic unconscious is *not* crucial for understanding or treating psychopathology, even if attention must be paid to causal factors lying beneath the surface of consciousness; and second, contrary to what Skinner's theory holds, cognitive causes of some kind or other must be admitted, whether or not conditioning factors are also important in explaining clinical phenomena. Once we go beyond these very abstract claims, we find some general theories, but not ones that even purport to cover all clinical phenomena.

Assessment I am largely in agreement with the above methodological, evaluative, and philosophic views. In particular, I agree entirely with Hans Eysenck, Albert Bandura, Joseph Wolpe, and other behavior therapists who have championed the rigorous, scientific study of clinical phenomena. As to the sort of empiricism accepted by most behavior therapists –

the insistence that all except trivial theoretical and outcome hypotheses be supported by firm empirical evidence before they are accepted – this is, as I noted, hardly unique to a behavior therapy paradigm. In so far as it needs defense, it can be supported, first, by undermining certain post-modernist clinical epistemologies that challenge the need for empirical inquiry, and, second, by appealing to an objectivist epistemology. I did both of these things in Chapter 4.

I turn next to issues that are not primarily evaluative or philosophical, except that the first is conceptual.

The Nature of Behavior Therapy

Behavior therapy is obviously not a single therapy, but is it one *kind* of therapy? This is a question not about the meaning of words but about certain techniques: Do they have a common nature? As to the definitional question, some writers dispose of it by stipulation. For example, some stipulate that they will use the expression "behavior therapies" to mean "conditioning therapies"; others use it to mean "those procedures regularly and frequently called behavioral in the literature" (see Sweet and Loizeaux, 1991: 161). For some purposes, such definitions are adequate, but they leave unanswered the question: Do the therapies that are typically called "behavior therapies" have any theoretically interesting properties in common (other than their being sorted under a single label)?

In the 1970's, there was a relatively small number of behavior therapy techniques. Yet, even then, it was difficult to say what they and only they had in common. David Barlow (1978) reports that prominent psychiatrists and psychologists tried during this period to come up with a satisfactory definition during long and arduous board meetings of the AABT (the Association for the Advancement of Behavior Therapy). He characterizes these discussions as "interminable and fruitless." A consensus was eventually reached, but the AABT definition was so elastic that it could fit dynamic techniques as well as behavior therapy (Erwin, 1978: 36). I proposed a theory-neutral account which may have drawn the lines in the right places *then*, but I doubt that it would work today, given the proliferation of new techniques.

How many behavior therapy techniques exist today? The *Dictionary of Behavior Therapy Techniques* (Bellack and Hersen, 1985) lists approximately 158 such therapies. What is the prospect for isolating important characteristics that are shared by all and only these techniques? I am skeptical that this can be done at all, but let us look at some possible approaches.

The most natural way of picking out the behavior therapies would be to tie them to their underlying theory, or theories if there is more than one. One problem, however, is that different theorists can offer competing theories about why a therapy works. Systematic desensitization is said by Joseph Wolpe to work through conditioning mechanisms, and by

Albert Bandura through cognitive factors. Should the therapy, then, be classified as "behavior therapy" or "cognitive behavior therapy," or even as "cognitive therapy"?

We could say that the decision should depend on who is right. If Wolpe's explanation is the correct one, then systematic desensitization falls in the "behavior therapy" category, otherwise in the cognitive classification. However, taking this approach leads to new problems. If we first have to show that a particular theory correctly explains why a therapy works, if it works, before we can classify it, then many of the behavior therapies cannot presently be classified. In many cases, the theoretical explanation of how the therapy works has yet to be established. Furthermore, what do we do with a therapy that was clearly suggested by a certain theory, but the theory turns out to be wrong? If that is the fate of Freudian theory, for example, and psychoanalysis works when it works because of conditioning factors, should we say that it is really a kind of behavior therapy?

Furthermore, if we do not yet have an all-compassing theory for the entire field, can we even be confident that there is such a theory waiting to be discovered? I am sympathetic to the views of those (such as Staats, 1983) who would like to unify the field of behavior therapy, but I doubt that there is any empirical evidence so far that would justify our being confident that this can be done. As far as what we know today, is it not just as likely that separate theories will be needed to explain the workings of different behavior therapies as that a single theory will explain all? In any event, the question remains: How do we *now* explain what makes something a form of behavior therapy?

Hans Eysenck (1987a) has an interesting but, I believe, modest proposal. First, he argues that the concept of neurosis is still useful despite its abandonment by some psychiatrists (it was, for example, dropped from DSM-III, the third edition of the *Diagnostic and Statistical Manual of Mental Disorders* of the American Psychiatric Association). Eysenck cites factor analytic studies indicating that the concept picks out a distinct group of non-psychotic disorders. He then theorizes that the different types of neuroses arise through a process of Pavlovian conditioning, and can be eliminated through a process of Pavlovian extinction. The behavior therapies, then, are those that are used in treating neuroses and which work through conditioning mechanisms.

What about non-psychotic disorders that do not arise through conditioning? Eysenck suggests that existential fears, worries, and doubts *might* be examples. If that turns out to be the case, then, he proposes, they may not be classified as neuroses.

There is nothing circular in Eysenck's proposal. First, find out through empirical study if a distinct set of various non-psychotic clinical problems have theoretically interesting properties in common as to their origin and suitability for a certain type of treatment. Use the term "neurosis," then, as a technical term that applies exactly to these disorders.

What do we say, however, about those behavior therapies that are used to treat neurotic disorders (as defined by Eysenck) but do not work through conditioning mechanisms? If Bandura and Adams (1977) are right, one of the best-known of all behavior therapy techniques, systematic desensitization, would not qualify as behavior therapy on Eysenck's proposal. Furthermore, what of those behavior therapy techniques that are used to treat "existential" doubts and worries, or in general, non-neurotic disorders? Apparently, we would have to say that these too are not really behavior therapies. But, then, many of the 158 techniques listed in the *Dictionary of Behavior Therapy Techniques* would not be behavior therapies.

Eysenck's proposal, then, is in the end a modest one. It provides a way of picking out only some, and perhaps very few, of what behavior therapists call "behavior therapy." It does not address the problem of saying what most or all behavior therapies have in common. I suppose that Eysenck might say that there is no problem here because these other therapies are not really instances of behavior therapy. However, I know of no way of arguing for this thesis that is not question-begging. In the end, it may be better simply to subdivide the behavior therapies, and call some of them by a different name. For example, those picked out by Eysenck's criteria might be called "the conditioning behavior therapies."

Another approach is to identify the behavior therapies by their being "behavioral." The problem then becomes: How do we distinguish techniques that are behavioral from those that are not? Hallam (1987) raises this question, but in the end he does not answer it. His idea (page 327) is that a therapy is properly called "behavioral" when it is based on a "behavior theory." What is that? Hallam's answer is that such a theory holds that behavioral observations are the factual basis from which constructs are inferred and subsequently tested. This contrasts with theories that employ behavioral observations merely to test hypotheses about internal/subjective constructs.

Even at the level of theories, this classification is of dubious value. Is social learning theory a behavioral or a non-behavioral theory? It places heavy emphasis on the role of beliefs of a certain sort in explaining behavioral change, but it does not employ behavioral observations *merely* to test hypotheses about mental states. Even theories such as those proposed by Beck and Ellis purport to explain some behavior. In fact, even psychodynamic theories that claim to explain both behavior and mental states would qualify as behavioral on Hallam's criterion: They do not use behavioral data merely to test hypotheses about mental states.

In any event, even if there are some theories that come out as non-behavioral on Hallam's criterion, this at best provides a contrast between theories, not therapies. The proposal will not work at all unless it can be shown that all or most of the behavior therapies, *and they alone*, are based on theories that qualify as "behavior" theories in Hallam's technical sense.

We might also try to draw a distinction in terms of the aims of therapy. For example, Martin (1987: 453) assumes that behavior change forms *the* goal of behavior therapy. As a matter of sheer empirical fact, this is untrue. Behavior therapists who seek to rid the client of feelings of anxiety or obsessive thinking are trying to change both behavior and mental states.

Even if, contrary to fact, the aim of all behavior therapists were merely behavior change, that would be a fact not about behavior therapy but about the intentions of certain therapists. Therapists with a different orientation could use exactly the same therapies but with a different intention. So, to single out a certain therapeutic aim is not to pick out a certain sort of *therapy*.

There may be some other way to explain what is "behavioral" about the behavior therapies, but there is an obvious problem to be overcome. What are called "behavioral" and "cognitive" features are intermixed in both cognitive and behavior therapies, and even in therapies that are generally classified as neither, such as interpersonal therapy. It is not easy to sort out these features in such a way that we can say: Those that have this particular assortment are the behavior therapies; those that have a different mix are not.

The problem of saying what behavior therapy is is hardly the most pressing or interesting problem for contemporary behavior therapists. Yet it is useful now and then to reflect on what glues the field together. My own view is that it is primarily a commitment to the philosophical, methodological and evaluative views that I discussed earlier. If we ask what justifies calling certain *techniques* and not others "behavior therapy," then I believe that today the only reasonable answer is: Nothing, except that this is what they are called by those who identify themselves as behavior therapists.

Theoretical Issues

First, one theoretical issue that continues to reverberate throughout the behavior therapy literature concerns the role of conditioning. If we exclude applied behavior analysts, then the majority of behavior therapists agree that cognitive and emotional factors have causal consequences that have to be taken into account. That has not prevented many behavior therapists from continuing to talk about a "conditioning view of behavior" (Martin, 1987: 453). In many cases, this sort of talk appears hard to justify. For example, Martin (page 451) notes that today's "conditioning research" is partly about cognitive representations and information processing that involves learning about the causal structure of the world. Does this constitute, however, an enlargement or an abandonment of a conditioning point of view? That depends on exactly what Martin has in mind.

She makes the reasonable point (1987: 455) that under certain conditions, the terms "automatic" and "unmediated" can be applied to convey the directness of the stimulus–response connections. In such cases, it is plausible to apply the concept of conditioning. Martin also points out, however, that under other conditions the effects of knowledge about contiguity seem to provide additional control over "conditioned respond-ing." My question is: In these latter cases, what justifies calling the responses "conditioned responding"? If in these cases, the organism learns (or at least thinks that it has learned) that there is a causal connection between doing something and some consequence, and decides, on the basis of this belief and its motivation, either to act or not act, then the connection is neither unmediated nor automatic. Why, then, call the response a "conditioned" response? It is as if "conditioned" is being equated with "acquired," so that any acquired response becomes by definition a conditioned response. This creates the illusion that con-ditioning research has a lot more to do with behavior therapy than it really does. This may not be how Martin is using the term "conditioning," but if it is not, what is the justification for its extension to cases where the response is mediated and not automatic?

The same sort of problem arises in Dickinson's (1987) excellent account of animal conditioning and learning theory. He points out that in the last 20 years almost every aspect of the traditional view of conditioning has been challenged. Even the simplest forms of conditioning appear to involve cognitive processes; learning can occur without reinforcement within the conditioning paradigm; and even where reinforcement oper-ates, strict contiguity between the response or stimulus and the reinforcer is neither necessary nor sufficient for conditioning (1987: 57–8). He concludes (page 61) that at least some forms of conditioning reflect the acquisition of knowledge about the relationship between the events involved rather than the simple strengthening of a stimulus–response link.

My question again is: In such cases, why call the response "con-ditioned"? Dickinson's answer appears to be the following. He distin-guishes (1987: 77) between the "empirical phenomenon of conditioning" and a certain outmoded theoretical explanation of it. As he notes, the contemporary approach recognizes a role for representation and beliefs about predictive and causal relationships *even* in the case of animal con-ditioning. This is important, he contends, because it means that the conditioning model is not necessarily at variance with the increasing recognition of the role of mental processes in psychiatric disorders.

What, however, does this distinction that Dickinson tries to draw amount to? Suppose that my boss gives me extra money for raising my work output, and she tells me that this will be done in the future. I think it over, and decide that I need the extra money, and so I work longer hours and repeat my high output performance. Is this an example of the "empirical phenomenon of conditioning" that is to be given a cognitive explanation, or is it rather not an example of conditioning at all? If one says the first, then I ask again: What, other than the fact that it is an acquired response, justifies the use of the term "conditioning" here? If one agrees that it is not conditioning, then what is different about this sort of case and cases illustrating "the empirical phenomenon of conditioning" that are to be explained cognitively? In short, the description of a response as "conditioned" has a built in explanation; namely, that it was caused by conditioning factors. Once that explanation is rejected, logic demands that the description be withdrawn.

Talking about a "second signalling system," or of verbal responses as reinforcers, or of mental events obeying the same conditioning laws as other responses, all fail to respond adequately to the issue. No doubt, sometimes when people think, they do so mechanically and associatively. Someone hears the word "homosexual" and automatically thinks "pervert." We can speak reasonably here of a sort of conditioning. That is not true in general, however. If a scientist appraises a scientific theory, and notices a flaw in the reasoning of its proponents, and thinks, consequently, that the theory lacks support, this is not an example of conditioning. If I figure out that if I do such and such, I will probably get something I value, and then decide that it is worth the time and effort, my thinking process does not obey laws of conditioning; there are no such known laws that are applicable to this sort of case.

I am not suggesting that making room for cognitive factors always crowds out conditioning explanations. It depends on the weight that is given to the respective factors. On Eysenck's (1987a) conditioning theory, for example, cognitive factors play a role in the development of neurosis, but the conditioning factors that are postulated are of primary importance. For example, a man may be afraid to ride on an elevator because of a traumatic experience that "incubates" in the way that Eysenck's theory suggests. The client may believe that riding in an elevator is not really risky, but that belief does him no good. It is counteracted by the lingering effects of the pairing of the traumatic elevator ride and the bad experience. So, it does seem reasonable in such a case to speak of conditioning.

A second, and related, theoretical issue concerns the extent to which problems treated by behavior therapists are due to conditioning. Joseph Wolpe (1993) estimates that about two-thirds of maladaptive fears are classically conditioned and one-third cognitively based. On the basis of this estimate, he concludes (page 142) that this is the putative ratio of cases calling, respectively, for classical conditioning and cognitive correction. He thus challenges the cognitivists, such as Beck and Ellis, who, according to Wolpe, "infiltrated" the behavior therapy movement during the 1980's, and who think that cognitive errors are the basis of all maladaptive anxieties.

In an earlier paper (1981), Wolpe cites war neuroses as a classic example of a single trial fear conditioning. After seeing comrades mutilated while machine-gun fire predominates, the soldier has tremendous anxiety aroused within him. When he returns home, his anxiety is automatically aroused by sounds resembling machine-gun fire. As Wolpe puts it, no cognitive error is involved. This is an example of one trial conditioning, but, Wolpe points out, the conditioning can come in stages. As an example, he cites the fear of public speaking that is based on numerous anxiety-based experiences.

One question that can be raised about Wolpe's argument concerns its intended scope. Behavior therapists now treat a tremendous variety of problems. Which of these is Wolpe talking about? He mentions (1981) psychosomatic disorders, sexual inadequacies, agoraphobia, insomnia, neurotic depression, and fear of public speaking. This would embrace a relatively large number of cases, but it should be mentioned in passing that it also omits quite a lot of sorts of cases treated by behavior therapists.

Leaving this issue aside, how good is the evidence for Wolpe's estimates? He cites two studies: Ost and Hugdahl (1981) and Wolpe (1981). Although both are interesting, neither together nor separately do they provide any firm evidence for Wolpe's estimates.

Ost and Hugdahl studied only phobias, which may be the most favorable sorts of cases for a conditioning etiology. Moreover, what they found (1981: 444), through the use of questionnaires, is that 57.5 per cent (not two-thirds) of their subjects *ascribed* their phobias to conditioning experiences. To go further and infer that these clients were correct, we would not only have to trust the accuracy of their memory; we would also have to take their theorizing at face value and not demand from them any supporting evidence. How in general, not merely in a few clear-cut cases, do the subjects know what caused their phobias to originate?

In the second study, Wolpe (1981) extracted from his alphabetical files 40 cases with a central complaint of unadaptive fear. He and his assistant then "jointly determined" whether the fear was autonomically conditioned or cognitively based (page 38). It is not clear, however, how they were able to do this merely by inspecting the records. They present no evidence that in the cases judged to be ones of autonomic conditioning there was no cognitive error, and that the fear, as in the war neuroses, was unmediated and automatic.

Wolpe raises an important issue, though, and he may be right about the sorts of problems he is discussing, but unless there is better evidence, his estimates are mere conjectures at this stage. Furthermore, there is another premise in his argument that can be questioned: that if the estimates are approximately correct, then they provide the putative ratio of cases calling for classical conditioning as opposed to cognitive correction.

As a small child, I fell off my bike at high speed, and landed on my teeth. Five years passed before I would ride a bike again. If my memory is accurate, this looks like a case where the fear of bike riding was directly conditioned; no cognitive error, to use Wolpe's words, was involved. Yet I later developed beliefs about the dangers of bike riding, and these were subsequently challenged by friends and family members. What changed my mind (here I speculate) was not any rational argument, but watching other children ride their bikes without harm befalling them.

One case would prove little even if I could be sure that I had the facts right. I use it only to illustrate a point: Even if no cognitive error is involved initially, beliefs that are developed later may play an important role in maintaining the phobia. If Bandura's self-efficacy theory applies to a large number of phobias, then regardless of their etiology, what maintains them is the subject's belief about what will happen if one approaches the phobic object. Bandura is not recommending that one simply try to argue the subject out of his or her conviction, nor does his theory have this implication. However, the research in support of his theory presents a challenge to the premise that if the problem arose from conditioning, then cognitive correction is not needed. Cognitive correction may still be needed, but not necessarily through the use of the sort of cognitive techniques that Wolpe is challenging.

My point, in fact, is neutral concerning Wolpe's conclusion about the methods of Beck and Ellis, but it does bear on part of his argument. Although theory can guide us in selecting techniques, we need more than information about etiology to tell us which sort of techniques are likely to work in a given case. In addition, we do not yet have enough hard evidence to be confident about the exact percentages of cases in which conditioning factors or cognitive factors are paramount.

Third, Sweet and Loizeaux (1991), in a very interesting paper, also raise a doubt about the growing popularity of cognitive techniques. They, like Wolpe, ask the question (page 160): "Does the specific addition of a purely cognitive therapeutic procedure enhance the outcome of behavioral treatment methods for actual patient populations?" The evidence they accumulate appears to say "no." Most of the studies they review show an equivalence between cognitive-behavioral therapy and behavioral procedures alone, although behavior therapy was superior in two studies to treatments with a cognitive component.

Based on this evidence, Sweet and Loizeaux challenge two claims: (1) that by switching from behavioral to cognitive techniques we gain more than a modest amount of therapeutic efficacy; and (2) that where cognitive techniques are effective, the specifically cognitive elements help account for their efficacy. Given that only a "modicum" of clinical benefit has been added in the 20 years that the cognitive therapy movement has been in place, the authors suggest (page 159) that the wholesale adoption of cognitive procedures is unmerited.

Although questions could be raised about the quality of some of the studies that are reviewed and the way that they were divided up (the behavioral ones were picked out simply by their being *called* "behavioral"), let us assume that these issues in the end make no important difference to the Sweet-Loizeaux argument. On that assumption, I would not challenge any of their main conclusions. In fact, I would go further than they do and ask whether either Beck's or Ellis' procedures have been shown to be effective at all in treating any sort of clinical problem (although I am not suggesting that these techniques are ineffective; the point concerns what has been demonstrated to date). Earlier I raised some doubts about the alleged demonstrations of effectiveness of Beck's procedures, graver doubts with respect to Ellis' techniques, and even more doubts about whether either set of procedures has been shown to be more effective than a credible placebo in treating depression or any other clinical disorder. This goes beyond doubting that these sort of cognitive techniques are demonstrably more effective than behavioral ones, or whether the cognitive elements add any degree of effectiveness.

I do, however, wish to raise a theoretical issue, one that is tangential to Sweet and Loizeaux's argument but is nonetheless important. As an aside, they appeal to their evidence to challenge not only the "wholesale" adoption of cognitive procedures but also cognitive terminology and explanations (1991: 180). Such wholesale use of cognitive terminology may be unwarranted, but, for reasons I gave earlier, the extension of "conditioning" terminology is also misguided in many cases, giving the false impression that behavior therapy has a closer connection to conditioning than it really does. As to the theoretical issue, the data reviewed by Sweet and Loizeaux are neutral on the question of what originally caused or what now maintains pathological states. The "essential" identifying ingredient, they say (page 161), in the techniques they pick out as cognitive is the use of *verbal* methods, such as disputation, to attack underlying cognitions. However, if such verbal methods prove useless (this has not yet been established) that is neutral on the theoretical question of what maintains the disorders. On social learning theory, certain expectations play an important role in maintaining many sorts of clinical disorders, but the theory does not imply that verbal methods will be very helpful in changing the relevant beliefs. Bandura and other social learning theorists have consistently maintained that performance-based procedures are needed. If that proves correct, and attempting to argue a client out of his or her deviant beliefs proves ineffective, that does nothing to refute Bandura's theory.

Sweet and Loizeaux also cite non-outcome evidence to suggest that the majority of maladaptive anxiety responses are classically conditioned. Their evidence, however, comes solely from the studies of Wolpe (1981) and Ost and Hugdahl (1981). I have already explained why this evidence ought not to persuade.

Fourth, issues about the respective causal roles of conditioning and cognitive factors arise in still another way in discussions of the major competing theories in the field: Bandura's social learning theory and Eysenck's conditioning theory. As already indicated, the first places heavy emphasis on expectations (what Bandura calls "self-efficacy expectations"); the second allows for the operation of both cognitive and genetic factors, but the main emphasis is on conditioning factors (see Bandura, 1995; Eysenck, 1987a, 1987b). Both of these theories have empirical support, but there are also, not surprisingly, unanswered empirical questions – for example, see the issues raised in the commentary on Eysenck (1979b) and

Eysenck's replies. Although I will not argue this, it seems to me that, because of these unanswered questions, we are not yet warranted in accepting either theory. Perhaps it is misleading even to ask about accepting either theory in its entirety. The more appropriate question may be: For exactly which clinical disorders and treatments are the causal mechanisms postulated by the respective theories operative?

Regardless of their degree of empirical support, neither Bandura's nor Eysenck's theory purports to cover all of the techniques that are called "behavior therapies," nor all of the clinical problems treated by behavior therapists. There is no such all-encompassing theory at the present time, and as suggested earlier, no such theory may ever be formulated. The lack of such a theory, however, is not reason by itself to adopt a purely technological point of view that neglects theory altogether. An alternative is to develop mini-theories that may explain the maintenance of only one or two disorders, or the workings of only one or two behavior therapy techniques. To some extent, this is already being done – see some of the papers in Barlow (1993). There are also theories of wider scope now available; see the papers in O'Donohue and Krasner (1995).

Therapeutic Effectiveness

I intend to argue in the final chapter that the proper standard for judging therapeutic effectiveness requires the use of a placebo control (or some adequate substitute). Many behavior therapists now disagree with this standard, but *if* it is correct, it is reasonable to ask: How many of the approximately 158 techniques listed in the *Dictionary of Behavior Therapy Techniques* (Bellack and Hersen, 1985) have been shown to be effective according to this standard? Very few (my guess would be fewer than 20). However, some who are skeptical about the effectiveness of psychotherapy suggest that *none* of its forms has been shown to be effective (Epstein, 1995: 85–6). Such extreme skepticism goes too far: Some forms of behavior therapy have met the rigorous requirements for demonstration of effectiveness. One example is the use of behavior therapy in treating the very difficult problem of obsessive compulsive disorder; in a number of studies, it has been shown to be more effective than a pill-placebo (see some of the studies reviewed in van Balkom et al., 1994). Other examples can be found in Barlow (1993), such as cognitive-behavioral group therapy, which has outperformed a sugar pill in the treatment of social phobias (Hope and Heimberg, 1993). Still other behavior therapies, such as cognitive-behavior therapy for bulimia nervosa, have been developed only recently, but the preliminary evidence is very encouraging (Wilson and Pike, 1993; Wilson, 1996).

7

Psychoanalysis and the Psychodynamic Therapies

As noted in Chapter 3, there is more than one psychoanalytic theory; significant parts of Freud's version have been rejected by those contemporary analysts who embrace object relations theory or self psychology. One also needs to distinguish orthodox, long-term psychoanalytic therapy from the newer short-term psychoanalytically oriented psychotherapies, or, as they are often called, the "dynamic psychotherapies." Still, some parts of Freudian theory and elements of his therapy continue to have great influence in the field of psychotherapy. I shall begin with Freud's views.

FREUDIAN THEORY AND THERAPY

Freudian theory is sometimes spoken of as if it were a single theory, but in fact it is a collection of theories that in varying degrees are independent of one another. Some are important in some contexts but not others. What is most germane to psychotherapy is the so-called "clinical theory." Exactly which propositions should be included here is not so clear; what follows is an attempt to identify *some* of the major hypotheses.

The Dynamic Unconscious

Clearly, the idea of the unconscious is extremely important to Freud's clinical theories; yet it is well known that the unconscious was not discovered by Freud. Many Freudians reply that what he discovered was the existence of the *dynamic* unconscious. This is different from the unconscious of common-sense psychology, which Freud referred to as the "preconscious," and from the "cognitive unconscious" postulated by contemporary cognitive psychologists. Scholars disagree about how to characterize the differences, but some link the idea of a dynamic unconscious to repression: The ideas, wishes, urges, and so on buried in the unconscious remain there because they continue to be repressed. Others disconnect the two concepts, and explain the dynamic unconscious in terms of inaccessibility to consciousness unless there is a successful psychoanalysis (for two very good discussions of the issues, see Eagle, 1987; Erdelyi, 1985).

Some Freudians speak of the unconscious as merely a "useful fiction," but if this means that there is no dynamic unconscious in any sense, then most of Freudian theory is false. Something that does not exist cannot cause neuroses, or affect our dreams, or contribute to our forgetting names, or making linguistic slips. What is true, and perhaps this is what is meant, is that there is no need to think of the unconscious as an *entity*, any more than one need speak of consciousness as a "thing." With respect to the dynamic unconscious, all that is needed to make sense of Freud's clinical theory is the postulation of dynamic unconscious mental processes, events, or states.

It is also not necessary for a Freudian to take sides on the question of the ultimate ontological status of unconscious mental events. Whatever Freud's view of the matter was, a contemporary Freudian can say they are identical with brain events, or hold the dualistic view that their relation to brain events is either causal or correlational.

It is hardly necessary to stress the significance of the idea of a Freudian unconscious. In terms of influence, it must surely rank as one of the most fertile ideas of the twentieth century. Particularly relevant to psychotherapy, however, are the implications of Freud's views about the unconscious for the origin and treatment of psychoneuroses. To mention just one, if most psychological disorders are maintained by causes that lie deeply buried in our unconscious, there is an initial presumption that cognitive and behavioral treatments that fail to make contact with them will be either superficial or harmful, although in the end only the empirical data will decide the value of these rival therapies.

The Theory of Dreams

In *The Interpretation of Dreams* (1900, *SE* 4 and 5), Freud holds that all dreams are wish fulfillments, although in his later writings, he speaks of "attempts" at wish fulfillment. The key wishes are repressed during the infantile period (although wishes from later life that are not repressed can also make a difference); they affect dream content in the following way. Dreams serve a sleep-preserving function, but that function is interfered with by wishes emanating from the unconscious that are unacceptable to the ego. Because a person's usual defenses are weakened during sleep, the ego is forced to compromise: sleep continues, and the repressed wishes are allowed into consciousness as the person dreams, but only in a disguised form. So, there is something akin to censorship: the dreamer is allowed to become aware of something that reflects a repressed infantile wish, but not in a recognizable form.

Freud thus distinguishes between the manifest and latent content of a dream; namely, the collection of dream images experienced by the dreamer and their underlying meaning. Many of the items that appear as part of the manifest content are symbols, most of which are sexual in nature. In addition to interpreting the dream symbols, an important technique used by Freudian therapists in deciphering the dream is to have the dreamer free associate about its manifest content. At least in theory, an analyst can thus figure out the latent content and ultimately learn about the dream's unconscious determinants.

Personality Types and Stages of Sexual Development

According to orthodox Freudian theory, each of us goes through four stages of sexual development. In the first year of life, the child passes through the oral stage, during which the mouth is its primary source of pleasure. During the next three years, the anal stage, the child's interest shifts to the anus. How it responds to such things as toilet training, defecating, and in general the use of its bowels can have an important effect on personality development. Roughly, from 3 to 5, the child passes through the phallic period, and its genitals become of major concern. There is then a latency period until puberty when an interest in sexual things re-emerges.

How the child reacts during the various stages of sexual development may play a crucial role in the development of the adult personality. A child may become fixated at one stage, or because of later problems may regress to it. In his "Character and anal erotism" (1908, *SE* 9), Freud describes the constellation of traits causally linked to the anal stage. The anal character consists essentially of three traits: obstinacy, parsimony, and orderliness. Other Freudians — most notably, Abraham (1924) — have also delineated an oral character.

The Oedipal Phase and the Castration Complex

Approximately, between the ages of 3 to 5, the male child develops a desire to possess his mother sexually, and sees his father as his chief rival. Soon, however, partly because of threats he receives in reaction to his masturbation, the boy comes to fear that his father will cut off his penis. If he can recall seeing genitals of females, he will infer that these females have been castrated and this will enhance his fear that he will be the next victim. Thus, the child develops castration anxiety. As a consequence, the Oedipal period comes to an end. The boy ceases his sexual advances to his mother, and begins to identify with his father.

When the female child discovers that men have a penis and she does not, she concludes that she has been castrated. She turns against her mother, whom she blames for this state of affairs, and develops a desire for a penis, or "penis envy." She then shifts her affection toward the father, whom she fantasizes as impregnating her. The Oedipal phase comes to an end for the female, not because of fear of castration, but because of fear of loss of love.

The Theory of Repression and Resistance

In his early writings, Freud sometimes uses "repression" as a synonym for "defense"; in later works, repression counts as but one kind of defense, but by far the most important. It plays a crucial role in Freudian explanations of the etiology of the psychoneuroses, dreams, and parapraxes. Indeed, as Grünbaum points out (1984: 3), Freud saw the idea of repression as the "cornerstone" of the whole structure of psychoanalysis (1914, *SE* 14: 16).

Scholars disagree about the exact definition of "repression," but at a minimum repression involves the keeping out of consciousness threatening or painful material. A related idea is that of "resistance." As Freud notes (1923 [1922], *SE* 18: 246), if in the course of analytic work one attempts to make repressed impulses conscious, one becomes aware of the repressive forces in the form of resistance on the part of the patient. A crucial step in the therapy is the overcoming of these resistances.

Other Freudian defense mechanisms include: denial, reaction-formation, projection, and displacement. In denial, the ego wards off something from the external world which it feels as painful; it does this by denying some perception that brings knowledge of such a demand on the part of reality. When engaging in reaction-formation, the subject develops an attitude or behavior that is the opposite of the one being defended against. In projection, one attributes to someone else characteristics of oneself that one unconsciously rejects. Displacement involves the ego's protecting against instinctual demands of the id by redirecting aggression originally aimed at someone or some thing, and redirecting it toward someone else or some other thing.

The Etiology of Psychoneuroses and Slips

After he substituted free association for hypnosis, Freud noticed a pattern as he reached further back into the patient's puberty or childhood. "Eventually," he writes, ". . . it became inevitable to bow before the evidence and recognize that at the root of the formation of every symptom there were to be found traumatic experiences from early sexual life" (1923 [1922], *SE* 18: 243). In cases of "actual neuroses," Freud concluded that the disorders could be traced to contemporary abuses in the patient's sexual life, and in the psychoneuroses, the symptoms were due to sexual events of early childhood. The symptoms of the latter disorders, Freud concluded, are "compromise formations," that is, they are indirect expressions of repressed ideas or wishes associated with the early traumatic sexual traumas.

Slips of the tongue and other parapraxes, in so far as Freudian theory purports to explain them, are analogous to neuroses. They are caused by repressed wishes, and also constitute compromise formations.

The Transference

Freud's key theoretical claim concerning the transference is that in the course of an analysis, the patient sees the analyst as the reincarnation of some important figure of the patient's childhood or past, and as a consequence transfers toward the analyst positive or negative feelings that were formerly directed toward the figure from the past (1940, *SE* 23: 174–75). As Laplanche and Pontalis (1973: 455) succinctly phrase the thesis, "In the transference, infantile prototypes re-emerge and are experienced with a strong sensation of immediacy."

Freud thought the concept of transference to be of great importance for his therapeutic enterprise, and contemporary analysts generally hold that a resolution of the patient's transference is a key element in a successful analysis.

The above ideas constitute only a small part of Freudian theory, but they are a very important part. Here is how Freud himself described what he called the "corner-stones" of psychoanalytic theory:

> The assumption that there are unconscious mental processes, the recognition of the theory of resistance and repression, the appreciation of the importance of sexuality and of the Oedipus complex – these constitute the principal subject-matter of psycho-analysis and the foundations of its theory. No one who cannot accept them all should count himself a psycho-analyst. (1923 [1922], *SE* 18: 247)

Classical Psychoanalytic Therapy

Psychoanalytic therapy has changed in many ways since Freud developed it, but there are some important constants, such as the following. Freud himself stressed the importance of overcoming the patient's resistances, and most contemporary Freudians would agree. A second important distinguishing feature is the attempt by the analyst to *interpret* the slips, dreams, free associations, and other behavior of the patient in order to discover the unconscious determinants of the clinical disorder, if that is what is being treated. At least two caveats, however, are needed. First, some analysts see their key task as doing something other than treating (what used to be called) psychoneuroses. For example, some would stress character reformation instead. Second, some analysts view their interpretations merely as useful clinical devices, not as accurate portrayals of what caused the client's current state.

A third important ingredient in standard psychoanalysis is making conscious the repressed wishes and pathological ideas that lie beneath the surface of the client's problems. A fourth important feature is the attempt to resolve the transference. Although there are a number of different types of dynamic therapies, some of which but not others include key Freudian ingredients, any therapy that fails to include most of the foregoing factors cannot qualify as classical psychoanalysis.

METHODOLOGY

As with other clinical paradigms, there are some distinctive methodological assumptions that analysts tend to share, even if not everyone agrees
with each one. One such assumption, obviously, is that free association
can be reliably used as an investigative tool. As one philosopher nicely
expresses the point, Freud assumed that it is intrinsic to symptoms and
dreams that they are invariably formed by the patient along an "associ-
ative pathway" leading from a desire that the patient can no longer act on
to the symptom or dream (Wollheim, 1993: 104). It was Freud's expectation that in his free associations the patient would retread this path, or
one sufficiently related to it, although in the opposite direction. By
following this path, the analyst in turn can uncover important evidence
concerning the patient's unconscious mental life.

Another important methodological assumption, one that behavior
therapists and cognitivists tend to reject, concerns the probative value of
clinical case studies. Analysts have traditionally taken the position that
such studies not only have heuristic value but also have significant evidential worth. In fact, many hold that experimental evidence and the data
from everyday life are greatly inferior to the evidence obtained from
clinical settings in the treatment of clients.

PHILOSOPHY

There is a vast amount of philosophy that has been written about Freud's
work. Much of it concerns such issues as the nature of the unconscious,
our concept of the self, the mind–body problem, and free will and
determinism. There is no need to explore such issues here where the
focus is on the assessment of Freud's theories and therapy. There *is* a body
of philosophic work, however, that is directly relevant because it concerns
the standards for weighing the Freudian evidence.

Some of this work concerns the scientific status of Freudian theory. As
is well known, some philosophic critics of Freud, notably Karl Popper
(1962) and Ernest Nagel (1959), argue that most of Freudian theory is
untestable in principle. What they generally conclude is not that Freud
was mistaken but that his theories are pseudo-scientific, or at least non-
scientific. These arguments of Popper and Nagel have now been answered
(see Erwin, 1988b; Grünbaum, 1993). Most if not all of Freudian theory is
testable at least in principle, and much of it in practice. The attempt by
philosophers to discredit Freudian theory *without looking at the actual
evidence* was a convenient short cut but it led nowhere.

Other philosophers have paid more attention to the existing evidence
but have argued that it is a mistake to judge it by standards appropriate to
the natural sciences. This raises an important philosophic issue. If we
cannot agree about the very criteria for evaluating the evidence, we can

look at the same body of data and reach opposite conclusions about what is right and wrong in Freud's work. Three major views about standards can be found in the recent work of philosophers.

The Hermeneutic Model

The idea that psychoanalysis either is or should be a hermeneutic science can be traced back to the work of the psychiatrist-philosopher Karl Jaspers (1963). There are a variety of hermeneutic positions, but one holds that Freudian theory is primarily about meanings rather than causes (Ricoeur, 1970). Some who take this position treat the analyst's interpretations as analogous to the reading of a text. Consequently, it is argued, it is an error to judge them by standards that are employed in judging causal hypotheses of the natural sciences. Just as in reading a text, ultimately insight and intuition can and must be appealed to in judging Freudian hypotheses (see Taylor, 1979, 1985).

The Meaning Affinity Model

On this view, when Freudian theory talks about unconscious wishes and desires, it *is* talking about causes; however, where there is a similarity in meaning between propositions about symptoms, dreams, or actions and propositions about wishes and desires, we can reasonably infer a causal connection. To take an example from everyday life, suppose I say, "He is getting a drink of water." There is a similarity in content between that proposition and "He wants to get a drink of water." So, it is argued, when I notice the similarity in meaning, I am warranted inferring a causal connection, in this case between the desire for the drink and the action of getting a drink of water.

The Folk Psychology Model

The term "folk psychology" is used by philosophers to refer to common-sense psychology. Some have argued that Freudian theory is an extension of this psychology; consequently, whatever epistemic standards govern the latter also apply to the former. For example, suppose that I notice that a man is putting his sweater on. If I also know that the temperature has just dropped, I can infer that he is doing this *because* he wants to become warmer. Surely, to be confident that my explanation is correct, I do not have to do a controlled experiment and check to see if there generally is a causal connection between desiring to be warmer and putting one's sweater on. What, then, does justify my inference?

On one view, such folk psychology explanations provide an "understanding from within," and they are to be evaluated by a distinctive standard, one not appropriate for judging research in, say, particle physics or cancer research (Nagel, 1995). To understand someone else's thoughts, feelings, or behavior "from within" requires that we make sense of the phenomena, even if only "irrational sense," from the agent's point of view, by using our own point of view as an imaginative resource (Nagel, 1995). In providing Freudian explanations, it is argued, we do pretty much the same thing (Nagel, 1995). We put ourselves, so to speak, "in the shoes" of other people, and make sense of their symptoms and responses by attributing to them beliefs, desires, feelings, and perceptions – with the difference that these are aspects of their point of view of which they are not consciously aware.

VALUES

It is not clear that being a Freudian commits one logically to basic values that are different from those of non-Freudians, nor is there empirical evidence, at least that I am aware of, that Freudians as a class tend to hold basic values that are distinctive. Many Freudians, moreover, insist that the practice of psychoanalysis should be value free. If, however, we talk about non-basic values, ones based on empirical and theoretical beliefs, then we can identify some values that tend to be distinctive of a Freudian paradigm.

One is the idea that the analyst ought to be morally neutral with respect to what the client reports or does, although virtually all analysts would agree that there are extreme cases where this rule is not applicable. This assumption is not held by Freudians alone, but it is less likely to be held by therapists in some other schools, particularly those who are members of the clergy. Other values concern outcomes. Analysts are less likely than cognitivists or behavior modificationists to value a change in the client's cognitions or behavior, unless the change is accompanied by insight into the cause of the client's problems. Many analysts view symptomatic change as not very beneficial, and perhaps even harmful. Some place little emphasis on the client's so-called "presenting problem," and tend to stress character change or the achievement of autonomy. (For an attempt to identify other distinctive psychoanalytic values, see Wallwork, 1991.)

Evaluating the Freudian Evidence

There is a tremendous amount of evidence that bears on Freudian theory, but once the correct standards for evaluating that evidence are identified, it is possible to see clearly what the trends are. For that reason, the philosophic issues about evidential standards are important if not crucial.

The distinctive evidential standards that philosophers have proposed for evaluating Freud's claims have at least one thing in common: they are in some sense lower than the standards used not just in physics or chemistry but also in organic medicine. Let us look briefly at the three major models identified earlier: the Hermeneutic, Meaning Affinity and Folk Psychology Models.

The hermeneutic model fails for several reasons. First, Freudian theory does talk about the meaning of symptoms, dreams, and the like, but this is not *linguistic* meaning. Consequently, it is illicit to infer that because we can interpret a text merely by appealing to intuition, we can do likewise when interpreting a symptom or dream. Second, in talking about meaning, Freudian theory generally makes implicit causal claims. If I explain the meaning of a slip of the tongue, for example, in terms of a repressed wish, I am implying a causal claim – namely, that the wish affected what the person said. Suppose that the man had such a wish, but it made no difference whatsoever to what he uttered. In that event, the wish would definitely not be the true meaning of the slip.

Suppose, to take another example, that an analyst says that the latent meaning of the client's dream is that he has a repressed wish to have sex with a significant figure from his early life. That claim presupposes a causal hypothesis: that the repressed wish made a difference to the manifest meaning of the dream. In general, the fact that Freudian theory makes claims about meanings does not mean that it does not also make implicit causal claims. Hence, there is no basis for concluding that because many of its hypotheses concern meanings that they are exempt from being evaluated by standards for judging causal hypotheses.

Philosophers who accept the Meaning Affinity Model generally agree that Freudian hypotheses are causal, but they take meaning similarities to be a "mark" of causal connection. For that reason, they also conclude that Freudian theory should be judged by evidential standards inappropriate for judging causal hypotheses in other sciences. This view should also be challenged. If I see a man getting a drink, I am generally warranted in inferring that he is doing this because he desires a drink. There is no need, however, to postulate a mysterious epistemological connection between meaning and causation. We have lots of evidence from our own case and that of others that people generally drink water because they desire a drink.

The element of truth in the meaning similarity theory is that most of the time we need no experimental evidence to confirm hypotheses about people's motives. The reason, however, is not because of the presence of meaning connections; it is rather because we can draw on a vast fund of background evidence. In simple cases, we know from our experience and the experience of others that when people drink water, or go to sleep, or eat their dinner, it is because they have certain desires and intentions. There is no need, then, to postulate special evidential standards for such cases, unless all we mean is that we do not need to meet an experimental standard. When we go beyond such simple cases, as we do when we say that all dreams are the result of attempts at wish fulfillments or when we postulate that psychoneurotic symptoms are caused by repressed wishes, our fund of common-sense evidence is insufficient to warrant the hypotheses. (For arguments that meaning similarities are of no help here, see Grünbaum, 1993; Erwin, 1996: chapter 1.)

On one important version of the Folk Psychology Model, we warrant common-sense causal hypotheses by "understanding from within" (Nagel, 1995). This view also encounters serious problems when extended to the psychoanalytic case. It is true that by reflecting on what we would do in a certain sort of case, we can imaginatively reconstruct what might have motivated the agent. To know, however, whether the motive we come up with was the agent's actual motive, we need observational evidence.

Consider the case of the man who puts on his sweater, an example used by Nagel (1995). There are certain empirical presuppositions that have to be met before we can reasonably infer what his motive was, although these presuppositions generally go unnoticed. First, we need reason for thinking that the behavior was intentional. If we had evidence that the man's action was accidental or due to a brain lesion, the common-sense inference would be dubious.

Second, we often need reason to think that the postulated motive *generally* affects this sort of behavior in the described way. If I say that the man put on his sweater to impress me, I need more than the thought that this is how I would act in such circumstances. Part of the reason for attributing to the man the desire to become warmer is that we know that this sort of desire typically does make a difference in the sort of circumstances under discussion. As Grünbaum puts it in his (1994a) reply to Nagel, we need evidence that in a reference class, c, the incidence of Ys (say, putting on one's coat) in the class of Xs (say, desiring to be warm) is different from its incidence in the class of non-Xs. We have such background evidence to draw on in the case of the man putting on his sweater.

A third presupposition is that there be no competing factor, be it a reason or something else, that is just as likely to have been the cause of the action. If it is equally likely that I gave a homeless man 10 dollars for either of two reasons (but not both), either to help him or to impress my girlfriend, then "putting myself in his shoes" does not support one explanation rather than another.

There is, finally, a fourth presupposition in Nagel's simple case. We are taking for granted that the man had a desire to get warmer. If we had no reason to believe that, we would not be warranted in moving from "This reason would justify the action from the agent's point of view" to "This reason caused, or was a partial cause, of the action." In general, we are obviously not entitled to infer that X caused Y without having some good reason for thinking that X occurred or was present.

If even one of the above empirical presuppositions is missing, the imaginative use of what we would do in such a case makes the causal inference problematic. Yet, in typical cases in which Freudian theory is potentially applicable, one or more of these presuppositions does not hold. When people have a particular sort of dream, or commit a slip of the tongue, or develop neurotic symptoms, do we have evidence that they are *intentionally* doing these things? We might if we had prior evidence for Freud's theory of repression, but Nagel (1995) is not assuming that we do; if he had such evidence, we would not need to appeal to some special evidential principle to support Freudian theory. A second crucial presupposition also generally fails in the Freudian cases. Even if we had evidence that slips, dreams, and so on are generally intentional (something that I deny), is there good evidence that they are typically preceded by repressed wishes? The history of attempts to demonstrate the existence of repression (see Holmes, 1990) strongly suggests otherwise. Without such evidence, a third presupposition of common-sense psychology is not met: we have no good reason, in applying Freudian theory to a particular case, for believing that repressed wishes generally make a difference to the occurrence of dreams, slips, or neuroses. Finally, quite often, when we try to explain something in Freudian terms, there are competing explanations of equal or greater plausibility.

I conclude, then, that the fact that we can often reasonably make a causal inference in cases such as that of a man putting on a sweater gives us no reason to think that we should use any special evidential standards in judging Freudian causal hypotheses. There are other attempts to argue for the application of distinctive folk psychological standards in assessing Freudian theory, but these too are failures (see Erwin, 1996: chapter 3).

There may well be some standards that are peculiar to certain sciences (although typically they are not standards for evaluating evidence), but the epistemic standards that I argued for in Chapter 4 apply to causal hypotheses in any discipline. That is, such standards as the differential principle and Salmon's principle for assessing causal relevance (see Chapter 4) apply to all hypotheses that say that one event or factor is generally causally relevant to another.

What is the result if we apply such natural science standards in evaluating the Freudian evidence? The overall conclusion is the one that Adolf Grünbaum argues for persuasively in his 1984 book: In general, Freud's theoretical hypotheses cannot be warranted without experimental evidence, although epidemiological data might suffice in certain cases. One reason (although hardly the only one) that clinical evidence is generally of little evidential value in supporting Freudian theory – even if it is extremely interesting for other purposes – is that the differential principle generally cannot be met in a clinical setting. That is, without some sort of experimental controls, we generally cannot discount a credible rival hypothesis: that the verbal reports and behavior of the client are the result of unwitting suggestion. This point, of course, needs to be argued in detail (see Erwin, 1996: 95–106).

There have been a number of attempts to rebut Grünbaum's arguments about the contamination of the clinical data by suggestion and about other matters, but these criticisms have been answered (Erwin, 1993). Furthermore, additional support for his verdict about the need for experimental evidence is provided for in Erwin, 1996: chapters 1–3 (see also Grünbaum, 1986, 1993).

Assuming that experimental evidence is generally needed for confirmation of Freudian theory, that shifts the burden of proof to the
Freudian experimental evidence. Paul Kline (1981) and Fisher and
Greenberg (1985) review between them more than 1500 Freudian
experimental studies, almost all of which were published before 1980.
There have also been systematic Freudian research programs (such as
Silverman, 1976; Weinberger and Silverman, 1987) that were begun in
the late 1970's or 1980's. What does all of this experimental evidence
show? I review it in Erwin (1996) and conclude that it fails to provide
firm support for any distinctively Freudian theoretical hypothesis (for a
more favorable judgment, see Kline, 1981; Fisher and Greenberg, 1985;
but see as well my reply to their arguments in Erwin, 1996).

How does all of this affect the epistemic standing of Freudian theory?
After reviewing virtually all of the best evidence, from any source, I
conclude (Erwin, 1996: chapter 7) that virtually no part of Freudian
theory that is distinctively Freudian has been confirmed. The main
possible exceptions are the existence of a dynamic unconscious and
repression, but *not* Freudian claims about how either of these contribute to
the workings of dreams, the occurrence of parapraxes, or the development
of symptoms. This is a harsh verdict, although a similar conclusion has
been reached by others (Eysenck, 1985) including some psychoanalysts,
but if it is thought to be counter-intuitive, I refer the reader to the
relevant arguments (Erwin, 1996; Grünbaum, 1993; Macmillan, 1991).

I turn next to some newer versions of psychoanalysis.

The Newer Psychoanalytic Theories

Many psychoanalysts are themselves skeptical of many of Freud's theoretical claims, and have embraced in whole or in part one of the newer
psychoanalytic theories. The three main contenders are ego psychology,
object relations theory, and self psychology.

Some of the various claims of these theories do not go beyond
common-sense psychology, but for those that do, what is *their* supporting
empirical evidence? In a recent review, Morris Eagle (1993) cites evidence
in support of a few claims of object relations theory: that an interest in
objects is an autonomous inborn natural propensity that appears in
humans at birth or shortly thereafter; that the infant–mother attachment is
based on an autonomous need for "contact comfort"; that the inter-
ruption of physical contact between infant and mother leads to abnormal
development; that there is in humans an inborn "attachment" system; and
(what appears to be a trivial claim) that we are inherently "object-seeking
creatures."

What, however, of the specific hypotheses about the nature and etiology
of psychopathology; the nature of mental functioning; and hypotheses
about effective treatment? The verdict of Eagle's careful review (1993) is

that there is no firm evidence for any of these hypotheses of object relations theory, or ego psychology, or self psychology.

To some degree, the hypotheses of these newer theories *compete* with one another in so far as they concern the cause or treatment of psycho-pathology. The differential principle (see Chapter 3) thus requires that in so far as the respective psychoanalytic competition is just as plausible as the theory being considered, each of these theories needs evidence to discount the others. Each also faces competition from plausible non-psychoanalytic rivals, such as various cognitivist and conditioning theories.

It is also important to stress that the epistemic situation facing the distinctive causal hypotheses of the newer psychoanalytic theories is approximately the same as that confronting traditional Freudian theory. The very same arguments that show that either experimental or longitudinal studies are required for confirmation of Freudian theory (Grünbaum, 1984, 1993; Erwin, 1996) will show the same for the distinctive etiological claims of the newer psychoanalytic theories. At least there is a large body of experimental studies of Freud's theoretical claims. Where is there a similar body of experimental evidence allegedly supporting object relations theory, ego psychology, or self psychology? There is no such body of evidence. The conclusion must then be that, although psychoanalysis has moved on to newer grand theories, the key epistemic problems have not been resolved. The newer psychoanalytic theories resemble Freudian theory in the following respect: they are mainly collections of unsupported conjectures.

Some supporters of the newer theories, especially object relations theory, see the demand for experimental support as a legacy of a discredited logical positivism. They turn instead to a postmodernist epistemology. For reasons given in Chapter 4, this sort of epistemology is unreliable, and provides no escape from the demand for rigorous empirical evidence before we give our allegiance to mere conjectures.

The Psychodynamic Therapies

Many who use some form of psychodynamic therapy care less about which psychoanalytic theory, if any, is true than whether their therapy works at least for certain types of clients and outcomes. What does the evidence show about this issue?

Here we have to distinguish sharply between long-term (on average three years or more) orthodox psychoanalysis and the newer, short-term psychodynamic therapies, sometimes called "psychoanalytically orientated psychotherapies." Concerning the orthodox model, evidence of effectiveness is extremely poor, although not everyone agrees with this assessment. For example, a relatively recent report on efficacy issued by the American Psychoanalytic Association (Bachrach et al., 1991) reaches a more optimistic conclusion. On the basis of their review of a number of formal studies, they conclude (page 911) that the evidence confirms that patients suitable for analysis derive benefits from it. However, the criteria Bachrach et al. (1991) use in their evaluation of the evidence are demonstrably inadequate.

The authors list five criteria for evaluating research on treatment outcomes, such as the need to demonstrate that the treatment being evaluated is taking place, the requirement that the patient be suitable for treatment, and so on. The criteria do not require, however, that the psychoanalytic outcome measures be shown by independent means to correlate with outcomes of real benefit to the client. Nor do the criteria require that a study be *experimental* (with random assignment to treatment and comparison groups, and the inclusion of at least a no-treatment or wait-list control group). In fact, none of the studies that the authors review is an experimental study, and for that reason alone, they are all too weak to confirm claims of effectiveness.

The need for experimental evidence arises partly because of the necessity to satisfy the epistemic standards discussed in Chapter 3. First, Salmon's principle requires at least a comparison between treated and non-treated controls in order to confirm that a therapy generally makes a positive difference. Second, the differential principle requires that we discount credible rival explanations to our outcome hypotheses. For the types of non-psychotic problems typically treated by analysts, there are generally at least two credible hypotheses that need to be defeated. The first says that factors external to the therapeutic situation caused most or all of the therapeutic gains; the second says that placebo factors were the operative causal factors. Most psychotherapy researchers agree about the need to discount the first rival, but not everyone agrees about the placebo hypothesis. This issue will be taken up in the final chapter, where I argue that there is need to discount placebo factors.

It should also be noted that, given the history of psychotherapy research, a single experimental study is not likely to settle very much. If our question is not "Has the use of analysis ever produced a significant therapeutic benefit?" but rather "Is analysis, when employed by a trained therapist, *generally* effective in treating a certain type of patient with a certain type of problem in a certain type of clinical setting," then a *body* of experimental evidence will be needed to answer the question with assurance.

I conclude, then, that to provide firm evidence that psychoanalysis is generally effective in producing a certain type of benefit for a certain type of client, we generally need experimental evidence. At present, there is no such body of evidence.

In contrast to (orthodox) psychoanalysis, there are a number of controlled studies of short-term psychodynamic psychotherapy (STPP). So, here the situation is more encouraging, particularly since controlled research is continuing. Yet some significant reservations are needed here as well.

The first concerns the nature of STPP. Luborsky et al. (1993: 6) view short-term dynamic psychotherapy as an early split-off from psycho-analytic treatment, "copying the parent" in its principles but being shorter. However, there are many different types of dynamic therapy; Koss and Butcher (1986) identify more than 20 variants. Not all "copy the parent," to any great extent. Thus, apart from any other problems, recent meta-analytic reviews of dynamic therapy may be averaging the results of different types of therapies, some of which are quite unlike psychoanalysis. To take but one example, 4 of the 11 studies of "dynamic" therapy in the Crits-Christoph (1992) review employed interpersonal therapy, which bears little resemblance to psychoanalysis. It would clearly be misleading to say of this therapy that it "copies the parent" in its principles, if the parent is said to be psychoanalysis. Crits-Christoph acknowledges the point when he writes of interpersonal therapy that it "may be quite distant from the psychoanalytically oriented forms of dynamic therapy more commonly practiced" (1992: 156).

More importantly, although the results have been generally positive, the research record for STPP is somewhat mixed. For example, in their (1975) landmark paper, Luborsky et al. had 33 comparisons of psycho-therapy (excluding behavior therapy) to no-treatment. In 20 of these, the psychotherapy group did better than the no-treatment group, but in 13 comparisons, there was a tie (Luborsky et al., 1975: 1003). This does not constitute clear and unequivocal evidence for the effectiveness of STPP even if other problems are ignored.

In two recent meta-analyses (Luborsky et al., 1993; Crits-Christoph, 1992) the results were favorable, but in a third (Svartberg and Stiles, 1991), the results were again mixed.

Svartberg and Stiles (1991) review 19 clinically relevant comparative outcome studies of short-term psychodynamic psychotherapy published between 1978 and 1988. Nine of the studies contained a no-treatment comparison (in four studies, of patients awaiting psychotherapy and in five studies, of patients not awaiting psychotherapy). In eight of the studies, STPP was compared to a form of cognitive therapy or cognitive-behavior therapy (in some cases in addition to a no-treatment condition).

Overall, STPP demonstrated a small but statistically significant superior-ity to wait-list patients at post-treatment, but even this meager result is suspect. Svartberg and Stiles note (page 711) that STPP shows its superiority to no-treatment controls predominantly in methodologically poor studies.

STPP also showed significant but small-sized inferiority to alternative treatments (cognitive therapy and cognitive behavior therapy) at post-treatment, and close to a large-sized inferiority at 1-year follow-up. Svartberg and Stiles estimate (1991: 711) that patients will increase their chances of improvement (assessed at 1-year post-testing) from 33 per cent (STPP) to 67 per cent by undergoing a form of psychotherapy other than STPP.

Third, STPP has not yet demonstrated its ability to outperform an inexpensive, credible placebo such as a sugar pill plus minimal therapist contact. In the very few studies of dynamic therapy where a placebo control was included (for example, Brill et al., 1964; McLean and Hakstian, 1979), the clients receiving the dynamic therapy improved approximately to the same degree as those receiving the placebo treatment (see Prioleau et al., 1983, for discussion).

CONCLUSION

Proponents of psychoanalysis have, at various times, claimed that their treatment is effective for a large number of clinical problems. In Bachrach et al. (1991), Table 1 (page 877) lists more than 30 clinical disorders treated by analysts, including anxiety, hysteria, compulsion, neurosis, depression, sexual impotence, transvestism, bronchial asthma, and character disorders. The existing evidence, however, fails to substantiate the claim that psychoanalysis is generally effective in treating any of these problems. Many analysts will respond that their first priority is not the elimination of symptoms, but is rather the provision of some other type of benefit such as insight, an increase in autonomy, or character change. However, in the absence of properly controlled experiments, the verdict must be the same for these benefits as with respect to symptom remission: there is little, if any, good evidence that the therapy is generally effective in producing any of these other sorts of therapeutic benefit – and no evidence at all that if it does contribute to the production of any such benefit, its contribution is typically greater than that of an inexpensive, credible placebo. This last verdict, of no evidence of superiority to a credible placebo, applies as well to the short-term psychodynamic therapies.

I am not arguing with respect to any particular sort of benefit that orthodox, long-term psychoanalysis is ineffective, only that there is no good evidence that it is effective. If that is true, what should a patient do? The first reasonable move is to look to alternative, cheaper therapies that are supported by good evidence. However, for certain types of problems, such as reformation of character, there may be no alternative to psychoanalysis. So, a patient might reasonably wish to gamble on psychoanalysis for this sort of problem even if there is no evidence that a beneficial payoff is likely. In addition, certain patients enter therapy to explore their feelings or to talk to someone for an extended duration, or for some other reason. So, whether a particular patient should undergo psychoanalysis depends on other issues besides effectiveness.

Epilogue

8

The Crisis in Psychotherapy

Is there a crisis in the field of psychotherapy? If growth is the criterion, the opposite appears to be true. The field is flourishing. Consider the numbers, at least for the United States.

In 1959, only 2500 members of the American Psychological Association listed specialties in either clinical or counseling psychology. By 1988, this number had increased to approximately 40,000 (Dawes, 1994: 12). Although the growth rate for psychiatrists was slower, the membership of the American Psychiatric Association grew from 10,000 members in 1959 to 34,000 in 1989. Compared to both groups, there were even larger growth rates among social workers who practice psychotherapy.

It seems reasonable to infer that this great growth in the number of professional psychotherapists reflects a growing demand for services, as well as a high degree of consumer satisfaction. Studies of consumer satisfaction with psychotherapy that were done in the early 1980's did, in fact, find a high level of satisfaction. More recently, a poll of 4000 readers of *Consumer Reports* (1995) found that most were highly satisfied with their psychotherapy.

On another criterion, the field is also doing quite well. It is generally not perceived, at least by the educated public, as being dominated by the sort of pseudo-science that is characteristic of such fields as astrology and psychic-counseling. There was at one time much skepticism about the effectiveness of psychotherapy, but the doubts have greatly diminished. Few would argue that we do not need more empirical work to determine which are the optimal treatments for specific kinds of clinical problems and clients, but the issue of whether psychotherapy is generally effective is considered settled by the work of Smith et al. (1980).

In 1980, they published a meta-analytic review of over 400 controlled studies of psychotherapy and concluded that virtually all forms are quite effective, and, furthermore, are about equally effective (Smith et al., 1980). Based on their data – and much more has accumulated in the past 15 years – it is estimated that approximately 80 per cent of those undergoing psychotherapy improve as a result of it.

Even some who had been quite skeptical are now convinced. For example, one severe critic of many aspects of the field of psychotherapy, Robyn Dawes, was dubious about the degree of random assignment to treatment and control groups in many of the studies reviewed by Smith et al. So, he and a colleague re-analyzed the data, and found to their surprise that it did not matter whether the studies had true random assignment or not (Landman and Dawes, 1982). Dawes now agrees that psychotherapy in its "multitude of forms" is generally effective (Dawes, 1994: 38). One leading methodologist puts the point about as forcefully as it can be put:

> A new experiment to learn whether psychotherapy works in general is manifestly not worth doing given the meta-analytic results of Glass (1976) and his colleagues (Smith, Glass, and Miller, 1980). Until their meta-analytic work resolved the issue, the question of whether psychotherapy worked in general was indeed controversial. It is controversial no longer. (Rosenthal, 1994: 131)

If there is any reason at all to speak of a "crisis," some would point to the growing scarcity of resources for meeting the demand for services. In the United States, insurance companies have become increasingly unwilling to pay for any psychotherapy except short-term treatment. The likely slowing of growth in Medicare, Medicaid, and other government programs is likely to mean that even fewer funds for psychotherapy will be available in the near future. If we put aside, however, the issue of paying for services, a seemingly powerful case can be made, on the basis of growth, consumer satisfaction, and perceived effectiveness, that the psychotherapeutic field, far from being in a state of crisis, is faring quite well.

WHY THERE REALLY IS A CRISIS

Despite widespread perceptions about progress in the field, there *is* a crisis, an intellectual crisis, that needs to be discussed. For there to be such a crisis, its existence need not be perceived by anyone (although a minority of commentators, without using the term "crisis," have argued for something like its existence; see Kline, 1992a; Eysenck, 1992).

Consider the state of organic medicine 100 years ago. On two counts, the problems were severe enough to justify talk of a crisis, whether or not anyone perceived the seriousness of the problems. First, how effective were most medical treatments at that time? According to some commentators, most, if not all, were no more effective than a credible placebo (Shapiro and Morris, 1978). Second, what did medical expertise consist of? It did not consist of the ability to use medical treatments more effectively than credible placebos; for there generally were no such treatments. A well-trained physician might, for example, know better than the average layman where to place the leeches that were sometimes used in medical treatments, but why consider this medical expertise if the use of leeches generally did not help the patient? A partial defense of medical expertise, however, might be provided. Even given the poor state of medical knowledge that existed in the nineteenth century, the average physician probably knew more about the anatomy of the human body than did the average layman.

How analogous is the current state of psychotherapeutic knowledge to the medical knowledge of 100 years ago? On both of the criteria that I mentioned, the analogy is almost exact. Most of the various forms of psychotherapy, *as far as anyone knows*, are not more effective than credible placebos; psychotherapeutic expertise, *as far as anyone knows*, does not generally consist of knowledge about how to wield techniques that can routinely outperform a credible placebo. At least, this is what I intend to argue.

How Good is the Evidence of Effectiveness?

As just suggested, many who claim that the effectiveness issue has been settled rely primarily on the meta-analysis of Smith et al. (1980). This is hardly the only evidence that could be brought into play, but it is a good place to start.

The authors calculated over 1700 "effect sizes" for more than 400 controlled studies of psychotherapy and found that the average effect size was .85. The effect size for each outcome measure for each study was calculated by subtracting the control group's average score on that measure from the treatment group's average score and dividing the result by the standard deviation for the control group. The results have been interpreted as showing that the average person receiving psychotherapy is better off at the end of it than 80 per cent of those not receiving it (Glass and Kliegl, 1983).

There have been a number of criticisms of the reasoning of Smith et al. (Eysenck, 1983; Erwin, 1984, 1994a; Wilson, 1985). Some have been answered, some not.

One persistent issue concerns the lumping together of studies of very different methodological quality, diverse clinical populations, and different clinical problems. This objection is sometimes referred to as the "apples-and-oranges" criticism. After all, it is objected, is not the comparison of the very different sorts of items grouped together by Smith et al. like comparing apples and oranges? The defenders of meta-analysis have an answer: In order to generalize about fruit, it is perfectly appropriate to combine apples and oranges (Dawes, 1994: 51). This response is correct, but it fails to answer a different criticism, one that applies not to the comparison but to certain inferences that are commonly drawn on the basis of the comparison.

Consider an example of holistic medicine (sometimes called "alternative medicine"), which has become popular in the United States. One such holistic treatment utilizes mental imagery in treating cancer. In an allegedly successful case, a patient with throat cancer was advised to visualize the rays of his radiation treatment and his body's white blood cells demolishing his tumor cells. The patient did this, and the cancer went into complete remission. This sort of imagery treatment is said by its proponents to be quite effective in treating various sorts of cancerous tumors. As one critic puts it, on this view, you can "dream your cancer away."

There are outcome studies of this imaging treatment; for a critical review, see Friedlander (1985). Suppose that we were to combine them with studies of more conventional treatments for throat cancer, such as chemotherapy or radiation treatment, and were to calculate the average effect size for all of the studies. If it were positive, we might conclude that the average cancer treatment is effective in treating throat cancer. This proposition, however, does not by itself entail the additional proposition that image therapy is effective for this problem. This is a purely logical point about the logical implications of the statement about averages. If the studies of image therapy are so flawed that no causal inferences can be drawn, then we do not know, at least not from these data, that this sort of therapy is an average cancer treatment in the relevant respect, namely, in respect to its capacity to cure throat cancer. There is no logical connection, then, between the statement about the average cancer treatment and the proposition about the effectiveness of image therapy. An additional argument is needed to bridge the logical gap between the two propositions. The same sort of logical chasm exists between the proposition that the average psychotherapy works and the proposition that a particular form of it works.

Smith et al. (1980) do have an additional argument. They divided their studies up, separating the good ones from those having a poor methodological design. They then checked to see if the results of each type of study were different, found that they were roughly the same, and used this finding to justify giving both sorts of studies equal weight. This is the justification that is generally given for such liberal meta-analytic treatment of poor studies. Thus the statisticians Hunter and Schmidt, after noting that judgments of methodological quality are often very subjective, write concerning the question of how to treat inferior studies:

> Therefore, the question should be decided empirically by meta-analyzing separately the studies judged methodologically strong and weak and comparing the results. If they differ, one should rely on the "strong" studies; if they do not, then all studies should be used. (1990: 480–1)

Or, as Dawes puts it, when he and Landman re-analyzed the Smith-Glass (1977) data, they found that it "didn't matter whether the studies had had true random assignment" (Dawes, 1994: 54).

In saying that it "didn't matter," Dawes means that the outcomes were the same whether or not there was random assignment. In that sense, it did not matter, but from an epistemological standpoint, it may have mattered quite a bit. Suppose that the effect size for our studies of image therapy were found to be roughly the same as for radiation treatment, but that in the image therapy studies there was no random assignment to treatment or control groups. Instead, the advocates of image therapy simply picked for treatment only those who were *also* undergoing radiation treatment; they then assigned the remaining untreated patients to the control group. Given this flawed selection process, no evidence was provided that image therapy is useful in treating cancer, despite the empirical finding that the lack of random assignment "made no difference" to the effect size.

Hunter and Schmidt say that the question of how to treat poor studies is to be answered empirically, but how precisely are we to do this? We re-analyze our data and find that studies with epistemological characteristics X, Y, or Z have approximately the same outcomes as those lacking all of these characteristics. But how does this answer the epistemological question of whether all studies should be given equal weight? It does not, as will be shown by the following.

Suppose that X, Y, and Z are all "defeaters." By that I mean that the presence of any one of them defeats any attempt to infer a causal connection between therapy and outcome. Hunter and Schmidt, and Smith et al., talk of the "subjectivity" of many judgments of methodological quality, but there is nothing subjective about the claim that certain design characteristics are defeaters. For example, if there is no evidence that the therapy being studied was actually used, that fact alone bars a causal inference that the putative cause helped bring about the outcome. If there is no evidence that any of the outcome measures correlate with the putative effect, this fact alone prevents a causal inference that the putative effect was caused by the therapy. If the control group, for whatever reason, is so deficient that it fails to rule out an equally plausible rival to the outcome hypothesis being tested, then that fact alone is a defeater. I am not suggesting that proponents of meta-analysis are unaware of these obvious facts, but I am suggesting that the valid complaint that many methodological judgments are subjective can mislead: There clearly are some objective rules for disqualifying studies of psychotherapy outcomes. The fact that some judgments of quality of design are subjective is no justification for following the epistemological strategy recommended by some proponents of meta-analysis of treating sound and unsound studies equally if their trends are the same. I am also arguing that the presence of defeaters bars that epistemological strategy.

To return to my hypothetical case, we compare our inferior studies having the properties X, Y or Z, which are all studies of therapy of type A, and find that the effect sizes are the same as those of the superior studies, which are all of therapy type B. So we follow the methodological advice to include the deficient studies in our meta-analysis. However, we now encounter exactly the same problem faced with the image therapy studies. Our overall results may support the conclusion that psychotherapy on average is effective, but we cannot get from that conclusion to the additional conclusion that the A-type of psychotherapy studied in the X, Y, Z studies is effective to any degree at all. These defective studies have failed to provide any evidence that therapy A is effective in treating anything; consequently, we have no warrant for believing that this type of therapy is like the average psychotherapy with respect to effectiveness.

Suppose that the good and bad studies were all of the same therapy, therapy B, but the clinical problems were different. For example, the X, Y, Z studies might have all dealt with depression, and the superior studies with phobias. In that case, we encounter a different but analogous problem. From the conclusion that therapy B on average produces a therapeutic benefit, we cannot infer that it helps with depression in particular unless we have support for the proposition that depression is an average benefit in the relevant respect.

It might be replied that all of this is merely hypothetical; none of it shows that the studies reviewed by Smith et al. were, in fact, too defective to permit causal inferences. However, I am not yet addressing that question. I am answering only the epistemological point that if we find that a design flaw "makes no difference" in that studies with it have the same sort of outcomes as studies without it, then we are justified in giving the studies equal weight. My reply, in brief, is this: If the flaw makes such an epistemological difference that all evidence of causation is lacking, then there is no justification for giving equal probative weight to studies having and not having the flaw.

It should also be mentioned that there is good reason to suspect that many of these early studies reviewed by Smith et al. did contain defeaters. The reason concerns the prevalence of defeaters in so many outcome studies of psychotherapy that were carried out in the period under review. To take but one example, as was noted in Chapter 5, a fatal flaw in later meta-analytic reviews of rational emotive therapy was the lack of evidence that exactly that therapy was actually used in the studies that were analyzed. This design flaw is not unusual; it is a defect of many psychotherapy outcome studies even today. It was especially prevalent during the period when the studies analyzed by Smith, Glass, and Miller were done. To take another example, as noted in Chapter 6, many of the psychoanalytic outcome measures of the studies reviewed by Bachrach et al. (1991) were of dubious validity. This problem, too, is not unusual; it was and is present in many outcome studies even today.

It should also be stressed that the epistemological problems that need to be overcome are not limited to insuring that the therapy being evaluated was actually used and that there really was a beneficial outcome. In an excellent discussion of the problems, Paul Kline details what he calls "a depressing catalogue of problems which have not yet been overcome" (1992a: 64). He lists 19 such problems, including the ones that I have mentioned, as well as problems about spontaneous remission, variance among therapists, problems of patient diagnosis, and patient–therapist interaction. Because of the failure to overcome these problems, Kline concludes (page 83) that the case for the effects of psychotherapy remains to be made. Contrary to what Rosenthal (1994: 131) says, then, the claim that psychotherapy works in general *is* still controversial, and, as will be argued shortly, it *ought* to be controversial.

Kline is not suggesting that any single study needs to overcome all 19 problems, but he does conclude that if a study is not free from fault, it is difficult to know what value to attach to it. It is this fact, he argues, that makes questionable all meta-analytic studies of psychotherapy (Kline, 1992b: 96).

A proponent of meta-analysis could reply that not all 19 problems are equally serious. Some are what I called "defeaters"; some are not. Consequently, if it can be shown that the epistemological defects are minor, we might be able to determine what value a study has: It might provide *some* evidence of effectiveness despite the flaw. Nevertheless, the burden of proof is on those who do a meta-analytic review, and use the results to argue for certain causal inferences. For reasons already given, it is not enough to do what Smith, Glass, and Miller do – namely, argue that the good and bad studies have roughly the same effect sizes.

Because Smith et al. (1980) fail to meet the above burden of proof – that is, they fail to show that the studies they review overcome the epistemic problems listed by Kline – many of the standard conclusions drawn from their work are simply unsupported. In particular, their first major conclusion, "Psychotherapy is beneficial, consistently so and in many different ways" (1980: 183), is unsupported if it implies that each of the types of psychotherapy that were studied is effective. *A fortiori*, the data fail to support the even more general proposition that most of the more than 400 different types of psychotherapy now available are effective in producing at least one type of clinical benefit.

Could we not, at least in principle, take another look at the studies analyzed by Smith et al., and demonstrate that the epistemological problems discussed by Kline were overcome? Perhaps no single study did this, but there might be a pattern of evidence that we can point to. If we were to do this, we would have to make the very qualitative methodo-logical decisions that Smith et al. were trying to avoid, the ones that they and some other supporters of meta-analysis claim are subjective. No matter; the problems cannot be avoided if we wish to support causal inferences. However, given the number of epistemological problems (19 or more), the number of studies (400 plus), and the number of effect sizes (over 1700), this would be a very complex undertaking. Still, I do not claim that *in principle* it could not be done. What I do claim is that it has not been done. Consequently, the burden of proof has not been met by the Smith, Glass, and Miller review.

I now want to argue that even if we were to do the extremely complex review just mentioned, we would most likely not find that all of the epistemic problems had been resolved. One problem in particular was clearly unresolved: the failure to show that with real clinical problems, a particular sort of psychotherapy is more effective than a credible placebo. I pick this problem not because it is of singular importance, but because it arises with almost all meta-analytic reviews of psychotherapy. If it turns out to be either inconsequential or resolved, that will still not be enough; the other problems will remain.

PLACEBOS AND PLACEBO CONTROLS

In 1983, Prioleau et al. (1983) published a re-analysis of the Smith et al. data, but excluded studies of behavior therapy. They located 513 of the original 520 studies (there are more than 500 because the original set also included drug studies), but judged that only 40 contained a placebo control. Of these 40, 8 were discarded either because of serious design flaws or because of inability to calculate effect sizes. The only studies showing significant effects for psychotherapy were ones not using real clinical patients. The authors conclude that for real patients, there is no evidence from the Smith et al. studies that the benefits of psychotherapy are greater than those of placebo treatment.

Glass et al. (1983) have several replies. First, they claim that the authors' concluding speculation that future research will not provide evidence of superiority to a placebo is based on an "intuitive model" of how verbal psychotherapy should perform, but the model, they claim, is *ad hoc* and unconvincing. This may be right but the point bears only on what Prioleau et al. clearly label as "speculation," a prediction about what future evidence will show. The argument for their *main* conclusion, that the data of Smith et al. provide no evidence that the benefits of psychotherapy for real patients are greater than a placebo, does not in any way presuppose the intuitive model rejected by Glass et al.

A second charge is that Prioleau et al. commit a serious error in their reasoning in that they fail to distinguish between what is true of psychotherapy and what is true of *the literature of psychotherapy research*. Again, this point might be relevant to the concluding speculation about what future research will show, but it does nothing to undermine the main argument cited above. That argument *is* directed at a portion of the psychotherapy literature, namely, the Smith et al. review. There is no error here on the part of Prioleau et al.

A third complaint is that Prioleau et al. discount a study showing a large superiority of verbal psychotherapy over placebo (Coche and Flick, 1975) because of a failure of replication (Coche and Douglas, 1977). "That logic," Glass et al. complain (1983: 293), "is asymmetrical, to put the matter kindly. What is really at issue are Prioleau et al.'s expectations for empirical regularity in psychotherapy research." This is a completely muddled response. The reason for the discounting is not the expectation of an empirical regularity. It is, rather, the reasonable assumption that the evidence from the initial study was negated by the attempted but failed replication. We might, of course, be able in any particular case to explain away the failure to replicate, and do so in a manner consistent with the original data retaining their probative worth. In the absence of such a salvaging maneuver, however, the new data offset the old data (as dictated by the differential principle of confirmation defended in Chapter 4). Contrary to what is considered good scientific practice in other sciences, psychotherapy researchers routinely accept favorable results as evidence even when there is no attempt at replication. This is bad enough, but Glass et al. apparently wish to go one step further, on the grounds that one should not expect empirical regularities in psychotherapy research. Even in the rare case where there *is* an attempt to replicate, accept the original evidence as probative even if the attempt fails. This is not good scientific advice.

A fourth objection is that Prioleau et al.'s "impeachment" of 21 studies of students nominated or selected for therapy is arbitrary. However, Prioleau et al. excluded these studies for a good empirical reason, which they explain (1983: 283): Both the students and their problems were unrepresentative of the sorts of patients or problems encountered in either institutional or outpatient settings.

A final objection is that there are newer studies showing large positive effects of verbal psychotherapy compared to a placebo. Glass et al. (1983) claim to have found 12 such additional studies. However, they cite only one (Comas-Díaz, 1981), and that study contains a wait-list control but no placebo control. Brody (1983) replies that at the time of publication, 1983, there were no such additional studies of neurotic outpatients involving (non-behavioral) psychotherapy and placebo comparisons.

In brief, none of these objections of Glass et al. does anything to answer the main argument of Prioleau et al. (1983).

I will take up again the last question raised by Glass et al. (1983): Are there new relevant placebo comparisons that lie outside the data set analyzed by Smith et al. (1980)? However, even if it turns out that there are, and they are enough to turn the issue around, that does not affect the conclusion of Prioleau et al. (1983): That the evidence most often cited for the general effectiveness of psychotherapy in "its multitude of forms" (Dawes, 1994: 38) – namely, the evidence reviewed by Smith et al. (1980) – fail to support the hypothesis that for real patients any type of psychotherapy, excluding behavior therapy, generally provides benefits greater than a placebo.

Before asking about new evidence, a constraint needs to be laid down. It is fairly easy, but also irrelevant, to show superiority of a psychotherapy to a placebo that is less believable than it. Is rolfing an effective treatment for anxiety (for a discussion of what rolfing is, see Erwin, 1985)? Well, there is at least one experimental study in which rolfing did better than a placebo in treating anxiety (Weinberg and Hunt, 1979). But what does this show if the placebo was clearly ineffective? If we are trying to control for expectancy of cure, as well as other placebo factors, then at the very minimum the placebo must be at least as credible as the therapy. This condition was apparently not met in the rolfing study. After five weeks of placebo treatment, the subjects showed no improvement; in fact, their condition got worse.

The history of this subject needs to be kept in mind. For example, there were a number of controlled studies in the 1960's and early 1970's in which systematic desensitization outperformed various placebos, but significant doubts were raised about the credibility of the placebos (Borkovec and Nau, 1972; Nau et al., 1974). So, newer studies were done using more plausible placebos, but then the consistency of the results vanished. Some of the newer studies found systematic desensitization superior to the placebo, but others did not (Erwin, 1978: 9).

Ideally, a placebo control should control for a number of factors that might plausibly explain improvement, such as therapist attention, demand for improvement, and therapeutic rationale. At a minimum, it must be at least as credible to the patient as the therapy to which it is being compared. Many of the pseudo-therapies used in psychotherapy research have not met this minimal condition.

Although credibility of a particular procedure will vary somewhat with different clients and clinical problems, a pill placebo plus minimal therapist contact has been found to be a credible and useful placebo control in many situations. It is for that reason that it was used in the NIMH collaborative study of depression (Elkin et al., 1989). It provides a standard of sorts for the adequacy of a placebo control, even though other placebos can serve the same epistemic purposes, and even though a pill procedure may fail to be believable to some patients.

To return to the issue raised by Glass et al.: Does the evidence now available show that clients receiving specific psychotherapies generally improve more than those in placebo groups? Two leading outcome reviewers say "yes" (Lambert and Bergin, 1992), and cite three studies to back up their claim. These studies (Blanchard et al., 1980; Miller and Berman, 1983; Quality Assurance Project, 1983), whatever their value, do little to support the claim of the general superiority of psychotherapy to placebo. To take the first example, Blanchard et al. (1980) reviewed studies of a very unrepresentative clinical problem. The clinical problem was tension headache. The reviewers found that frontal EMG biofeedback alone, or relaxation training, or a combination of the two were significantly superior to medication placebo or psychological placebo. This provides little or no evidence that most standard sorts of psychotherapy are generally more effective than a credible placebo in treating such common problems as depression, alcoholism, or anxiety.

The second review (Miller and Berman, 1983) provides no evidence at all concerning credible placebos. The placebos used in the studies they review, either because they lacked credibility or because they had some other defect, did no better than wait-list controls. For that reason, Miller and Berman decided to combine the results of the placebo and wait-list control groups – see their discussion (1983: 43). The remaining report (Quality Assurance Project, 1983) provides no breakdown of placebo results that would permit assessment of efficacy.

It would be unfair to place much weight on a single comment by Lambert and Bergin (1992), one that might have been intended as an offhand remark. It is not unfair, however, to ask about what the total outcome evidence shows: Does it support the proposition that most psychotherapeutic techniques, when used with certain types of clients and problems, can routinely outperform a credible placebo? The answer is: No. It is not that there are no studies at all with satisfactory placebo controls, but finding a few studies here and there is not sufficient especially when there is also contrary evidence. As I pointed out in Chapter 5, there are studies with placebo controls of a few behavior therapy techniques, but that does not even show that most of the 158 behavior therapy techniques (Bellack and Hersen, 1985) can outperform a credible placebo, let alone that most of the hundreds of non-behavior therapies can. Would anyone seriously contend that, because several medical treatments for high blood pressure have been shown to be superior to placebo, it is reasonable to infer that *most* medical treatments, including so-called "alternative" medical procedures, will be just as effective no matter what the clinical problem?

One difference, some may argue, is that there is evidence that different medical procedures have different effects, but the reverse is true for psychotherapy. All psychotherapies, it is often claimed, are roughly equal in effectiveness (Luborsky et al., 1975; Smith et al., 1980). Consequently, if some can be shown to be generally more effective than a credible placebo, then that is a basis for concluding that most are. This widely accepted thesis of equal effectiveness should be challenged (see Rachman and Wilson, 1980), but suppose that this is what the current evidence does indicate, leaving aside those few behavior therapies that are demonstrably superior to placebos. In that case, the evidence is neutral on the issue that I am discussing. The equivalence data are consistent with the proposition that most psychotherapies are equally effective *and* superior to a credible placebo, but they are just as consistent with the proposition that most psychotherapies are equivalent in their *inability* to outperform placebos. The evidence cited for the equivalence thesis does not support the first proposition over the second. The finding that a few behavior therapies can consistently outperform a credible placebo is very weak evidence, even in the absence of any counter-evidence, that most psychotherapies have the same capabilities. Consequently, I ask again: Would finding that a few procedures can do better than placebos enable us to infer that most of the other 400 plus psychotherapies can do the same? It would not, any more than an analogous finding would provide such support in the field of medicine.

Furthermore, it is not true that there is no contrary evidence. If anything, the history of psychotherapy research shows that when a psychotherapy finally confronts a credible placebo, it rarely wins. The record was mixed, for example, in the systematic desensitization studies I cited earlier. The placebo group also did about as well as the treatment group in the Brill et al. (1964) study of psychoanalytically orientated psychotherapy, and there was a similar finding in the NIMH collaborative study (Elkin et al., 1989). In the latter study, two psychotherapies, Beck's cognitive therapy and interpersonal therapy, both of which have a far more impressive research record than the overwhelming majority of psychotherapies, were compared to a pill-placebo plus minimal therapist contact in treating depression. The results for the two psychotherapies and the placebo were approximately the same. Would the results have been different if, for example, dynamic therapy of some sort had been substituted for one of the psychotherapies? That is not likely. In comparisons to cognitive therapy, dynamic therapies have done worse (Svartberg and Stiles, 1991) than the cognitive therapy.

There is also reason to believe that the effects of credible placebos have been underestimated in both psychotherapy and drug research (Roberts et al., 1993; Brown et al., 1992). One reason is that clients can often detect the difference between a pill placebo and active drug by noting the absence of side effects of the former. In a study of the newer antidepressants, which have fewer side effects and where it is harder to tell who is getting the active drug, Brown et al. (1992) found placebo response rates close to 50 per cent rather than the more usual 33 per cent.

There are earlier studies that also bear on this issue. Thomson (1982) reviewed 75 double-blind placebo controlled studies of tricyclic antidepressants completed between 1958 and 1972, and found that all but 7 used an "inert" placebo, one that does not mimic the active drug in terms of side effects. The remaining 7 used atropine as a placebo, a drug that is inactive for depression but which produces a variety of sensations, thereby making it a more credible placebo. Of those studies using the inactive pill comparison, 59 per cent found a superior therapeutic effect for the tricyclic drug, but in only 1 of the 7 studies (14 per cent) where the "active" placebo was employed was the tricyclic able to do better than the placebo.

Greenberg and Fisher (1989) review other research of this sort and conclude (page 26) that the active placebo is more effective than an inactive placebo. This has several important implications. One obvious one is that where a pill-placebo is employed in psychotherapy studies, the value of the psychotherapy is likely to be overstated unless an active pill-placebo is used. Second, as Greenberg and Fisher (1989) argue at length, the effectiveness of drug treatments for depression, including Prozac, has been overstated. That, in turn, reduces the impressiveness of the finding that cognitive treatments of depression often do as well as drug treatments (see Hollen et al., 1991; and Chapter 5 of this book for a skeptical discussion of these comparisons). Third, the power of placebos in treating psychological problems has probably been underestimated. If that is true, then that provides one more reason for doubting unsubstantiated claims that most of the psychotherapies can routinely outperform a credible placebo.

Can most psychotherapies, then, generally provide benefits greater than credible placebos? I am not arguing that their inability to do this has been demonstrated. As of now, however, there is no good reason to believe that they can. In this one respect, the situation is like that of organic medicine 100 years ago: As far as anyone knows, with the exception of relatively few behavior therapies, psychotherapy provides no benefit greater than that typically provided by credible placebos. Future research may alter this verdict, but as of now, it stands unrefuted.

Does this conclusion matter? Greenberg and Fisher note (1989: 22) that "It goes without saying" that unless a drug treatment produces a therapy result substantially exceeding that obtained from placebo and/or spontaneous recovery it has little value. However, it does not "go without saying" in the field of psychotherapy. A very common position is that: (1) it does not matter whether a form of psychotherapy can outperform a placebo, and (2) a placebo control is inappropriate in judging psychotherapeutic outcomes. Is this implied lower standard warranted for the field of psychotherapy? Let us look at its most common defenses.

One defense is conceptual. In organic medicine, it is argued, a placebo is a treatment that by definition works for psychological reasons. However, we do not want to count a *psychological* therapy as a placebo merely because it works for psychological reasons. This conceptual problem, however, has been resolved by the work of the philosopher Adolf Grünbaum, who has provided an explication of the placebo concept that renders the concept useful in both medical and psychotherapy research. Suppose that a therapeutic theory specifies that therapy t's characteristic treatment factors $f1$, and $f2$, and $f3$ are remedial for disorder d. On Grünbaum's (1994b) analysis, therapy t is a placebo for disorder d if and only if none of the characteristic factors is remedial for d. We are not forced to say, then, that a psychological therapy is a placebo merely because it works for psychological reasons. It is a placebo for a certain disorder only if its characteristic treatment factors have no effect on that sort of problem.

A second reason commonly given for not employing placebo controls in psychotherapy research is that placebos are not inert. Indeed they are not; if they were, of what epistemic value would they be? However, they are not inert in drug research either. They are *physiologically* inert for, say, the treatment of depression, but as the research demonstrates, they often have a remedial effect on the depressed patient. More precisely, it is not that the pill itself has the effect; rather, it is the enhancement of the patient's belief in its efficacy (or some other placebo factor) that has the effect. However, there is no difference here between using a pill-placebo as a control for drug treatment of depression or for a psychological treatment. In both cases, the pill, or rather enhancement of the patient's confidence in it, has therapeutic effects.

A third commonly given reason is that in comparing a placebo to a psychotherapy, we are really comparing two *psychological* treatments. This is correct, but what follows from this? It does not follow that to have value a psychotherapy need not be able to outperform a placebo, nor does it follow that a placebo control is not needed.

A related response is that in psychotherapy, the expectancy of cure is part of the treatment. This does nothing, however, to justify the lower standard. Expectancy of cure is present in psychotherapy if the treatment is credible to the client; indeed, the concern is that this is the sole factor that is effective. However, generation of the expectancy is not one of the characteristics that typically define a psychotherapy. If I stipulate that systematic desensitization consists of a relaxation procedure and an image hierarchy, creating expectation of cure is not one of the specified ingredients. If it turns out that none of the specified ingredients makes any difference, and that all improvement is due to the patient thinking that the therapy will work, then the therapy is not effective.

One can, of course, build expectation of cure into the very specification of what the therapy is. I can say that "psychoanalysis," as I define it, consists of the interpretation of dreams and slips, the overcoming of resistances, the working through of the transferences, *and* creation or the enhancement of the client's expectation of cure. But the same thing can be done with drug treatment. My drug treatment consists of giving the patient Prozac and creating the expectation of cure. Would this trivial move answer Greenberg and Fisher's point about a drug treatment having no value if it cannot outperform a placebo? It would not. We would now want to know which ingredient of the stipulatively defined treatment is effective: the drug or instilling the expectation. Why would it be different for psychotherapy? Anyone is free to stipulate that generating expectation of cure is one of the defining factors of psychoanalysis or a certain type of behavior therapy, but that does nothing to show that it is not imperative to find out if creation of the expectation is the sole effective ingredient. In short, none of these reasons for using a lower standard in psychotherapy research shows what it purports to show.

One reason for including a placebo control (or some epistemologically adequate alternative) in psychotherapy research is the same as in drug research. If all we know is that the clients in the therapy group improved more on average than those in a no-treatment or wait-list control, then we are not in a position, without additional information, to infer that any of the ingredients that make up the therapy had any positive effect. We would still need to show, whether in drug or psychotherapy research, that it was not the expectation on the part of the patient (plus other placebo factors) that made all of the difference. The therapeutic procedure consists of certain elements; if none of them makes any clinical difference with respect to a particular problem, then the *therapy* is impotent for that problem.

It is tempting to respond that showing that a therapy is effective in treating a disorder and showing that its constituent factors are effective are two different things. But are they? What is the difference? If systematic desensitization consists of a relaxation procedure and transversing an image hierarchy, what is the difference between saying that these factors either singly or in combination have a certain effect and saying that the therapy has the effect? The therapy is just the ensemble of these factors. Other things are present when the therapy is employed: the client makes a decision to do something about his or her problem, which may in itself be morale-enhancing; the client has certain beliefs about the therapy and its likely effects; there may be a so-called demand for improvement; the therapist pays some attention to the client; and so on. However, if all improvement is due to the operation of these factors, in what sense was the *therapy* responsible?

It could be said that the therapy at least made a difference in the following respect. Even if the therapist provides a rationale for using the therapy, the therapy cannot appear to be some strange procedure such as voodoo, unless the patient finds voodoo plausible. So, the features of the therapy play some role in determining whether the client will trust it, and that confidence in turn makes a difference. I concede this point, but it applies equally well to pharmacological procedures. Even if a drug is physiologically inert for a certain illness, we can give some meager credit to the drug for at least appearing to be effective, even if the outcome is a placebo effect.

As already noted one can build such factors as generating the expectation of cure, or therapist attention, or demand for improvement into the very definition of the therapy, but then it becomes imperative to find out whether these factors are the only effective ingredients. Why? For several reasons.

One reason is cost-effectiveness. A pill-placebo, to take but one example of an inexpensive procedure, provides the above-mentioned factors (expectancy of cure, and so on) if it is accompanied by minimal therapist contact. Yet it lacks the bad side effects of many active drug treatments, and is cheaper, briefer, and easier to administer than almost all psychotherapies. If for a certain problem, such as non-psychotic depression, the pill-placebo procedure is just as effective, what are the grounds for not using it? In Erwin (1994b), I suggested that it might be preferable to drugs and standard psychotherapies for certain depressed clinical populations, such as the spinal-cord injured who must take a variety of other medications that sometimes interact with drugs for depression. Brown (1994) provides a more detailed and persuasive argument for using a pill-placebo as therapy (see the critical replies in the same journal, and Brown's responses).

A second reason to find out if psychotherapies generally can do no better than an inexpensive, simple-to-use placebo concerns therapist education. What is the rationale for much of the standard training in using psychotherapies if such treatments cannot outperform a credible placebo?

A third reason concerns public policy issues. Funds for treatment of mental health disorders are limited, and are becoming scarcer. Why should society pay for a drug treatment for depression, say, if it turns out that that particular drug is no more effective than a cheaper pill that has no bad side effects? The same sort of question arises for any sort of psychotherapy that cannot be shown to be more effective than a pill-placebo. Why should society pay for the more expensive treatment?

I conclude that the first part of my analogy with the state of nineteenth-century medicine is almost exact. As was true then of almost all medical procedures, the overwhelming majority of the more than 400 psychotherapy procedures have not yet been shown to be more effective with real patients than a credible placebo. I turn now to the second part of my analogy: therapeutic expertise.

THERAPEUTIC EXPERTISE

Concerning the comparison of nineteenth-century medical expertise and current psychotherapeutic expertise, there is this disanalogy. Except for the medically trained (in most cases, this means psychiatrists), there is no reason to believe that the average psychotherapist knows more about the anatomy of the human body than the average educated lay person. So, on that criterion, the average psychotherapist does worse than his or her nineteenth-century counterpart. That need not matter if the expertise of psychotherapists consists of their superior knowledge of something else, namely, either human behavior or the human mind. But is there knowledge of the latter sort generally shared by psychotherapists?

When we examine current psychotherapeutic theories, what we find is a great variety of theories that tend to conflict with one another. Even within the circle of dynamic theories, orthodox Freudian theory clashes with the theories of self psychology, which in turn conflict at various points with object relations theory, which rivals ego psychology. Each of these theories, in turn, must contend with operant conditioning theory, Gestalt psychology, various cognitivist theories, and a myriad of mini-theories of various sorts. Given the many inconsistencies, these theories cannot generally be true; consequently, they cannot generally be known to be true. *Some* psychotherapists may rely on well-supported clinical theories, just as *some* may use techniques demonstrably superior to credible placebos. What cannot be true, however, given the great diversity of conflicting psychotherapeutic theories, is that psychotherapeutic expertise generally consists of theoretical knowledge about human behavior or the mind.

On this second criterion, then, that of expertise, psychotherapists may do even worse than medical doctors of the nineteenth century. However, that depends on whether psychotherapeutic expertise does not consist of something else besides theoretical knowledge or knowledge of use of techniques. One possibility is that psychotherapists possess, as some put it, a "clinical wisdom." This may be correct, but it is sobering to realize that the new "psychic counselors," those who are part of the psychic network advertised on American television, can also claim a fund of clinical wisdom. How do we know that such talk is not just hollow verbiage unless we can specify more precisely what the alleged wisdom consists of, *and* then demonstrate that psychotherapists generally possess it? It might be possible to do both things, but I am unaware that this joint task has been carried out by anyone. Until it is, speaking of clinical wisdom fails to advance the discussion.

There is, however, a more obvious way to break down my analogy. Many psychotherapists would point to their training and experience as the key constituents of their expertise. I have partly anticipated this reply: Both for nineteenth-century physicians and contemporary psychotherapists, neither their training nor expertise has given them any edge over a lay person in using techniques demonstrably superior to placebos (leaving aside a few behavior therapy or cognitive-behavior therapy techniques). It can be replied, however, that even if specific techniques have not, except in a few cases, proved their superiority to placebo treatment, experienced and well-trained therapists still produce superior outcomes compared to non-professionals. How they do it is one matter, but that they have this therapeutic edge is undeniable. Or, is it? Let us look at the evidence.

Durlak (1979) reviewed 42 studies comparing professional and paraprofessional psychotherapists. Of these studies, 41 out of 42 failed to show the superiority of the professional psychotherapist. After Nietzel and Fisher (1981) criticized Durlak's argument, Hattie et al. (1984) did a meta-analysis of 39 of the original studies. Based on the data from these studies, the authors conclude (page 540) that paraprofessionals are at least as effective as, and in many instances more effective than, professional counselors.

Berman and Norton (1985) argue that some of the 39 studies reviewed by Hattie et al. are inappropriate. After omitting the problematic studies, Berman and Norton still found (page 405) no evidence that professionals are more effective than para-professionals. They go on to ask whether training makes a therapist more effective, and conclude: "On the basis of current research evidence, we would have to concede that the answer is no" (page 405). Additional evidence is available from other studies. This evidence has recently been reviewed in Christensen and Jacobson (1994), who reach the following verdict, after discussing the improvements in methodology and refinements of the evidence: "Yet, whatever refinements are made, whatever studies are included or excluded, the results show either no differences between professionals and paraprofessionals or, surprisingly, differences that favor paraprofessionals" (page 9).

Methodological problems, as already noted, have been raised with some of the existing studies. For that reason, I am not arguing for the stronger conclusion that professional psychotherapists generally do no better than non-professionals. Rather, I am asking if there is good reason at the present time, based on the current evidence, to think that they generally do have this ability. The answer is no.

I conclude that the second part of my analogy is also almost, if not entirely, exact: As far as is known, the average nineteenth-century physician was not more expert than the average educated lay person in using procedures more effective than a placebo; the same is true of most psychotherapists. I agree that the relevant expertise might consist of something else. In the case of physicians of the last century, at least they could rightly claim superior knowledge of anatomy. Perhaps one can point to one or more respects in which psychotherapists, too, *generally* have expertise not widely possessed by educated lay persons. I have not tried to rule out that possibility altogether. However, if one points to clinical wisdom or ability to do better in helping people with clinical problems, the case for either sort of psychotherapeutic expertise has not yet been made.

GROUNDS FOR OPTIMISM

Despite the current problems, there are reasons to be optimistic. There is nothing inherent in the field of psychotherapy that guarantees that clinical theories and problems must be discussed with neither clarity nor precision. There is no necessity for accepting theoretical speculations entirely ungrounded in observational evidence. There is no need, and as argued in chapter 4 no good reason at all, to accept the postmodern epistemologies currently popular in the field, epistemologies that devalue experimental research and which are likely to inhibit the development of a genuine science of psychotherapy. High-quality experiments are difficult, but obviously not impossible.

Furthermore, rigorous research has produced some impressive results. False clinical theories have been discredited; some weak therapies have been discarded. Although it is quite difficult to prove superiority to a credible placebo, in at least some cases, that has been done. Furthermore, there are therapies which are quite promising even if they have not yet met that standard, including interpersonal psychotherapy, some of the cognitive therapies, and some of the behavior therapies. Progress has also been made in other areas such as in diagnosis and in measuring outcomes.

In addition, there is a sense in which for many people, psychotherapy is the only game in town. If we exclude the relatively small number of psychological problems that have an optimal drug solution, the only thing left for many people is psychotherapy, defined broadly to include all psychological therapies. Even if placebo factors explain most of the beneficial effects, and that has not been established, many people who undergo psychotherapy appear to be better off at the end of the process, no matter what caused the good results. Perhaps they could obtain such benefits from talking to spouses or friends, or to their clergy, or even to the "psychic counselors" who advertise on American television, but many people do not want to do any of these things. For these people, professional psychological treatment, whatever its defects, is all that is left.

Finally, in both counseling and psychotherapy, there are often elements that clearly are of value to many people, including a warm, caring relationship and the provision of sound advice. When people are troubled, and for whatever reason pharmacological treatment is inappropriate, these elements can be of great value. Even where psychotherapy cannot "Raze out the written troubles of the brain," it can still do good.

References

Abraham, K. (1924) 'Contributions to the theory of the anal character', in *Selected Papers of Karl Abraham* (1965). London: Hogarth Press and Institute of Psycho-Analysis.

Akhtar, S. (1989) 'Kernberg and Kohut: a critical comparison', in D. Detrick and S. Detrick (eds), *Self Psychology: Comparisons and Contrasts*. Hillsdale, NJ: The Analytic Press. pp. 329–62.

Alloy, L. and Abramson, L. (1988) 'Depressive realism: four theoretical perspectives', in L. Alloy (ed.), *Cognitive Processes in Depression*. New York: The Guilford Press.

American Psychiatric Association (1994) *Diagnostic and Statistical Manual of Mental Disorders*. 4th edn. Washington, DC: American Psychiatric Association. (Called DSM-IV.)

Annis, H. and Davis, C. (1988) 'Assessment of expectancies', in D. Donovan and G. Marlatt (eds), *Assessment of Addictive Behaviors*. New York: The Guilford Press. pp. 84–111.

Arnkoff, D. and Glass, C. (1992) 'Cognitive therapy and psychotherapy integration', in D. Freedheim (ed.), *The History of Psychotherapy*. Washington, DC. pp. 657–94.

Ayllon, T. and Azrin, N. (1964) 'Reinforcement and instructions with mental patients', *Journal of the Experimental Analysis of Behavior*, 7: 327–31.

Bachrach, H., Galatzer-Levy, R., Skolnikoff, A. and Waldron, S. (1991) 'On the efficacy of psychoanalysis', *Journal of the American Psychoanalytic Association*, 39: 871–916.

Baldwin, M. and Satir, V. (eds) (1987) *The Use of Self in Therapy*. New York: The Haworth Press.

Bandura, A. (1982) 'The self and mechanisms of agency', in Jerry Suls (ed.), *Psychological Perspectives on the Self*, vol. 1. Hillsdale, NJ: Lawrence Erlbaum Associates. pp. 3–39.

Bandura, A. (1991) 'Self-efficacy conception of anxiety', in R. Schwarzer and R. Wicklund (eds), *Anxiety and Self-focused Attention*. New York: Harwood. pp. 89–110.

Bandura, A. (1995) 'Exercise of personal and collective efficacy in changing societies', in A. Bandura (ed.), *Self-efficacy in Changing Societies*. New York: Cambridge University Press. pp. 1–45.

Bandura, A. and Adams, N. (1977) 'Analysis of self-efficacy theory of behavioral change', *Cognitive Therapy and Research*, 1: 287–310.

Barlow, D. (1978) 'Foreword', in E. Erwin, *Behavior Therapy: Scientific, Philosophical and Moral Foundations*. New York: Cambridge University Press.

Barlow, D. (ed.) (1993) *Clinical Handbook of Psychological Disorders: a Step-by-Step Treatment Manual*. 2nd edn. New York: The Guilford Press.

Basch, M. (1989) 'A comparison of Freud and Kohut: Apostasy or Synergy?', in D. Detrick and S. Detrick (eds), *Self Psychology: Comparisons and Contrasts*. Hillsdale, NJ: The Analytic Press. pp. 3–22.

Bass, E. and Davis, L. (1994) *The Courage to Heal: a Guide for Women Survivors of Child Sexual Abuse*. New York: HarperCollins. (1st edn., 1988.)

Beck, A. (1967) *Depression: Causes and Treatment*. Philadelphia: University of Pennsylvania Press.

Beck, A., Emery, G. and Greenberg, R. (1985) *Anxiety Disorders and Phobias: a Cognitive Perspective*. New York: Basic Books.

Beidel, D. and Turner, S. (1986) 'A critique of the theoretical bases of cognitive-behavioral theories and therapy', *Clinical Psychological Review*, 6: 177–97.

Bellack, A. and Hersen, M. (eds) (1985) *Dictionary of Behavior Therapy Techniques*. New York: Pergamon Press.

Bellack, A. and Hersen, M. (eds) (1993) *Handbook of Behavior Therapy in the Psychiatric Setting*. New York: Plenum.

Bergmann, F. (1977) *On Being Free*. Notre Dame, IN: University of Notre Dame Press.

Berman, J. and Norton, N. (1985) 'Does professional training make a therapist more effective?', *Psychological Bulletin*, 98: 401–6.

Biglan, A. (1993) 'A functionalist contextualist framework for community interventions', in S. Hayes, L. Hayes, H. Reese and T. Sarbin (eds), *Varieties of Scientific Contextualism*. Reno, NV: Context Press. pp. 251–76.

Biran, M. and Wilson, G.T. (1981) 'Treatment of phobic disorders using cognitive and exposure methods: a self-efficacy analysis', *Journal of Counseling and Clinical Psychology*, 49: 886–9.

Blanchard, E., Andrasik, F., Ahler, T., Teders, S. and O'Keefe, D. (1980) 'Migraine and tension headache: a meta-analytic review', *Behavior Therapy*, 11: 613–31.

Bonjour, L. (1985) *The Structure of Empirical Knowledge*. Cambridge, MA: Harvard University Press.

Borkovec, T. and Nau, S. (1972) 'Credibility of analogue therapy rationales', *Journal of Behavior Therapy and Experimental Psychiatry*, 3: 257–60.

Brandt, R. (1979) *A Theory of the Good and Right*. New York: Oxford University Press.

Braude, S. (1991) *First Person Plural: Multiple Personality and the Philosophy of Mind*. London: Routledge.

Brewer, W. (1974) 'There is no convincing evidence for operant or classical conditioning in adult humans', in W. Weimer and D. Palermo (eds), *Cognition and the Symbolic Processes*. Hillsdale, NJ: Lawrence Erlbaum Associates.

Brill, N., Koegler, R., Epstein, L. and Forgy, E. (1964) 'Controlled study of psychiatric outpatient treatment', *Archives of General Psychiatry*, 10: 581–95.

Brody, N. (1983) 'Author's response: Where are the emperor's clothes?', *The Behavioral and Brain Sciences*, 6: 303–8.

Brown, W. (1994) 'Placebo as a treatment for depression', *Neuropsychopharmacology*, 10: 265–9.

Brown, W., Johnson, M. and Chen, M. (1992) 'Clinical features of depressed patients who do and do not improve with placebo', *Psychiatry Research*, 41: 203–14.

Cashdan, S. (1988) *Object Relations Therapy: Using the Relationship*. New York: W.W. Norton & Co.

Catania, A.C. (1973) 'The psychologies of structure, function, and development', *American Psychologist*, 28: 434–43.

Chisholm, R. (1994) 'On the observability of the self', in Q. Cassam (ed.), *Self-knowledge*. New York: Oxford University Press. pp. 94–108.

Christensen, A. and Jacobson, N. (1994) 'Who (or what) can do psychotherapy: the status and challenge of nonprofessional therapies', *Psychological Science*, 5: 8–14.

Coche, E. and Douglas, A. (1977) 'Therapeutic effects of problem-solving for hospitalized patients', *Journal of Clinical Psychology*, 33: 820–7.

Coche, E. and Flick, A. (1975) 'Problem-solving training groups for hospitalized patients', *Journal of Psychology*, 91: 19–29.

Comas-Díaz, L. (1981) 'Effects of cognitive and behavioral group treatment on the depressive symptomatology of Puerto Rican women', *Journal of Consulting and Clinical Psychology*, 49: 627–32.

Consumer Reports (1995) 'Mental Health: does therapy help?', 60: 734–9.

Crews, F. (1995) *The Memory Wars: Freud's Legacy in Dispute*. New York: A New York Review Book.

Crits-Christoph, P. (1992) 'The efficacy of brief psychotherapy: a meta-analysis', *The American Journal of Psychiatry*, 149 (2): 151–8.

Davison, G. (1976) 'Homosexuality: the ethical challenge', *Journal of Consulting and Clinical Psychology*, 44: 157–62.

Dawes, R. (1994) *House of Cards: Psychology and Psychotherapy Built on Myth*. New York: The Free Press.

Day, W. (1976) 'The concept of reinforcement-history and explanation in behaviorism', in S. Leigland (ed.), *Radical Behaviorism: Willard Day on Psychology and Philosophy*. Reno, NV: Context Press. pp. 117–22.

Dennett, D. (1984) *Elbow Room: the Varieties of Free Will Worth Wanting*. Cambridge, MA: The MIT Press.

Dennett, D. (1991) 'The origin of selves', in D. Kolak and R. Martin (eds), *Self and Identity: Contemporary Philosophical Issues*. New York: Macmillan.

Dickinson, A. (1987) 'Animal conditioning and learning theory', *Theoretical Foundations of Behavior Therapy*. New York: Plenum Press. pp. 57–79.

Dobson, K. (1989) 'A meta-analysis of the efficacy of cognitive therapy for depression', *Journal of Consulting and Clinical Psychology*, 57: 414–19.

Doppelt, G. (1988) 'The philosophical requirements for an adequate conception of scientific rationality', *Philosophy of Science*, 55: 104–33.

Dryden, W. (1991) *A Dialogue with Albert Ellis: Against Dogma*. Philadelphia: Open University Press.

Durlak, J. (1979) 'Comparative effectiveness of paraprofessional and professional helpers', *Psychological Bulletin*, 86: 80–92.

Dworkin, G. (1988) *The Theory and Practice of Autonomy*. New York: Cambridge University Press.

Eagle, M. (1984) *Recent Developments in Psychoanalysis: a Critical Evaluation*. New York: McGraw-Hill.

Eagle, M. (1987) 'The psychoanalytic and the cognitive unconscious', in S. Stern (ed.), *Theories of the Unconscious and Theories of the Self*. Hillsdale, NJ: Analytic Press.

Eagle, M. (1993) 'The dynamics of theory change in psychoanalysis', in J. Earman, A. Janis, G. Massey and N. Rescher (eds), *Philosophical Problems of the Internal and External Worlds: Essays on the Philosophy of Adolf Grünbaum*. Pittsburgh: University of Pittsburgh Press. pp. 373–408.

Elkin, I., Shea, T., Watkins, J., Imber, S., Sotsky, S., Collins, J., Glass, D., Pilkonis, P., Leber, W., Docherty, J., Fiester, A. and Parloff, M. (1989) 'National Institute of Mental Health treatment of depression collaborative research program', *Archives of General Psychiatry*, 46: 971–82.

Ellickson, P., Bell, R. and McGuigan, K. (1993) 'Preventing adolescent drug use: long term results of a junior high program', *American Journal of Public Health*, 83: 856–61.

Ellis, A. (1962) *Reason and Emotion in Psychotherapy*. Secaucus, NJ: Citadel.

Ellis, A. (1993) 'Reflections on rational-emotive therapy', *Journal of Consulting and Clinical Psychology*, 61: 199–201.

Ellis, A. and Bernard, M. (1986) 'What is rational-emotive therapy (RET)?', in A. Ellis and R. Grieger (eds), *Handbook of Rational-Emotive Therapy* (Vol. 2). New York: Springer. pp. 3–30.

Epstein, W. (1995) *The Illusion of Psychotherapy*. New Brunswick, NJ: Transaction Publishers.

Erdelyi, M. (1985) *Psychoanalysis: Freud's Cognitive Psychology*. New York: Freeman.

Erwin, E. (1978) *Behavior Therapy: Scientific, Philosophical and Moral Foundations*. New York: Cambridge University Press.

Erwin, E. (1984) 'Establishing causal connections: meta-analysis and psychotherapy', *Midwest Studies in Philosophy*, IX: 421–36.

Erwin, E. (1985) 'Holistic psychotherapies: what works?', in D. Stalker and C. Glymour (eds), *Examining Holistic Medicine*. Buffalo, NY: Prometheus Books.

Erwin, E. (1988a) 'Psychoanalysis and self-deception', in B. McLaughlin and A. Rorty (eds), *Perspectives on Self-deception*. Berkeley, CA: University of California Press. pp. 228–45.

Erwin, E. (1988b) 'Cognitivist and behaviorist paradigms in clinical psychology', in D. Fishman, F. Rotgers and C. Franks (eds), *Paradigms in Behavior Therapy: Present and Promise*. New York: Springer. pp. 109–40.

Erwin, E. (1988c) 'Testing Freudian hypotheses', in D. Batens and J. van Bendegem (eds), *Theory and Experiment*. Boston: D. Reidel Publishing Co.

Erwin, E. (1993) 'Philosophers on Freudianism: an examination of replies to Grünbaum's *Foundations*', in J. Earman, A. Janis, G. Massey and N. Rescher (eds), *Philosophical Problems of the Internal and External Worlds: Essays on the Philosophy of Adolf Grünbaum*. Pittsburgh: University of Pittsburgh Press. pp. 409–60.

Erwin, E. (1994a) 'The effectiveness of psychotherapy: epistemological issues', in G. Graham and L. Stephens (eds), *Philosophical Psychopathology: a Book of Readings*. Cambridge, MA: MIT Press. pp. 261–84.

Erwin, E. (1994b) 'Psychotherapeutic treatments of depression in the spinal cord injured'. Paper read at Annual Meetings of American Association of Spinal Cord Injury Psychologists and Social Workers. Las Vegas, NV.

Erwin, E. (1996) *A Final Accounting: Philosophical and Empirical Issues in Freudian Psychology*. Cambridge, MA: MIT Press.

Erwin, E. and Siegel, H. (1989) 'Is confirmation differential?', *British Journal for the Philosophy of Science*, 40: 105–19.

Eysenck, H.J. (1979a) 'Behavior therapy and the philosophers', *Behavior Research and Therapy*, 17: 511–14.

Eysenck, H.J. (1979b) 'The conditioning model of neurosis', *The Behavioral and Brain Sciences*, 2: 155–99.

Eysenck, H.J. (1983) 'The effectiveness of psychotherapy: the specter at the feast', *The Behavioral and Brain Sciences*, 6: 290.

Eysenck, H.J. (1985) *Decline and Fall of the Freudian Empire*. New York: Viking.

Eysenck, H.J. (1987a) 'Behavior Therapy', in H.J. Eysenck and I. Martin (eds), *Theoretical Foundations of Behavior Therapy*. New York: Plenum Press. pp. 3–35.

Eysenck, H.J. (1987b) 'The role of heredity, environment, and "preparedness" in the genesis of neurosis', *Theoretical Foundations of Behavior Therapy*. New York: Plenum Press. pp. 379–402.

Eysenck, H.J. (1992) 'The outcome problem in psychotherapy', in W. Dryden and C. Feltham (eds), *Psychotherapy and Its Discontents*. Philadelphia, PA: Open University Press. pp. 100–24.

Fairbairn, W.D. (1952) *Psychoanalytic Studies of the Personality*. London: Tavistock Publications and Routledge & Kegan Paul.

Feldman, M. and MacCulloch, M. (1971) *Homosexual Behavior: Therapy and Assessment*. Oxford: Pergamon Press.

Fine, A. (1993) 'Indeterminism and freedom of the will', in J. Earman, A. Janis, G. Massey and N. Rescher (eds), *Philosophical Problems of the Internal and External Worlds: Essays on the Philosophy of Adolf Grünbaum*. Pittsburgh: University of Pittsburgh Press. pp. 551–72.

Fisher, S. and Greenberg, R. (1985) *The Scientific Credibility of Freud's Theories and Therapy*. New York: Columbia University Press. (1st edn., 1977.)

Follette, W. and Houts, A. (1992) 'Philosophical and theoretical problems for behavior therapy', *Behavior Therapy*, 23: 251–61.

Foster, J. (1991) *The Immaterial Self: a Defense of the Cartesian Dualist Conception of the Self*. New York: Routledge.

Frank, R., Elliot, T., Corcoran, J. and Wonderlich, S. (1987) 'Depression after spinal cord injury: is it necessary?', *Clinical Psychology Review*, 7: 609–30.

Frankfurt, H. (1969) 'The principle of alternate possibilities', *The Journal of Philosophy*, 66: 829–39.

Freud, S. (1953–1974) *The Standard Edition of the Complete Psychological Works of Sigmund Freud (SE)*, 24 vols, tr. J. Strachey. London: Hogarth Press.

Friedlander, E. (1985) 'Dream your cancer away: the Simontons', in D. Stalker and C. Glymour (eds), *Examining Holistic Medicine*. Buffalo, NY: Prometheus Books.

Friman, P., Allen, K., Kerwin, M. and Larzelere, R. (1993) 'Changes in modern psychology: a citation analysis of the Kuhnian displacement thesis', *American Psychologist*, 48: 658–64.

Gergen, K. (1985) 'The social constructionist movement in modern psychology', *American Psychologist*, 40: 266–75.

Gergen, K. (1994) *Toward Transformation in Social Knowledge*. London: Sage. (1st edn., 1982.)

Gerwirtz, J. (1971) 'The roles of overt responding and extrinsic reinforcement in "self" and "vicarious reinforcement" phenomena and in "observational learning" and imitation', in R. Glaser (ed.), *The Nature of Reinforcement*. New York: Academic Press.

Gibbard, A. (1990) *Wise Choices, Apt Feelings: a Theory of Normative Judgement*. Cambridge, MA: Harvard University Press.

Glass, G. (1976) 'Primary, secondary and meta-analysis of research', *Educational Researcher*, 5: 3–8.

Glass, G. and Kliegl, R. (1983) 'An apology for research integration in the study of psychotherapy', *Journal of Consulting and Clinical Psychology*, 51: 28–41.

Glass, G., Smith, M. and Miller, T. (1983) 'Placebo effects in psychotherapy outcome research', *The Behavioral and Brain Sciences*, 6: 293–4.

Glynn, S. (1990) 'Token economy approaches for psychiatric patients', *Behavior Modification*, 14: 383–407.

Gossette, R. and O'Brien, R. (1992) 'The efficacy of rational emotive therapy in adults: clinical fact or psychometric artifact?', *Journal of Behavior Therapy and Experimental Psychiatry*, 23: 9–24.

Graham, G. and Stephens, L. (eds) (1994) *Philosophical Psychopathology*. Cambridge, MA: MIT Press.

Greenberg, R. and Fisher, S. (1989) 'Examining antidepressant effectiveness: findings, ambiguities, and some vexing puzzles', in S. Fisher and R. Greenberg (eds), *The Limits of Biological Treatments for Psychological Distress: Comparisons with Psychotherapy and Placebo*. Hillsdale, NJ: Lawrence Erlbaum Associates. pp. 1–37.

Grünbaum, A. (1984) *The Foundations of Psychoanalysis: a Philosophical Critique*. Berkeley: University of California Press.

Grünbaum, A. (1986) Author's response. *The Behavioral and Brain Sciences*, 9: 266–81.

Grünbaum, A. (1993) *Validation in the Clinical Theory of Psychoanalysis: a Study in the Philosophy of Psychoanalysis*. Madison, CT: International Universities Press, Inc.

Grünbaum, A. (1994a) 'Freud's permanent revolution: an exchange', *New York Review of Books*, XLI: 54–5.

Grünbaum, A. (1994b) 'The placebo concept in medicine and psychiatry', in G. Graham and L. Stephens (eds), *Philosophical Psychopathology: a Book of Readings*. Cambridge, MA: MIT Press. pp. 285–324.

Haack, S. (1993) *Evidence and Inquiry: Towards Reconstruction in Epistemology*. Oxford: Blackwell.

Haaga, D. and Davison, G. (1993) 'An appraisal of rational-emotive therapy', *Journal of Consulting and Clinical Psychology*, 61: 215–20.

Hacking, I. (1995) *Rewriting the Soul: Multiple Personality and the Sciences of Memory*. Princeton, NJ: Princeton University Press.

Hallam, R.S. (1987) 'Prospects for theoretical progress in behavior therapy', in H.J. Eysenck and I. Martin (eds), *Theoretical Foundations of Behavior Therapy*. New York: Plenum Press. pp. 315–29.

Hamilton, N. (1988) *Self and Others: Object Relations Theory in Practice*. London: Jason Aronson, Inc.

Harman, G. (1982) 'Critical review: Richard Brandt: a theory of the good and right', *Philosophical Studies*, 42: 119–39.

Hartmann, H. (1950) 'Comments on the psychoanalytic theory of the ego', *The Psychoanalytic Study of the Child*, V: 74–96.

Hattie, J., Sharpley, C. and Rogers, H. (1984) 'Comparative effectiveness of professional and paraprofessional helpers', *Psychological Bulletin*, 95: 534–41.

Hayes, L. (1993) 'Reality and truth', in S. Hayes, L. Hayes, H. Reese and T. Sarbin (eds), *Varieties of Scientific Contextualism*. Reno, NV: Context Press. pp. 35–44.

Hayes, S. (1993) 'Analytic goals and the varieties of scientific contextualism', in S. Hayes, L. Hayes, H. Reese and T. Sarbin (eds), *Varieties of Scientific Contextualism*. Reno, NV: Context Press. pp. 11–27.

Hayes, S., Hayes, L. and Reese, H. (1988) 'Finding the philosophical core: a review of Stephen Pepper's *World Hypotheses*', *Journal of the Experimental Analysis of Behavior*, 50: 119–37.

Hayes, S., Hayes, L., Reese, H. and Sarbin, T. (eds) (1993) *Varieties of Scientific Contextualism*. Reno, NV: Context Press.

Held, B. (1995) *Back to Reality: a Critique of Postmodern Theory in Psychotherapy*. New York: W.W. Norton & Co.

Higson, P., Woods, P., Tannahill, M. and Ellis, N. (1985) 'The role of meals as a reinforcing event in a token economy programme', *British Journal of Psychiatry*, 147: 170–4.

Hollen, S., Shelton, R. and Loosen, P. (1991) 'Cognitive therapy and pharmacotherapy for depression', *Journal of Consulting and Clinical Psychology*, 59: 88–99.

Holmes, D. (1990) 'The evidence for repression: an examination of sixty years of research', in J. Singer (ed.), *Repression and Dissociation: Implications for Personality Theory, Psychopathology, and Health*. Chicago: University of Chicago Press.

Holmes, J. and Lindley, R. (1989) *The Values of Psychotherapy*. Oxford: Oxford University Press.

Hope, D. and Heimberg, R. (1993) 'Social phobia and social anxiety', in D. Barlow (ed.), *Clinical Handbook of Psychological Disorders: a Step-by-Step Treatment Manual*. 2nd edn. New York: The Guilford Press. pp. 99–136.

Horwich, P. (1990) *Truth*. Oxford: Basil Blackwell.

Hospers, J. (1950) 'Meaning and free will', *Philosophy and Phenomenological Research*, X (3): 307–27.

Houts, A. (1989) 'Contributions of the psychology of science to metascience: a call for explorers', in B. Gholson, W. Radish, Jr., R. Neimeyer and A. Houts (eds), *Psychology of Science: Contributions to Metascience*. New York: Cambridge University Press. pp. 47–88.

Houts, A. and Haddock, C. (1992) 'Answers to philosophical and sociological uses of psychologism in science studies. A behavioral psychology of science', in R. Giere (ed.), *Cognitive Models of Science. Minnesota Studies in the Philosophy of Science*, 15: 367–400.

Humphrey, N. and Dennett, D. (1989) 'Speaking for ourselves', *Raritan*, 9: 68–98.

Hunter, J. and Schmidt, F. (1990) *Methods of Meta-Analysis: Correcting Bias in Research Findings*. London: Sage.

Jaspers, K. (1963) *General Psychopathology*. Chicago: University of Chicago Press.

Jensen, J. and Bergin, A. (1988) 'Mental health values of professional therapists: a national interdisciplinary survey', *Professional Psychology Research and Practice*, 19: 290–7.

Jones, M. (1924) 'The elimination of children's fears', *Journal of Experimental Psychology*, 7: 383–90.

Kendall, P., Haaga, D., Ellis, A., Bernard, M., DiGiuseppe, R. and Kassinove, H. (1995) 'Rational-emotive therapy in the 1990's and beyond: current status, recent revisions, and research questions', *Clinical Psychology Review*, 15: 169–85.

Kernberg, O. (1976) *Object-Relations Theory and Clinical Psychoanalysis*. New York: Jason Aronson.

Kernberg, O. (1987) 'The dynamic unconscious and the self', in R. Stern (ed.), *Theories of the Unconscious and Theories of the Self*. London: The Analytic Press. pp. 3–25.

Klein, D. (1989) Review of *American Psychiatric Press Review of Psychiatry* (vol. 7), *American Journal of Psychiatry*, 146: 263–4.

Klein, M. (1990) *Determinism, Blameworthiness, and Deprivation*. New York: Oxford University Press.

Kline, P. (1981) *Fact and Fantasy in Freudian Theory*. New York: Methuen. (1st edn., 1972.)

Kline, P. (1992a) 'Problems of methodology in studies of psychotherapy', in W. Dryden and C. Feltham (eds), *Psychotherapy and Its Discontents*. Philadelphia, PA: Open University Press. pp. 64–86.

Kline, P. (1992b) 'Rebuttal', in W. Dryden and C. Feltham (eds), *Psychotherapy and Its Discontents*. Philadelphia, PA: Open University Press. pp. 96–9.

Kohut, H. (1971) *The Analysis of the Self*. New York: International Universities Press.

Kohut, H. (1977) *The Restoration of the Self*. New York: International Universities Press.

Kohut, H. and Wolf, E. (1978) 'The disorders of the self and their treatment: an outline', *International Journal of Psycho-Analysis*, 59: 413–25.

Koss, M. and J. Butcher (1986) 'Research on brief psychotherapy', in S. Garfield and A. Bergin (eds), *Handbook of Psychotherapy and Behavior Change*. New York: Wiley.

Kovel, J. (1978) *A Complete Guide to Therapy: From Psychoanalysis to Behaviour Modification*. Harmondsworth: Penguin.

Krasner, L. and Houts, A. (1984) 'A study of the "value" systems of behavioral scientists', *American Psychologist*, 39: 840–50.

Kuhn, T. (1977) *The Structure of Scientific Revolutions*. Chicago: University of Chicago Press. (1st edn., 1962.)

Lambert, M. and Bergin, A. (1992) 'Achievements and limitations of psychotherapy research', in D. Freedheim (ed.), *History of Psychotherapy: A Century of Change*. Washington, DC: American Psychological Association. pp. 360–90.

Landman, J. and Dawes, R. (1982) 'Psychotherapy outcome research: Smith and Glass' conclusions stand up to scrutiny', *American Psychologist*, 37: 504–16.

Laplanche, J. and Pontalis, J. (1973) *The Language of Psychoanalysis*. New York: Norton.

Leigland, S. (1993) 'Scientific goals and the context of justification', in S. Hayes, L. Hayes, H. Reese and T. Sarbin (eds), *Varieties of Scientific Contextualism*. Reno, NV: Context Press. pp. 28–33.

Lowe, C., Horne, P. and Higson, P. (1987) 'Operant conditioning: the hiatus between theory and practice in clinical psychology', in H.J. Eysenck and I. Martin (eds), *Theoretical Foundations of Behavior Therapy*. New York: Plenum Press. pp. 153–65.

Luborsky, L., Diguer, L., Luborsky, E., Singer, B., Dickter, D. and Schmidt, K. (1993) 'The efficacy of dynamic psychotherapies – Is it true that "Everyone has won and all must have prizes"?', in N. Miller, L. Luborsky, J. Barber and J. Docherty (eds), *Psycho-dynamic Treatment Research: a Handbook for Clinical Practice*. New York: Basic Books.

Luborsky, L., Singer, B. and Luborsky, L. (1975) 'Comparative studies of psychotherapy: is it true that "Everyone has won and all must have prizes"?', *Archives of General Psychiatry*, 32: 995–1008.

Lynch, V. (1991) 'Basic concepts', in H. Jackson (ed.), *Using Self Psychology in Psychotherapy*. London: Jason Aronson, Inc. pp. 15–25.

Lyons, L. and Woods, P. (1991) 'The efficacy of rational-emotive therapy: a quantitative review of the outcome research', *Clinical Psychology Review*, 11: 357–69.

McLaughlin, B. and Rorty, A. (1988) *Perspectives on Self-deception*. Berkeley, CA: University of California Press.

McLean, P. and Hakstian, A. (1979) 'Clinical depression: comparative efficacy of outpatient treatments', *Journal of Consulting and Clinical Psychology*, 47: 818–36.

Macmillan, M. (1991) *Freud Evaluated: the Completed Arc*. New York: North Holland.

Mahoney, M. (1989) 'Participatory epistemology and psychology of science', in B. Gholson, W. Radish, Jr., R. Neimeyer and A. Houts (eds), *Psychology of Science: Contributions to Metascience*. New York: Cambridge University Press. pp. 138–64.

Martin, I. (1987) 'Concluding comments on theoretical foundations and requirements in behavior therapy', *Theoretical Foundations of Behavior Therapy*. New York: Plenum Press. pp. 451–64.

Meterissian, G. and Bradwejn, J. (1989) 'Comparative studies on the efficacy of psychotherapy, pharmacotherapy, and their combination in depression: Was adequate pharmacotherapy provided?', *Journal of Clinical Psychopharmacology*, 9: 334–9.

Miller, R. and Berman, J. (1983) 'The efficacy of cognitive behavior therapies: a quantitative review of the research evidence', *Psychological Bulletin*, 94: 39–53.

Nagel, E. (1959) 'Methodological issues in psychoanalytic theory', in S. Hook (ed.), *Psychoanalysis, Scientific Method and Philosophy*. New York: Grove Press.

Nagel, T. (1974) 'What is it like to be a bat?', *The Philosophical Review*, LXXXIII: 435–50.

Nagel, T. (1995) *Other Minds: Critical Essays 1969–1994*. New York: Oxford University Press.

Nau, S., Caputo, J. and Borkovec, T. (1974) 'The relationship between therapy credibility and simulated therapy response', *Journal of Behavioral Therapy and Experimental Psychiatry*, 5: 129–33.

Neimeyer, R. (1993) 'An appraisal of constructivist psychotherapies', *Journal of Consulting and Clinical Psychology*, 61: 221–34.

Nicholson, B. (1991) 'Narcissism', in H. Jackson (ed.), *Using Self Psychology in Psychotherapy*. London: Jason Aronson, Inc. pp. 27–47.

Nietzel, M. and Fisher, S. (1981) 'Effectiveness of professional and paraprofessional helpers: a comment on Durlak', *Psychological Bulletin*, 89: 555–65.

Nisbett, R. and Ross, L. (1980) *Human Inference: Strategies and Shortcomings of Social Judgment*. Englewood Cliffs, NJ: Prentice Hall.

O'Donohue, W. and Krasner, L. (eds) (1995) *Theories of Behavior Therapy: Exploring Behavior Change*. Washington, DC: American Psychological Association.

Ornstein, A. and Orstein, P. (1984) 'Empathy and the therapeutic dialogue', *Lydia Rappoport Lectures Program*. Northampton, MA: Smith College School for Social Work.

Ost, L. and Hugdahl, K. (1981) 'Acquisition of phobias and anxiety response patterns in clinical patients', *Behavior Research and Therapy*, 19: 439–47.

Overskeid, G. (1994) 'Private events and other causes of behavior: who can tell the difference?', *The Psychological Record*, 44: 35–43.

Pepper, S. (1942) *World Hypotheses: a Study in Evidence*. Berkeley, CA: University of California Press.

Polkinghorne, D. (1992) 'Postmodern epistemology of practice', in S. Kvale (ed.), *Psychology and Postmodernism*. London: Sage. pp. 146–65.

Popper, K. (1962) *Conjectures and Refutations*. New York: Basic Books.

Prioleau, L., Murdock, M. and Brody, N. (1983) 'An analysis of psychotherapy versus placebo studies', *The Behavioral and Brain Sciences*, 6: 275–310.

Quality Assurance Project (1983) 'A treatment outline for depressive disorders', *Australian and New Zealand Journal of Psychiatry*, 17: 129–46.

Rachman, S. and Teasdale, J. (1969) *Aversion Therapy and Behaviour Disorders: an Analysis*. Coral Gables, FL: University of Miami Press.

Rachman, S. and Wilson, G.T. (1980) *The Effects of Psychological Therapy*. New York: Pergamon Press.

Ricoeur, P. (1970) *Freud and Philosophy*. New Haven, CT: Yale University Press.

Roberts, A., Kewman, D., Mercier, L. and Hovell, M. (1993) 'The power of nonspecific effects in healing: implications for psychosocial and biological treatments', *Clinical Psychological Review*, 13: 375–91.

Robins, C. and Hayes, A. (1993) 'An appraisal of cognitive therapy', *Journal of Consulting and Clinical Psychology*, 61: 205–14.

Robinson, H. (1993) *Objections to Physicalism*. New York: Oxford University Press.

Rogers, C. (1951) *Client-Centered Therapy: its Current Practice, Implications, and Theory*. New York: Houghton Mifflin Co.

Rogers, C. (1961) *On Becoming a Person*. Boston, MA: Houghton Mifflin.

Rogers, C. (1989a) 'B.F. Skinner', in H. Kirschenbaum and V.L. Henderson (eds), *Carl Rogers: Dialogues*. Boston, MA: Houghton Mifflin Co.

Rogers, C. (1989b) 'Client-centered therapy', in H. Kirschenbaum and V. Henderson (eds), *Carl Rogers: Dialogues*. Boston, MA: Houghton Mifflin.

Rorty, R. (1979) *Philosophy and the Mirror of Nature*. Princeton, NJ: Princeton University Press.

Rorty, R. (1995) 'Is truth a goal of inquiry? Davidson vs. Wright', *The Philosophical Quarterly*, 45: 281–300.

Rosenthal, R. (1994) 'Science and ethics in conducting, analyzing, and reporting psychological research', *Psychological Science*, 5: 127–34.

Rotgers, F. (1988) 'Social learning theory, philosophy of science, and the identity of behavior therapy', in D. Fishman, F. Rotgers and C. Franks (eds), *Paradigms in Behavior Therapy: Present and Promise*. New York: Springer. pp. 187–210.

Rothenberg, A. (1976) 'Why Nixon taped himself: infantile fantasies behind Watergate', *Psychoanalytic Review*, 62: 201–23.

Ryle, A. (1982) *Psychotherapy: a Cognitive Integration of Theory and Practice*. London: Academic Press.

Salmon, W. (1984) *Scientific Explanation and the Causal Structure of the World*. Princeton, NJ: Princeton University Press.

Salmon, W. (1989) *Four Decades of Scientific Explanation*. Minneapolis, MN: University of Minnesota Press.

Sass, L. (1992) 'The epic of disbelief: the postmodernist turn in contemporary psychoanalysis', in S. Kvale (ed.), *Psychology and Postmodernism*. London: Sage. pp. 166–81.

Schopenhauer, A. (1960) *Essay on Freedom of the Will*, tr. K. Kolenda. Indianapolis: Bobbs-Merrill. (First published in 1841.)

Searle, J. (1995) *The Construction of Social Reality*. New York: The Free Press.

Shapiro, A. and Morris, L. (1978) 'The placebo effect in medical and psychological therapies', in S. Garfield and A. Bergin (eds), *Handbook of Psychotherapy and Behavior Change* (2nd edn.). New York: Wiley. pp. 369–410.

Siegel, H. (1988) *Relativism Refuted: a Critique of Contemporary Epistemological Relativism*. Dordrecht, Netherlands: D. Reidel.

Silverman, L. (1976) 'Psychoanalytic theory: the reports of my death are greatly exaggerated', *American Psychologist*, 31: 621–37.

Skinner, B.F. (1957) *Verbal Behavior*. New York: Appleton-Century-Crofts.

Skinner, B.F. (1963) 'Behaviorism at fifty', *Science*, 140: 951–8.

Skinner, B.F. (1974) *About Behaviorism*. New York: Alfred A. Knopf.

Smith, D. (1982) 'Trends in counseling and psychotherapy', *American Psychologist*, 37: 802–9.

Smith, M. and Glass, G. (1977) 'Meta-analysis of psychotherapy outcome studies', *American Psychologist*, 32: 752–60.

Smith, M., Glass, G. and Miller, T. (1980) *The Benefits of Psychotherapy*. Baltimore, MD: Johns Hopkins University Press.

Spence, D. (1982) *Narrative Truth and Historical Truth*. New York: Norton.

Staats, A. (1983) *Psychology's Crisis of Disunity: Philosophy and Method for a Unified Science*. New York: Praeger.

Svartberg, M. and Stiles, T. (1991) 'Comparative effects of short-term psychodynamic psychotherapy: a meta-analysis', *Journal of Consulting and Clinical Psychology*, 59: 704–14.

Sweet, A. and Loizeaux, A. (1991) 'Behavioral and cognitive treatment methods: a critical comparative review', *Journal of Behavioral Therapy and Experimental Psychiatry*, 22: 159–85.

Taylor, C. (1979) 'Interpretation and the sciences of man', in P. Rabinow and W. Sullivan (eds), *Interpretive Social Science: a Reader*. Berkeley: University of California Press.

Taylor, C. (1985) 'Peaceful coexistence in psychology', *Philosophical Papers, I*. New York: Cambridge University Press.

Thompson, A. (1990) *Guide to Ethical Practice in Psychotherapy*. New York: John Wiley & Sons.

Thomson, R. (1982) 'Side effects and placebo amplification', *British Journal of Psychiatry*, 140: 64–8.

Tjeltveit, A. (1986) 'The ethics of value conversion in psychotherapy: appropriate and inappropriate therapist influence on client values', *Clinical Psychology Review*, 6: 515–37.

Van Balkom, A., van Oppen, P., Vermeulen, A., van Dyck, R., Nauta, M. and Vorst, H. (1994) 'A meta-analysis on the treatment of obsessive compulsive disorder: a comparison of antidepressants, behavior, and cognitive therapy', *Clinical Psychology Review*, 14: 359–81.

Van Fraassen, B. (1989) *Laws and Symmetry*. Oxford: Oxford University Press.

Van Inwagen, P. (1983) *An Essay on Free Will*. New York: Oxford University Press.

Van Inwagen, P. (1989) 'When is the will free?', in J. Tomberlin (ed.), *Philosophical Perspectives, 3, Philosophy of Mind and Action Theory*. Atascadero, CA: Ridgeview Publishing Co. pp. 399–422.

Von Eckardt, B. (1981) 'Evaluating the scientific status of psychoanalysis', *The Journal of Philosophy*, lxxviii: 570–2.

Von Foerster, H. (1984) 'On constructing a reality', in P. Watzlawick (ed.), *The Invented Reality*. New York: Norton. pp. 41–61.

Von Glaserfeld, E. (1984) 'An introduction to radical constructivism', in P. Watzlawick (ed.), *The Invented Reality*. New York: Norton. pp. 17–40.

Wallwork, E. (1991) *Psychoanalysis and Ethics*. New Haven, CT: Yale University Press.

Warner, R. (1991) 'A survey of theoretical orientations of Canadian clinical psychologists', *Canadian Psychology*, 32: 525–8.

Watson, J.B. (1913) 'Psychology as a behaviorist views it', *Psychological Review*, 20: 158–77.

Weinberg, R. and Hunt, V. (1979) 'Effects of structural integration on state-trait anxiety', *Journal of Clinical Psychology*, 35: 319–22.

Weinberger, J. and Silverman, L. (1987) 'Subliminal psychodynamic activation: a method for studying psychoanalytic dynamic propositions', in R. Hogan and W. Jones (eds), *Perspectives in Personality: Theory, Measurement and Interpersonal Dynamics*, vol. 2: 251–87.

White, M. and Weiner, M. (1986) *The Theory and Practice of Self Psychology*. New York: Brunner/Mazel.

White, S. (1991) *The Unity of the Self*. Cambridge, MA: MIT Press.

Wilson, G.T. (1985) 'Limitations of meta-analysis in the evaluation of psychological therapy', *Clinical Psychology Review*, 5: 35–47.

Wilson, G.T. (1996) 'Treatment of bulimia nervosa: when CBT fails', *Behavior Research and Therapy*, 34: 197–212.

Wilson, T. and Pike, K. (1993) 'Eating disorders', in D. Barlow (ed.), *Clinical Handbook of Psychological Disorders: a Step-by-Step Treatment Manual* (2nd edn.). New York: The Guilford Press. pp. 278–317.

Winnicott, D.W. (1960) 'The theory of the parent–infant relationship', *International Journal of Psycho-Analysis*, 41: 585–97.

Wollheim, R. (1993) *The Mind and Its Depths*. Cambridge, MA: Harvard University Press.

Wolpe, J. (1981) 'The dichotomy between directly conditioned and cognitively learned anxiety', *Journal of Behavioral Therapy and Experimental Psychiatry*, 12: 35–42.

Wolpe, J. (1993) 'Commentary: the cognitivist oversell and comments on symposium contributions', *Journal of Behavioral Therapy and Experimental Psychiatry*, 24: 141–7.

Woods, P., Higson, P. and Tannahill, M. (1984) 'Token economy programmes with chronic psychotic patients: the importance of direct measurement and objective evaluation for long-term maintenance', *Behaviour Research and Therapy*, 22: 41–51.

Young, J., Beck, A. and Weinberger, A. (1993) 'Depression', in D. Barlow (ed.), *Clinical Handbook of Psychological Disorders: a Step-by-Step Treatment Manual* (2nd edn.). New York: The Guilford Press. pp. 240–77.

Name Index

Subject Index